Creating Rosie the Riveter

The University of Massachusetts Press
Amherst, 1984

Creating
Rosie the Riveter

Class, Gender, and Propaganda

during World War II

Maureen Honey

Copyright © 1984 by
The University of Massachusetts Press
All rights reserved
Printed in the United States of America
Second printing, with revisions, 1985
Library of Congress Cataloging in Publication Data
Honey, Maureen, 1945–
Creating Rosie the Riveter.
Bibliography: p.
Includes index.
  1. Women—United States—History—20th century.
2. Women in mass media—United States—History—20th century.   3. Women—Employment—United States—History—20th century.   4. World War, 1939–1945—Women—United States.   5. Women—United States—Social conditions.   6. Women in advertising—United States—History—20th century.   7. Women in fiction.   8. World War, 1939–1945—Propaganda.   I. Title.
HQ1420.H66   1984   305.4'2'0973   84-2596
ISBN 0-87023-443-9
ISBN 0-87023-444-7 (pbk.)

Portions of this book have appeared in earlier versions in the following articles:
"The Working-Class Woman and Recruitment Propaganda During World War II," *Signs* 8, no. 4 (1983); "The 'Womanpower' Campaign," *Frontiers: A Journal of Women Studies* 6, nos. 1/2 (1981); "New Roles for Women and the Feminine Mystique," *American Studies* 24, no. 1 (1983), © 1983 Midcontinent American Studies Association; "Images of Women in the *Saturday Evening Post*, 1931–1936," *Journal of Popular Culture* 10, no. 2 (1976); "Recruiting Women for War Work," *Journal of American Culture* 3 (Spring 1980).

To the women who made history
during World War II

Contents

Acknowledgments

THERE are several people who deserve special mention for the help they gave me in completing this study. I would like first to thank Russel Nye, who was my dissertation director at Michigan State University and guided me through the initial stages of the manuscript from which this book evolved. His enthusiasm for and skill in studying popular materials provided a major inspiration for undertaking this project. Barrie Thorne was also enormously helpful at this point, posing issues emerging from the research and pushing me to confront the questions it raised about the impact of propaganda. There are other people whose comments on the manuscript as it went through revision sharpened the theoretical focus of the work. Karen Anderson, Moira Ferguson, Richard and Pam Oestreicher all gave generously of their time to help me reformulate the topic while providing much needed encouragement to persevere. Muriel Cantor and Helen Moore gave me valuable feedback on my sampling procedure and made it possible for me to strengthen the rationale for selection of my material. In addition, the community of scholars that has developed around the World War II period has been an invaluable aid in my understanding of the subject. This includes Karen Anderson, Susan Hartmann, William Chafe, Leila Rupp, Ruth Milkman, Sherna Gluck, Eleanor Straub, Melva Baker, D'Ann Campbell, Sonya Michel, Lyn Goldfarb, Karen Beck Skold, Allan Bérubé, Paddy Quick, Joan Trey, Sally Van Wagenan Keil, Sheila Tobias, and Lisa Anderson. These scholars and others have retrieved from obscurity an extremely rich historical era.

I also thank the staffs of the National Archives, the Michigan State University library, and the University of Nebraska library for their help in procuring documents. The Instructional Media Center at the University of Nebraska and the Special Collections section of the Michigan State University library deserve specific mention for their help in making the illustrations for this book. I especially wish to thank the staff of the Macfadden Group, Inc. for allowing me to use their offices and collection of *True Story*. Without their cooperation, I could not have completed this research since confession magazines have not been collected in libraries. Thanks are also due Roma Rector who typed the initial draft of this manuscript and expressed great enthusiasm for the topic. I appreciate too the editorial advice and professionalism of the people at University of Massachusetts Press with whom it has been a great pleasure to work.

Finally, I am indebted to my friends and family whose support and affection carried me through to the final stages of this project. Without them, I might not have had the courage to keep trying.

Lincoln, Nebraska
February 1984

Introduction

MANY researchers have been drawn to the World War II period because demands of the wartime economy necessitated a dramatic reassessment of women's role in American life. Specifically, women were hired to fill positions normally occupied by men, jobs that not only paid higher wages than those in female fields but were thought to require "masculine" abilities and attitudes. The fact that a woman could step into a man's shoes and wear them rather comfortably posed an implicit challenge to traditional notions about femininity and female limitations. The question that has absorbed those of us focusing on the ideological dimension of this period is why the media's legitimation of female entry into male work failed to supplant the traditional image of women as homemakers, unsuited by nature for wielding power outside the domestic province, for competently manipulating the machinery at the heart of our industrial society, and for holding jobs normally allocated to male "breadwinners." Indeed, the great puzzle of the 1940s has been the paradoxical spawning of a reactionary postwar feminine mystique by a crisis that necessitated radical revision of traditional views.

In this study I am seeking to clarify those elements which defeated the potential of war work to legitimize women's entry into nontraditional occupations, to identify the ideological currents that invited women into men's sphere and yet flowed into the restrictive channels of traditional views about womanhood at the war's end. Where was the interface between praising women for their ability to perform public work competently and relegating them to the home because that is where their "natural" limitations and strengths placed them? How did the strong figure of Rosie the Riveter become transformed into the naive, dependent, childlike, self-abnegating model of femininity in the late forties and 1950s? Why did the public image of patriotic war workers eager to return home fail so completely to reflect the reality of women wanting to keep their jobs, given that the media must in part reflect the feelings and beliefs of consumers in order to be credible? Finally, what were the models available to working-class women during the war for forming nontraditional conceptions of women's work? Since they were, after all, the major source of labor power and the people most dramatically affected by female employment patterns, it is instructive to look at media designed especially for a working-class audience to see if our analyses of the media as a whole apply to them as well. These are the questions that informed this case study of wartime fiction, advertising, and propaganda.

Scholars disagree over the long-term impact of World War II on women's role in American life and over whether the war period should be characterized as a time of continuity or of dramatic change in definitions of woman's place.[1] William Chafe is at one end of the spectrum, concluding that the war accelerated the movement of women, especially married women, into the labor force, while Leila Rupp feels that the war had no permanent impact on their participation rate.[2] Karen Anderson agrees with Chafe that the war was an important turning point in that it began to make acceptable the notion that women could combine home roles and paid employment. She concludes, however, that women's secondary status within the labor force did not improve significantly and that the war's progressive impact was disappointingly weak.[3] Susan Hartmann believes that the war not only paved the way for homemakers to take on outside jobs but laid down important bases for emergence of the second wave of feminism. At the same time, she notes that other forces generated by the emergency undermined its potential to alter gender roles.[4]

While there is considerable disagreement over the war's liberating effect on women in the postwar world, it is generally conceded that various forces worked against the retention of most progressive changes adopted to encourage women's entry into nontraditional fields. These range from the exclusion of women from powerful policy-making bodies in government through war contractors' resistance to viewing women workers as permanent hires to the refusal of unions adequately to defend women's rights during reconversion.[5]

In searching for an explanation as to why the war failed more significantly to improve women's status, analysts have attempted to understand the complex and seemingly contradictory images of women that characterize the early 1940s. Specifically, they have sought to unravel the mystery of how those images could expand and contract public conceptions of woman's place within such a short period of time without confusing or alienating the population and without more seriously challenging the conservative ideology behind the sexual division of labor. Again, there is a range of opinion on this issue.

The first attempt to explain the postwar reaction was Betty Friedan's *The Feminine Mystique*, published in 1963.[6] Friedan's study was the first to recognize that a radical change had occurred in women's magazines in the postwar era. She pointed out that prior to World War II heroines from magazine fiction were self-actualizing achievers committed to following a dream, whereas the postwar heroine was devoid of goals for personal growth: "The image of woman that emerges . . . is young and frivolous, almost childlike; fluffy and feminine; passive; gaily content in a world of bedroom and kitchen, sex, babies, and home."[7] Advertising, articles, and fiction all abandoned the exciting world of adventure so characteristic of early magazines in favor of a mundane domestic playground which Friedan had come to view as a prison.

Friedan's explanation for this shift focuses on the social changes that occurred in the immediate postwar period when, she asserts, the insecurities and deprivations of the previous fifteen years made it tempting for people to retreat from the world into a domestic haven: "The American spirit fell into a strange sleep; men as well as women, scared liberals, disillusioned radicals, conservatives bewildered and frustrated by change— the whole nation stopped growing up. All of us went back into the warm brightness of home, the way it was when we were children and slept peacefully upstairs while our parents read, or played bridge in the living room, or rocked on the front porch in the summer evening in our home towns."[8] The traumas of the Depression and the war years had combined to produce in most citizens a desire for stability.

Friedan acknowledges, however, that other countries, even more traumatized by these events, failed to develop the mystique of feminine fulfillment through homemaking. She postulates that the American experience grew out of the ability of business to exploit such feelings in women in order to sell consumer products. While careful to point out that there was no high-level conspiracy to create the mystique, Friedan credits the plethora of domestic images to postwar sales strategies and the domination of women's magazines by male editors: "Somehow, somewhere, someone must have figured out that women will buy more things if they are kept in the underused, name-less-yearning, energy-to-get-rid-of state of being housewives."[9]

More recently, studies have sought to locate the origins of the feminine mystique in an earlier period. The most important of these is Leila Rupp's analysis of German and American propaganda from 1939 to 1945.[10] Rupp examines wartime images of women in government propaganda directives and women's magazines to see how the war affected traditional ideas about woman's place. She identifies several ways portrayals of war workers simultaneously urged the acceptance of women in male jobs and preserved their feminine identities. These ranged from comparing factory work to housework to using war workers as sex objects.[11] Rupp sharply contradicts Friedan's belief that the war's end precipitated an abrupt change in women's images. She concludes that, although the media's attention to working women was unprecedented in scope during World War II, fundamental changes in attitudes toward women did not occur as a result of the emergency: "Rosie the Riveter, like the flapper, was exotic in appearance, even perhaps in lifestyle. But the new image did not mean that the ideal American woman had changed beyond recognition. Beneath her begrimed exterior, she remained very much a traditional woman."[12]

Using a Marxist perspective, Ruth Milkman and J. E. Trey agree that wartime ideology continued to be based on prewar conservative values while noting that it reflects the intention and practice of capitalists to maintain gender divisions within the labor force even while they were hiring women to fill men's jobs. Though Trey states, as Milkman does not, that women were manipulated by the media into false consciousness of their roles as workers, both contend that tying war work to traditional female images was a logical direction for capitalist ideology to take because it reinforced women's inferior position in the work force at a time when material conditions challenged sexist work divisions.[13]

Rupp concurs that public images during World War II adapted to the temporary employment of women in male fields so as to leave traditional gender norms untouched. However, she roots the survival of traditional images in what she believes to be the inherently conservative nature of social attitudes, which change very slowly: "The economic role and the popular image of women may change drastically in the course of a modern war, but basic ideas about women's proper sphere, characterized by cultural lag even in the case of long-term economic developments, change little."[14]

Karen Anderson and Susan Hartmann advance yet a fourth perspective. They posit that the postwar yearning for stability identified by Friedan was an outgrowth of needs generated during the war period itself, needs that strengthened traditional gender roles. As Anderson says: "The postwar stress on traditional family roles and values for women did not constitute a dramatic break with wartime themes."[15] Both persuasively argue that disruptions to family life caused it to become highly valued and that women were expected to subordinate personal ambition in order to bolster the family unit.[16] These tendencies were accelerated, not initiated, by the demobilization period when social readjustment was occurring on a massive scale.

With the exception of Friedan, who does not discuss the war years, these analysts have demonstrated that there is a high degree of continuity in images of the early and late 1940s and that postwar conservative views of women were rooted in economic, social, and ideological structures that transcended the brief campaign to alter gender roles. My intention is not to dispute this consensus, although my data suggest that the prewar and war periods were significantly more egalitarian than the years that followed. Rather, I wish to focus attention on the complex dimensions of home-front propaganda and its significance for images of women. It is my contention that the picture we find of women during World War II cannot be fully understood without reference to the larger campaign that tried to solidify and mobilize the home front into an efficient production unit. The campaign to attract women into war production was part of a drive to weld the home front into an economic army, well disciplined, highly motivated by patriotism, and willing to make sacrifices for the good of American soldiers. This overriding propaganda goal subsumed the campaign to recruit women and largely shaped its direction; this was a goal, moreover, for which traditional ideas about women were well suited.

For a variety of reasons, war workers served as a symbol of the ideal home-front spirit, standing for national unity, dedication to the cause, and stoic pursuit of victory. This image both idealized woman as a strong, capable fighter infused with a holy spirit and undercut the notion that women deserved and wanted a larger role in public life. Because she was used to inspire energetic support of government programs, the war worker was shown as a paragon of virtue, capable of shouldering any burden and meeting any challenge. This aspect of her portrayal was a progressive movement toward the acceptance of women as equal partners in the struggle to preserve American institutions, to share in the hardships and rewards of public work at all levels.

Her apotheosis as a soldier-oriented, self-sacrificing martyr, however, reinforced notions about woman's traditional family role as supporter of the husband, without personal ambition or drive to make a lasting mark on the world. Such a view conflicted also with the feminist notion that women have a right to look after their own interests and promoted the idea of female self-subordination which feeds into the exploitation of women in and out of the home. Indeed, the notion that women had a right to be treated as individuals or to compete equally for positions of power ran counter to the major goal of war propaganda, which was to discourage individualistic, self-interested attitudes in order to produce a collective spirit of self-sacrifice on the home front. War work became a vehicle for women to shoulder their civic and moral responsibilities as good citizens rather than a way to become more independent and powerful.

Another dimension of the propaganda campaign to inspire civilian efforts which conflicted with the progressive notion that women could handle any man's job was the use of women as symbols of the besieged nation. To dramatize a conflict taking place on foreign soil, propagandists found in women the

personification of vulnerability they were looking for to concret-
ize and make real the message that civilians must help soldiers
protect American interests. Most often, this portrayal centered
upon a wife, fearfully trying to protect her family amid the ter-
rors of war. Though she was courageous and determined, it was
clear that she was ill equipped to defend herself and needed to
rely on masculine strength for her survival. The central role of
the family in wartime propaganda, with the vulnerable homemaker as its figurehead, led easily into the idealization of the
male breadwinner/female hearthkeeper at the end of the war.

Finally, women played the important role of preservers of
peacetime virtues and family life, which came to be equated
with security, stability, and prosperity. In addition to their courage and strength, they emerged as caretakers of national ideals
and normalcy, a role that echoed women's traditional function
as spiritual guides for the family. Having dramatized threats to
their well-being in order to inspire service to their country,
propagandists provided civilians with a vision of coming peace
and reassured them that a violent, brutal world had not destroyed human decency. Women, then children, came to stand
for those cherished qualities that had been snuffed out by car-
nage and danger: innocence, gentleness, idealism, continuity,
and safety. They were charged with preserving this vision for
soldiers caught up in the daily struggle to survive and with
mending the social fabric when peace was won. The role allocated to women in wartime propaganda, then, was a complicated mixture of strength and dependence, competence and
vulnerability, egalitarianism and conservatism.

These themes were all represented in both middle-class and
working-class magazines, although to varying degrees. One of
the more significant differences between the two groups is that
working-class women's fiction presented a weaker egalitarian
portrait of war workers than did middle-class stories. The former primarily featured characters in unskilled factory work or
female fields while middle-class heroines took up welding,
riveting, truck driving, and the like. Moreover, working-class
war workers were in subordinate positions to men whereas
their middle-class counterparts frequently wielded power over
male workers, at times taking charge of whole businesses. In
short, the feminist implications of war work were more likely

to be reflected in middle-class stories whereas in working-class literature heroines tended to identify proudly with the accomplishments of the working class as a whole rather than with their achievements as women.

There are a host of cultural factors that could have been responsible for this difference. In addition to these, story formulas with appeal for the two audiences and differing recruitment strategies led to an emphasis on different aspects of the government's campaign. This meant that in working-class periodicals there was a class rather than a gender emphasis in portrayals of war workers. Paradoxically, the wartime employment of women led to a more radical redefinition of female roles for an audience most likely to have remained in the home, but the real Rosie the Riveter found little affirmation of her ability to do a man's work in magazines aimed at her, nor did she see much indication that the war was a historic opportunity for escaping the female job ghetto. For us to view the war period, then, as a time when women were encouraged to believe they were capable of performing men's work is to ignore the fact that recruitment propaganda was significantly less egalitarian in working-class literature for women. We cannot therefore speak of a single wartime model of women workers in the media.

Although the major focus of this research is to clarify our understanding of a crucial moment in history when ideas about women underwent radical change, it also explores some important dimensions of popular culture—what functions it serves, what characteristics it has, what relationship it enjoys to the social realities from which it springs. One of these is that the use of formula fiction and advertising as propaganda highlights the extraordinary complexity and flexibility of media designed to have mass appeal. Advertisers tried to sell an image of war workers compatible with government programs, corporate marketing strategies, and women's interests even though some of these goals conflicted. Formula fiction writers wove a wide range of propaganda goals into their stories without losing a sense of what their audience wanted to hear. Their treatment of war workers, in particular, furnishes a striking example of how popular artists skillfully meshed contradictory currents in American life, sometimes creating images destructive to their audience's interests yet providing fantasies that carried great appeal. In addition, writers during World War II were able to incorporate didactic messages into sophisticated adult formulas without sacrificing their credibility or entertainment value. The campaign to mobilize women through popular fiction and advertising provides a model of how artists can attempt subtly to shape cultural attitudes, to effect a kind of social engineering through using frameworks with proven appeal. Whether this attempt indeed produced the desired results is impossible to prove, although some researchers have concluded that the implicit, value-laden messages of popular culture are especially effective because they are not consciously analyzed.[17] What is important is that media people and government officials *believed* their efforts would produce behavior that would help the wartime economy run smoothly and demonstrated that the media can be effectively coordinated to perform a wide array of functions.

Any study of propaganda raises questions about the impact of media messages on their audience. This is an issue of such complexity that the field has been clouded by a fog of controversy concerning the relationship of popular culture to attitude formation and behavior. In the early stages of research into the significance and effect of mass communication, people tended to see a cause-and-effect relationship between mass media and the consumer: media shaped the audience's attitudes through presenting values in attractive packages. Wilbur Schramm has characterized this approach as the "Bullet Theory," wherein media messages were seen as a "magic bullet" transmitting ideas rather automatically from sender to receiver: "the audience was typically thought of as a sitting target; if a communicator could hit it, he [or she] would affect it. This became especially frightening because of the reach of the new mass media. The unsophisticated viewpoint was that if a person could be reached by the insidious forces of propaganda . . . he [or she] could be changed and converted and controlled."[18] Schramm goes on to say that researchers gradually adopted a more complex model that characterized the audience as an active selective one, "a full partner in the communication process." Seen from this perspective, the power of the mass media or propaganda to persuade is limited by the already existing attitudes, values, experiences, and needs of the consumer, who tends to accept views from the media in agreement with his or her own: "the groups people [belong] to [lead] them to choose and react to messages in such a way as to defend the common norms of the groups they value."[19]

Most analysts of wartime popular culture agree with this perspective and caution against the temptation to attribute more power to the media than was the case. Leila Rupp, for example, rejects the view that women were manipulated into and out of the labor force by propagandists, stating that the most important factor in women taking a job was financial incentive.[20] Similarly, Susan Hartmann notes that although postwar media were largely controlled by men women voluntarily consumed their products. She therefore concludes that a responsive chord had been struck, one that spoke to women's problems in adjusting to peacetime: "The female imagery in the popular culture surely spoke to women's own ambivalence about their changing situation, an ambivalence produced not just by the novelty of their experiences, but by the failure of social and economic institutions to change in ways that would ease women's accommodation to different roles."[21]

Popular culture must, to some extent, reflect the assumptions, fantasies, and values of consumers in order to be commercially successful. As John Cawelti says of popular story types: "I think we can assume that formulas become collective cultural products because they successfully articulate a pattern of fantasy that is at least acceptable to if not preferred by the cultural groups who enjoy them. . . . When a group's attitudes undergo some change, new formulas arise and existing formulas develop new themes and symbols, because formula stories are created and distributed almost entirely in terms of commercial exploitation. Therefore, allowing for a certain degree of inertia in the process, the production of formulas is largely dependent on audience response."[22] Though we can attribute some of the traditional themes found in women's magazines to that portion of the audience which failed to enter the labor force, many of their consumers were wage earners, especially those of the confessions. We must assume, then, that some of the elements we find in wartime confession stories reflected the desires and feelings of many employed women, though they mirrored only some aspects of their experience while ignoring others.

Cawelti also points out that the degree to which popular literature can be said to reflect the world views of its readers is limited by the fact that literary experience is qualitatively different from how one responds to real life: "our experience of literature is not like any other form of behavior since it concerns events and characters that are imagined. Reading about something is obviously not the same thing as doing it."[23] That the readers of confessions, for instance, fantasized about male rescuers and found little affirmation of their ability to do a man's work does not mean that working-class women in the labor force failed to believe they had a right to and would benefit from high-paying blue-collar jobs in manufacturing. We know, for example, that many women employed in defense plants wanted to keep their war jobs, including 50 percent of those who had previously been homemakers, and that they resisted being channeled back into service and trade work.[24] Clearly, economic imperatives and the fulfillment of doing skilled work exerted a greater influence on women who had advanced during the war than did propaganda or private fantasies.

To recognize that wartime propaganda was not a purely top-down phenomenon that manipulated a gullible audience into betraying its own interests, however, does not mean that it had no damaging effects on employed women. Though war workers were not convinced that their role was to come into defense plants only to support the country, the fact that the media conveyed this message almost certainly persuaded the public as a whole that this was the case since many would have had no personal experience that countered the prevailing image. Although it is impossible to measure the effects of propaganda that reinforced myths about working women, the lack of a more congenial ideological framework undoubtedly made it more difficult for workers to mount an effective defense of their rights.

Finally, we ought not to minimize the power of images to frame the parameters of what people consider appropriate goals and behavior for themselves. Susan Griffin touches on the significance cultural images have for our self-conceptions in her analysis of the pornographic mind:

Human behavior is not universal . . . precisely because different cultures give us different forms through which to live our lives. Through culture, we learn what modes of behavior are acceptable expressions of our internal existences. . . . One might say that we can choose to reject cultural forms of behavior, and we can. But we have reason to accept these forms. When we speak or act through these forms we are understood. We are taken into the circle of humanity. . . . Images work a powerful effect on the mind. If we question in our hearts who we are, our minds throw up to our vision an image of ourselves. We seek a picture, a word, a name. We feel we do not know our own feelings unless they are named. And we inherit through culture the very names we give to feelings.[25]

The power of the media to reinforce is not a negligible one. Certainly, there is a large number of audience values that can be reflected and encouraged, many constellations in a group's ideological universe that can be made to sparkle while others are left in darkness. During World War II, economic, social, and political forces combined to produce a need for new images of women, those that showed wage work as a normal, vital part of female lives and that conveyed the message that women could and should occupy all types of jobs. The opportunity thus arose for women to be provided with "a picture, a word, a name" for conceptualizing themselves as nontraditional workers. Middle-class periodicals partially did that, although the message was undermined by others, while working-class magazines failed fully to encourage readers to enter a realm from which they had been actively barred. We cannot measure the impact such qualified permission had on any woman's life plans, yet certainly its progressive aspects helped protect those who entered man's sphere from self-doubt or the censure of friends, relatives, or male workers. That it was ultimately withdrawn entirely was a loss, not only to working women at the time but to the generation that followed and grew up without the social supports for training themselves to be other than secretaries, nurses, waitresses, or housewives.

This is a case study of the propaganda operation during World War II. It describes the impact of propaganda goals on images of women in magazine fiction and advertising in two mass circulation magazines: the *Saturday Evening Post* and *True Story*. There are sound reasons for focusing on these particular sources despite the inherent limitations involved in a case study, one of which is that any discussion of popular culture forces the researcher to select material for analysis. While I could have sampled a small amount of all media, I limited myself to one— magazines—because I wished to conduct an in-depth investigation of thematic directions as they developed in response to the war. By concentrating on one industry, I was able to familiarize myself with the complex machinery of the propaganda operation while at the same time noting the responses of editors, publishers, writers, and advertisers to see how they interpreted government requests for their audience. It is possible, indeed likely, that the participation of the magazine industry differed from that of other media, even though similar propaganda organizations were established for film, radio, and newspapers.[26] I did not feel, however, that this interfered with the major purpose of the study, which was to examine the interface between home-front propaganda and images of women during the war years, not to do a comprehensive analysis of popular culture. In addition, during the 1940s, magazines were one of the major forms of mass entertainment, and they enjoyed circulation figures high enough to make them important carriers of cultural values.[27]

Having decided on magazines as at least partly representative of portrayals of women, I elected to use a case-study approach rather than to attempt a broader-based but more superficial sampling of many magazines. An obvious disadvantage of this research strategy is that the publications in question may be so idiosyncratic as to be unrepresentative of the points one wishes to illustrate or of the group from which they are drawn. It may be, for instance, that the *Post* and *True Story* differed radically from other mass-circulation magazines in their treatment of war work. Partially offsetting this danger are two factors. The first is that both magazines were leaders of their fields during the war years. The *Post* was the best seller in the group of so-called family slicks while *True Story* was the big leader for the confessions.[28] Their leadership position makes plausible the possibility that other magazines imitated many of their features in order to insure mass appeal and makes unlikely their having been wildly out of line with what others in their areas were doing.

Second, all magazines were made aware of government propaganda needs, and there is evidence that the readiness of the *Post* and *True Story* to support home-front campaigns was shared by most periodicals of the day.[29] In addition, writers and advertisers were organized into propaganda groups independently of the magazines in which they were published and worked enthusiastically with the government to produce images of women that they felt were appropriate for wartime.[30] While the *Post* and *True Story* may have published writers others did not, it is reasonable to assume that the existence of a centralized propaganda bureaucracy fostered image consistency among other periodicals. Although every magazine has unique characteristics, I did not feel that normal variation would make unrepresentative the propaganda themes I found in these industry leaders.

Because I wished to see if class considerations had an impact on recruitment propaganda, I selected magazines that had clearly different socioeconomic markets but yet were widely read by women. Though it had begun as a man's magazine, by the 1920s the scope of the *Saturday Evening Post* had been broadened to include women and, like all periodicals aimed at a mixed audience, selection of its fiction was heavily weighted toward the tastes of female readers, who had been found to be the main consumers of magazine stories.[31] The *Post* was aimed at a wide group but one that the editors conceptualized as middle-class in outlook. Long before the war, its editorial direction had been defined by George Horace Lorimer, who envisioned his readers as successful, enterprising achievers able through hard work and ingenuity to move up the socioeconomic ladder.[32]

True Story, on the other hand, geared itself to the experiences of a working-class female audience, one whose concerns were largely ignored by other magazine publishers.[33] In contrast to the *Post*, which featured stories celebrating the virtues of middle-class life, *True Story* concentrated on the problems that hampered its readers from achieving the American dream. As the leading confession magazine of the twentieth century, it is an excellent representative of a formula designed to appeal specifically to working-class women. Both publications have been so marked by their class orientation that researchers have contrasted them to identify class differences in reading tastes.[34] While it would be difficult, perhaps impossible, to demonstrate that all readers of the *Post* came from the middle class and all purchasers of confessions like *True Story* were of the working class, their clear editorial directions allowed me to draw conclusions about class-differentiated portrayals of women during the war.

One other feature of these particular magazines made them attractive models of analysis: they both were heavily laden with formula fiction. I felt that fiction would provide me with a detailed picture of changing ideas about women, one that might differ in tone and complexity from the articles or editorials other analysts have studied. Formula fiction is a rich source of information about its readers' most deeply held values, wishes, and fears, for it expresses their innermost dreams in a satisfying way. It is for that reason a good indicator of widely shared cultural assumptions, myths, and symbols. As John Cawelti says: "By confirming existing definitions of the world, literary formulas help to maintain a culture's ongoing consensus about the nature of reality and morality. We assume, therefore, that one aspect of the structure of a formula is . . . confirming some strongly held conventional view."[35] Patricke Johns-Heine and Hans Gerth state this point another way: "Since the reader identifies . . . with a particular hero model, the fictional hero, together with his [or her] status, qualities, and achievements, becomes an important vehicle of social values. Heroes and heroines become the carriers of specific American traditions."[36] In addition, using fiction as a vehicle for propaganda is a potentially powerful technique because the reader is not examining the story in a conscious, rational way and may therefore be more receptive to the message.

I analyzed advertising as well because its visual impact is so powerful that I thought it warranted some attention. Readers who might fail to be reached by fiction would still absorb, even subconsciously, the messages of advertisements. In addition, advertising provides some of the same cultural information as does formula fiction because advertisers cannot afford to alienate potential consumers and so stay within conventional social frameworks. They also try to tie their products to pervasive dreams, which means that we can learn a good deal about common fantasies from studying the symbols they use. Because advertisers must seize the viewer's attention and communicate a detailed message in one picture with a few words, the images they use must of necessity evoke familiar myths with powerful emotional force. Though their impact is weakened by the viewer's skeptical regard for sales pitches, advertisements are nevertheless fairly accurate indicators of dominant attitudes and aspirations.[37]

Since advertisements are relatively easy to code, I elected to examine all of those in both magazines which concerned women. Selecting the relevant magazine fiction presented greater difficulties because it has not been indexed as are articles in the Reader's Guide to Periodical Literature, themes are not always obvious from the titles, and it is time-consuming to read. I therefore followed sampling procedures that are standard practice for content analysis.[38] The total number of stories I read from both magazines is well within the range of similar studies.[39] (For a discussion of the sample size and coding procedures for the fiction and advertising, see Appendix A.)

An intensive study of this sort cannot claim to be a comprehensive analysis of popular culture during the war years, but it has the advantage of thoroughly covering one important aspect of the propaganda campaign and revealing some of its subtler directions. Focusing on two magazines, moreover, allows for detection of trends that might otherwise go unnoticed because the researcher is well attuned to the story formulas and editorial policies under consideration.

Chapter 1 outlines the social and political context of the recruitment campaign and describes the propaganda groups that were most directly concerned with the magazine industry. The strategies used in the drive to mobilize women are discussed in some detail and are related to the major features of propaganda addressed to the population as a whole. In chapter 2 I focus on the Saturday Evening Post to investigate the response of writers, editors, and advertisers to government requests for assistance in the mobilization effort. I discuss the impact of propaganda organizations on story themes with proven appeal to a middle-class audience and identify the persuasive techniques used by advertisers to make war jobs, then homemaking, look attractive to women. Chapter 3 takes up the issue of propaganda directed at working-class women by focusing on the most successful magazine of the confessions group, *True Story*. Here I note the impact of class on the recruitment campaign and the limitations imposed by the confession formula on developing new images of women. Chapter 4 identifies the issues raised by contrasting images of war workers from magazines directed at middle-class and working-class women while attempting to explain the differences in treatment of the recruitment campaign. The Conclusion describes the dominant models of womanhood that emerged in these magazines during the war and explores their implications for widening or narrowing women's role in American life. It suggests that the war's failure to alter traditional ideas about female capacities was in part due to propaganda strategies for unifying the home front and to a top-down impetus for social change that left the new images vulnerable to swift annihilation.

1 Creation of the Myth

THE predominant media portrayal of women war workers was that they were young, white, and middle-class; furthermore, that they entered the labor force out of patriotic motives and eagerly left to start families and resume full-time homemaking. As historians have studied the war period, it has become clear that this image is almost completely false.[1] Contrary to popular belief, the women who entered war production were not primarily middle-class housewives but working-class wives, widows, divorcées, and students who needed the money to achieve a reasonable standard of living. Most of them had prewar experience in the labor force. A Women's Bureau survey of ten war production areas analyzed the work histories of employed women in 1944 and discovered that only 25 percent had less than two years' work experience. Almost half had been in the labor force at least five years and almost 30 percent at least ten.[2]

This report revealed, moreover, that only one third of women in war manufacturing plants described themselves as having been employed as housewives before entering war work. Many of these were home workers who had been in the labor force prior to Pearl Harbor but had withdrawn from the labor market due to the depressed state of the economy:

> When war conditions created the need for their work and an opportunity for employment, they again took their place among the working women. Despite the influx of many newcomers into the labor market during the war period, the group of wartime-employed women contained a markedly high proportion of women with extended work experience. Wartime employment for these women was not, therefore, a venture into something new but rather part of their continuing work experience.[3]

Further evidence that women in the wartime labor force were primarily working-class is that only 10 percent of women in war production centers had attended college, and fully 54 percent had not graduated from high school. In addition, half of the major production areas employed significant numbers of black women. In four of those, they comprised from less than 10 to 19 percent of the female work force and, in Baltimore, were one third of all women workers.[4] Moreover, war manufacturing industries drew roughly equal numbers of women from housework and other industry groups such as trade and domestic/personal service.[5] Undoubtedly, some of the women taking war jobs did so for patriotic reasons. However, given their extensive prewar work histories, it appears that war workers came primarily from the ranks of women who needed to earn a wage in peacetime as well, either to supplement family income or to support themselves.

The Impact of World War II on Female Employment Patterns

One of the primary negative effects the myth of the woman war worker has had is that it fails entirely to indicate the profound impact of the war on female job opportunities, nor does it convey the historic importance of women being hired for male jobs. From the earliest days of manufacturing, women have entered occupations that cannot attract male laborers because wages are too low, opportunities for advancement are insufficient, or working conditions are less attractive than other available work. The industries that have hired women generally operate on low profit margins and are nonunionized: service and trade (clerks, waitresses, laundry workers, telephone operators, domestics); and nondurable goods (apparel, textiles, food). Similarly, the professions that are dominated by women, nursing and public school teaching, have traditionally been at the low end of the salary scale for college graduates. In short, like minority and teenage workers, women are among the most exploited members of the work force.

That this has been a labor market that provides women with relatively poor work options is seen from the concentration of women in few occupational areas. In 1979, for instance, the vast majority of employed women fell into four job categories: clerical, service, professional/technical, and operative. Even with the recent implementation of affirmative action policies, only 9.9 percent of employed women were in traditionally male jobs while 68.5 percent were in female categories. It is largely due to this sexual segregation of the labor force that the median income for women workers is only 59.4 percent that of men's: "The most noticeable features of the American labor market are the industrial and occupational segregation of men and women. . . . In fact, this segregation is recognized as the single most important problem facing women in the labor force because it is intimately tied to women's lower earnings."[6] Partly because traditionally female employment has been in nonunionized, low-profit-margin, seasonal industries, women's wages are kept to a minimal level: "largely unorganized, practically unskilled, and victims of a tradition that places less value on women's work than on men's, women workers have been able to do little toward removing the unfair differentials that exist between women's and men's work."[7]

The primary advantage of the war to women workers was that it drained the labor force of male labor at a time when high industrial production was imperative. Indeed, the government later concluded that labor power was the most crucial factor in the success of the war production program.[8] Labor shortages were particularly acute in the skilled metal trades, aircraft, shipping, and small ammunition assembly—all fields that paid higher wages and offered more stimulating work than traditional female occupations. War industries fell into the high-wage, unionized, durable goods sector of the labor market, which had virtually excluded women workers prior to 1940. Due to the influx of women into aircraft, shipping, and ammunition manufacture, their numbers rose from only 8 percent of all durable goods production workers in 1939 to 25 percent in 1944.[9] Similarly, while only 15 percent of all women factory workers were in durable goods production in 1939, by 1943 fully 45.3 percent were engaged in such work.[10] By the end of 1943, women comprised 34.2 percent of all ammunition workers, 10.6 percent of those in steel production, 10 percent of all personnel in shipping, 8 percent of railroad workers, and 40 percent of people employed in the aircraft industry.[11] In addition, women went from 0.9 percent of all "craftsmen, foremen, and kindred workers" in 1940 to 1.5 percent in 1945, a small proportion of the total but a significant increase.[12]

Since wages in munitions plants and aircraft factories averaged 40 percent higher than those in female fields, the hiring of women in durable goods represented a significant step up the occupational ladder for women workers. In Detroit, a typical war production center, the average weekly take-home earnings of women in war industries were $40.35 whereas those of women in laundries, restaurants, hotels, retail and wholesale trade, and consumer goods industries ranged from $24.10 to $29.75.[13] As a result, massive shifts occurred in the labor force as women abandoned these fields to seek work in war production plants (see table 1). In the ten major war production areas, 50 percent of all women who had been in trade and personal service and 66 percent of those who had been employed in eating and drinking establishments shifted to war manufacture.[14] In the Puget Sound area, where many women found work in shipyards, the trade and service sector claimed 67 percent of all women workers before Pearl Harbor but only 42 percent by the end of the war.[15]

While the bulk of male and female workers remained in prewar sex-typed job categories, these figures indicate the great extent to which women were employed in the male sector of the labor market and benefited economically from the emergency. Women also entered male jobs in trade, service, and transportation, such as gas station attendants, truck drivers, and postal workers in addition to white-collar positions. A good example of the participation of women in nontraditional work is the Women's Air Service Pilots Association (WASP). Women who joined this paramilitary organization tested planes, towed targets for new recruits, ferried military equipment, and performed basic mechanical tasks on their airplanes. Though WASPs were discriminated against in many ways, their successful performance of a highly skilled, heavily male-identified role is representative of women's crossover into male spheres.[16]

The economic advantages to women of wartime hiring patterns, when viewed against a history of systematic exclusion from better-paying jobs, are one indication that the war meant more to women workers than an opportunity to defend the

Table 1   Women Changing Occupation Group,
          Pearl Harbor to March 1944

Occupation at time of Pearl Harbor	% of total employed women from occupation group who left between Pearl Harbor and March 1944 to enter another occupation group
Total, all occupations	14.7
Clerical workers	4.4
Proprietors, managers, officials	6.2
Professional and semiprofessional workers	6.6
Craftsmen, foremen, operatives, and laborers	8.6
Farmers, farm managers, farm laborers	24.2
Other service workers	29.3
Domestic service workers	29.5
Sales workers	32.9

Source: U.S. Department of Labor, Bureau of Labor Statistics, "Recent Occupational Trends," by Harold Wool and Lester Pearlman, Monthly Labor Review 65, (August 1947): 139–47.

country. Another is that surveys taken in 1944 revealed that 75 to 80 percent of women in war production areas planned to remain in the labor force after victory was won, and they wanted to keep the jobs they were then performing.[17] In late 1945 and early 1946, the Women's Bureau found evidence of worker dissatisfaction with being fired from war jobs and offered work in female fields. It described laid-off welders and riveters as "reluctant to return to household work [paid domestic work], and also to other services, and to the more unattractive and low-paid clerical and manufacturing jobs as well."[18] Another Women's Bureau study confirms the fact that many women were unwillingly channeled into prewar fields: "When jobs of the skill levels women have developed in war work are no longer available, the tendency is to refer them back to their earlier types of jobs, which many of them no longer desire."[19] The dominant image of the war worker's eager return to the home in the media belied the reality of women's resistance to losing their improved status in the work force as well as the fact that most needed to find alternative employment.

Despite some ineffectual protests from laid-off workers, women found themselves at the end of the war in nearly the same discriminatory situation they had faced prior to Pearl Harbor. While 45.3 percent of women production workers had been employed in higher-paying durable goods industries in November 1943, only 25 percent of these workers were in such jobs by November 1946.[20] (See figure 1.) There was a net drop of 0.5 million women in "craftsmen and foremen" positions after V-J Day, and the percentage of women in service work increased.[21] There is some evidence that the U.S. Employment Service referred white women to clerical jobs and low-paying unskilled work in manufacturing while channeling black women into domestic service and laundries.[22] While women previously employed in war manufacture were returning to the home, to school, and to female sectors of the labor force, large numbers of male wartime operatives moved up the occupational ladder into the rapidly expanding building trades or into skilled positions in manufacture of consumer goods. By April 1947 the prewar employment pattern had been reestablished and most employed women were clerical workers, operatives, domestics, and service workers.[23]

Government Attitudes toward Women Workers

Why did the historic opportunities for women to break out of the female job ghetto and their subsequent resistance to losing those opportunities fail to become part of the public story about war workers? How did the image of middle-class homemakers eager to do their bit for their country become established as the primary representation of this experience? In part, the image of war workers reflected incorrect assumptions about women workers at the highest levels of government and industry. Early plans to employ women reveal that federal policy makers, industry leaders, and war contractors assumed that the new hiring patterns necessitated by the labor shortage were temporary. They fully expected that new workers would be drawn from homes in which wives did not need to work and therefore would leave the labor market at the war's end. These assumptions provided a framework for the recruitment campaign that reinforced false beliefs about working women.

Early in 1942 several government and industry policy studies identified women as war labor reserves and discussed the util-

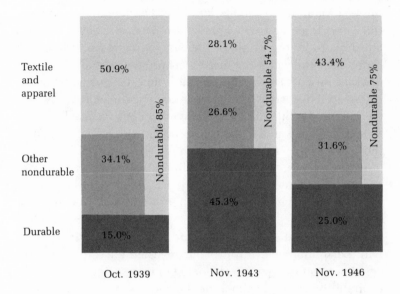

Figure 1   Distribution of women production workers in manufacturing industries. From U.S. Department of Labor, Bureau of Labor Statistics, "Postwar Labor Turn-Over among Women Factory Workers," by Clara Schloss and Ella Polinsky, *Monthly Labor Review 64* (March 1947): 411–19.

ity of having them available as a temporary source of workers. The Census Bureau, for example, made a detailed analysis for the War Manpower Commission (WMC) of potential entrants to the labor force and concluded that married women without children under ten would be the best source of workers for the duration of the war.[24] Another report produced by the War Production Board's Labor Division indicated that the government expected these women to leave as soon as the emergency was over: "There is little doubt that women will be required to leave their jobs at the end of the war to permit the return of men to their jobs as they are released from the armed forces."[25]

These reports, while they readily supported programs designed to facilitate the employment of women in jobs normally filled by men, evidence no concern for the fate of women workers once soldiers returned. In a study conducted by the National Industrial Conference Board, for example, interviews with personnel men in war plants revealed the following: "No consideration [was] given to the long-range social or economic desirability or implications of the increased employment of women."[26] Government and industry planners expressed concern over work conditions, equal wages, fair hours, and adequate living quarters for women workers, but it was clear that they saw women's role as temporary and gave precedence to male workers. A clear example of this priority system is a Labor Division policy statement which specified that defense training programs for women were not to be set up in industrial areas where great numbers of men were unemployed.[27] It was not until the middle of 1942, for instance, that women entered aircraft and shipfitting classes in Seattle because men were still entering those industries from the ranks of the unemployed.[28]

The early plans drawn up to deal with the labor shortage reflect long-standing myths about the role of wage labor in women's lives. The assumption has been that married women seek employment only to enable the family to buy "extras" and that single women work while waiting to get married, then drop out. Men, on the other hand, have been considered permanent workers, responsible for supporting a family. Policies that failed to consider the postwar employment opportunities for women war workers suggest that employers and government officials operated from a perspective that deemed wage labor as merely an adjunct to women's "real" role, which was full-time home-making. Recruiting married women into war production must have seemed to them an ideal solution to the problem of securing temporary workers. Another traditional assumption about women's work—the idea that woman's primary job is child rearing—is reflected in the reluctance of the WMC to recruit mothers of young children, even though it recognized that many of these women would be likely to enter the labor force. It made it official policy to employ young mothers as a last resort, and child care facilities were kept to a minimum throughout the war.[29]

The major advocate of working women's rights was the Women's Bureau, headed by Mary Anderson. It lobbied for enforcement of equal-pay regulations, upgrading of wages in consumer goods industries and other female-dominated fields, provision of adequate household services, and institution of gender-blind job classifications.[30] The Women's Advisory Committee to the WMC also pressed for a more progressive perspective, one which recognized that women most often entered the labor force out of economic necessity and that their interests deserved some protection. It went so far as to warn the WMC in 1944 that the initial expectations of war workers rested on incorrect assumptions about women who sought paying jobs: "Government and industry must not assume that all women can be treated as a reserve group during war only, nor should those who wish to stay in the labor market be accused of taking men's jobs. . . . any easy assumption that a great number of women will return to their homes is to be seriously questioned."[31] Neither the Women's Bureau nor the Women's Advisory Committee had enough power to implement such recommendations, however, and their attempts to alter the short-term orientation of government planners were futile.[32]

Even had they been able to exert more influence on the WMC, the efforts of women's groups in 1944 came too late to affect the image of war workers in the recruitment campaign, which had gotten fully under way by March of 1943. By the time surveys showed that most women in war plants planned to remain in the labor force beyond victory and desired comparable jobs, the early assumption that new workers would be drawn from the ranks of women whose career was homemaking had already been established as the dominant perspective in recruitment propaganda. In addition, the short-term orientation of war agencies to secure victory operated against viewing war workers as anything but emergency stand-ins.

The Office of War Information and the Magazine Industry

The image of women and war workers that developed during the war years was shaped also by propaganda campaigns on the home front, which were framed by the inaccurate belief that housewives without work experience would make up the bulk of new workers and naturally leave their jobs once things returned to normal. This belief dovetailed with other plans to foster home-front productivity to produce a misleading portrait of women who entered high-paying fields and to limit the impact of women's new roles on traditional conceptions about woman's place. Ties between propaganda groups and the media were extensive, and the popular portrayal of women's role in the war was greatly influenced by the joint efforts of government agencies and media personnel to see that the economy functioned as smoothly as possible.

There are two major reasons for the government's decision to engage in a massive propaganda effort. The first of these is that the powers of the government to influence or direct the economy were very limited. Although the New Deal had initiated many reforms such as the Social Security program, unemployment insurance, and the right to collective bargaining, for the most part the private sector governed itself. The role of Washington was to coordinate corporate activities in such a way as to prevent or at least contain the damage done by catastrophes such as the Depression.

In its role as overseer, the government could make suggestions to industry on how it should handle the labor shortage, but it had no way to enforce policies, a situation described by Eleanor Straub in her detailed account of labor policy during the war years. She relates, for example, the frustrations encountered by the War Manpower Commission and the War Department when they urged defense industries to hire women and minorities. Employers resisted their instructions to hire such workers in aircraft, shipping, steel, and other essential industries strapped for labor power. As late as the end of 1942, employers insisted that women were unsuitable for over half their labor needs. Despite continual pressure from the government, employers refused to remove prewar barriers against the employment of women until the last possible moment: "prejudices against women, blacks, aliens, and Jews in the labor force were often frequently deep-seated and employer specifications were often not modified until in-migration had strained community facilities to the breaking point."[33] Straub concludes that in order to have administered an effective labor program, the government would have had to take unprecedented measures to control industry, measures that would have interfered with the prerogatives of business to hire whom it pleased.

These steps, she asserts, the government was unwilling to take and, as a result, the program to get women into war production was not adequate to the task. Though the government could apply pressure on defense employers and the private sector as a whole through field offices and directives, it operated without powers to enforce WMC regulations. The best course open to it was publicity—contacting the public, enlisting its support in the labor drives, and trying to change the attitudes that had interfered with hiring women. Such an approach enabled the WMC and the War Department to bypass the cumbersome and ineffectual procedures to bring employers into line.

The second reason for relying primarily on propaganda to meet labor requirements was that the government hoped it could exert some influence on labor market patterns by providing an ideological framework compatible with wartime conditions. Through psychological manipulation and emotional appeals, propaganda could perhaps accomplish what enrollment and registration drives were failing to do: make more orderly the relationship between labor supply and demand. In addition, if production quotas were to be met, public resentment against dislocations dissipated, and the way paved for resumption of business as usual at the war's end, information to the media would have to be coordinated in such a way, so felt the government, that confusion would be kept to a minimum. It was thought that propaganda could help the government control public responses, not only to the labor shortage but to unsettling wartime phenomena as well—rationing, forced separations, housing shortages, strained community services, and overcrowded transportation facilities.

Despite the temptations to employ propaganda, however, there was initial government resistance to the idea. Allan Winkler argues that there were several reasons for this.[34] One is that propaganda was equated with falsehood and illegitimate manipulation, in part because the Creel committee of World War I was perceived to have distorted the truth about that conflict and to have whipped up war hysteria.[35] Perhaps the most telling source of resistance, according to Winkler, came from New Dealers who were reluctant to share their power with people they believed to be media hucksters and con men. Washington's power elite was in no way opposed to private enterprise, but it was uncomfortable with certain aspects of it, such as high-pressure sales pitches.

Resistance to waging a propaganda campaign weakened under the pressure of advertisers, business leaders, and media representatives for direction. In addition, it became increasingly clear to the administration that fiscal, economic, and labor policy needed an ideological framework. Prior to Pearl Harbor, for instance, there had been significant isolationist sentiment on the part of the public. Although after the Japanese attacked these feelings largely disappeared, there was still confusion over the purposes of the war, the reasons for rationing, and the seriousness of labor shortages in certain areas of the country. Communication between federal agencies and the media was unclear enough that some advertisers featured products whose sale would work against the production of war goods while others encouraged the public to hoard rationed material.[36]

The pressure became overwhelming to bring the communication system into closer alignment with the country's needs and to mobilize the population. As a result, the Office of War Information (OWI) was established in the summer of 1942. Roosevelt attempted to sidestep the controversy over using the media for propaganda purposes by asserting that OWI would merely disseminate information about government programs in a neutral way. To underline his objectives, he appointed as head of the operation Elmer Davis, a respected news reporter who was opposed to government control of the press: "This is a people's war, and to win it the people should know as much about it as they can. This Office will do its best to tell the truth and nothing but the truth."[37] This elaborate bureaucracy coordinated government policy with information sent to the media until victory was finally declared in the fall of 1945. Several bureaus were set up that were responsible for dealing with various media industries. Bureau chiefs kept track of war agency requirements through regular contact with government information officers and through an interdepartmental liaison staff which served as contact with war agencies for clarification of major policies. They sent detailed publications to, carried on extensive correspondence with, and visited representatives from the radio, print, and film industries.[38]

The War Advertising Council

Roosevelt's initial intention to downplay the propaganda function of OWI became its official image. However, the strong links with industries skilled in appealing to public tastes resulted in the transformation of government "information" into high-powered propaganda designed to produce appropriate attitudes and behavior in the population. Nowhere is this better illustrated than in the role played by advertisers in home-front campaigns. Prior to the establishment of OWI, leaders of the advertising industry approached government officials, through a "defense committee" set up in the spring of 1940, concerning the use of advertising in support of the Allies. They met with little success and, in response to the lack of federal support, formed the War Advertising Council (WAC) in November 1941. Its purpose was to enlist advertisers, companies, and the government in a drive to get the issues of the war before the public. James Webb Young of one of the leading agencies, Young and Rubicam, proudly boasted at that founding meeting of the vast powers held by the advertising industry: "We have within our hands the greatest aggregate means of mass education and persuasion the world has ever seen."[39]

Advertising had everything to gain by making this move. The most pressing problem before them was replacing accounts from consumer goods manufacturers who converted to war production. By June 1942, 29 percent of prewar production of consumer goods had been cut off due to conversion of manufacturing plants and to materials shortages.[40] Without products to sell, advertisers were faced with a projected loss of 80 percent of their business over the course of the war. To survive, they undertook a sales campaign that featured advertising as an essential feature of successful prosecution of the war. If advertisers could convince the government that their services would boost public morale, they would have something to sell at a time when consumer sales were down.

In his study of the War Advertising Council, Frank Fox explains the way interests of the advertising industry meshed with those of business in such a venture. Because companies were constrained from selling goods, they needed a way to keep their names before the public eye. It is Fox's contention that business also saw an opportunity in the emergency to strengthen the ideological supports of private enterprise through propaganda. He argues that the Depression had pushed many workers into open rebellion against capitalists' control of production and had resulted in a negative image of big business. Because the economy failed to provide adequately for people's needs, the massive hardships of the 1930s provoked a crisis of confidence in capitalism. Propaganda could speak to both of these problems by associating company names with patriotism and victory. Fox concludes that advertisers quickly grasped the key role they could play for corporate enterprises in improving their public image: "By the eve of Pearl Harbor, . . . advertising, the voice of free enterprise, [bore] the burden . . . of preserving the public's tolerance of, confidence in, and enthusiasm for the American institution of capitalism."[41]

Whether or not this was a primary goal, advertisers participated extensively in government campaigns. The recruitment of women into war production was one of its major projects, directed by OWI's Bureau of Campaigns. When Gardner Cowles was made director of OWI's domestic branch, he appointed a former marketing head from NBC and advertising director for Colgate-Palmolive, Ken Dyke, as chief of the bureau, and he became the WAC's principal contact with the government. Federal agencies funneled their publicity needs through his office to the council, which made suggestions for a campaign guidebook and contacted an advertising agency for copy and layout. It also found a sponsor for the ad or campaign and an agency to place the ads in appropriate publications.[42]

The council appointed a full-time consultant to the bureau, sent representatives to its bimonthly meetings with Cowles, and maintained regular contact with the War Manpower Commission through Raymond Rubicam of Young and Rubicam, who assisted Paul McNutt, a member of the WMC, with labor recruitment.[43] In addition to these direct links between the WAC and OWI, the Bureau of Campaigns attempted to coordinate government policy with magazine advertising through a monthly *War Guide for Advertisers*, which identified campaign dates, objectives, and promotional methods while providing samples of ad layouts. It is clear from the influx of businessmen and media personnel into Washington and the extensive communication network set up between OWI and advertisers that cooperation between government agencies, propaganda organizations, and private industry was close. The ties extended to Treasury Department rulings, which allowed war contractors to deduct publicity expenses from taxable income.[44] This key provision meant that businesses engaged in government contracts could run propaganda ads that were partially underwritten by the government.

Far from adhering to a neutral line, advertisers conceived their task as applying persuasive techniques developed for selling goods to promoting ideas that would support government aims. They argued persistently for the government to use what they considered their vast resources for influencing public opinion and behavior. The chair of the WAC, Chester La Roche, for instance, urged greater governmental control over media resources in this memo to Gardner Cowles:

For waging psychological warfare, our informational weapons have not been as highly developed as the fighting machines of the armed forces; . . . we, in the information field, are rapidly falling behind the Army. There cannot be total war effort unless the informational weapons at hand are properly used; . . . we have the brains, the experience, the coast-to-coast polling machines; we know the people, know how to make them read; know how to plan huge informa-

tional efforts; . . . and know how to coordinate every form
of media.

He saw the government's reluctance to utilize the media's power
as a serious misunderstanding of its role in wartime: "Our
channels of communication to the American people are the
most efficient in the world. Not to fully understand them, their
capabilities, is dangerous; not to use them to the fullest is to
hamper the war effort, the equivalent of a military error." La
Roche ended this lengthy plea with the suggestion that OWI re-
organize itself into a structure parallel to that of the army.[45]

What La Roche had in mind for "psychological warfare" was
to threaten the public with loss of political freedoms or worse if
it did not cooperate with government requests, an approach
that was to exert a reactionary influence on the image of women.
In this way he hoped to "create a background for the specific
directives of the government" that would "clear up misunder-
standings, overcome irritations, disarm unreasonable criticism,
and thus condition the public not only to make required sacrifices willingly but to make more than are actually asked."[46] La
Roche was convinced that if the government failed to use such
manipulative methods, most people would not cooperate. It is
not clear from the historical record whether Cowles officially
authorized the strategy La Roche so painstakingly outlined, but
advertisers and the Bureau of Campaigns adopted his plan to
infuse these emotional patriotic appeals into advertising that
concerned rationing, salvage, victory gardens, victory mail, absenteeism, and labor recruitment.

The War Advertising Council created ads encouraging women
to enter the labor force and the armed services throughout the
war, but the most extensive cooperation between OWI and the
council concerning female labor recruitment occurred in early
1944 when the national "Women in the War" program was
planned. This campaign, intended to last throughout the year,
aimed to recruit women into civilian work and military service.
The WAC asked advertisers to devote at least a portion of their
ads to the theme of women war workers and advised them on
appropriate appeals through booklets sent out in the winter of
that year. In addition to these guidebooks with their thematic

direction, the council provided the government with advertising agencies.[47]

This campaign is a good example of cooperation among the WAC, OWI, and government war agencies throughout the period. In November 1943 the Joint Army-Navy Personnel Board issued a directive requesting that OWI use all its facilities to recruit women into the armed forces. It noted that women were reluctant to join the newly formed women's services and urged that the media be used to change public attitudes about female enlistment.[48] The Bureau of Campaigns responded by contacting the News, Motion Picture, Graphics, Magazine, and Radio bureaus so that material could be adapted for different audiences. The News Bureau worked up special stories for the rural press, labor news, foreign language and black newspapers, women's pages, and business house organs while distributing human interest pieces to press syndicates. Films from federal agencies were given to distributors for dispersal to churches, schools, war plants, and citizen groups. In addition, theaters agreed to show Hollywood films made in support of the campaign. The army produced recruitment posters, which were delivered twice a month to stores by the Boy Scout Dispatch Bearer Service and mailed to all post offices and cooperating businesses. Public transportation supported the campaign through displaying car cards in vehicles, which were paid for by the War Manpower Commission, and the Outdoor Advertising Association provided posters to every community with a population of over twenty-five thousand. Under the National Spot and Regional Allocation Plan, radio stations agreed to transmit campaign messages on seventy-five programs a week for two months, and each station agreed to carry three announcements a day.[49] The WAC made a major effort to support this campaign, preparing ad guides for the Women's Army Corps, the navy, and the War Manpower Commission.

Ad agencies were highly dependent on war industries because their livelihood normally flowed from successfully promoting company products in peacetime. They took an especially strong interest in disseminating propaganda in order to survive until those products would once again be on the market. The council's unabashed enthusiasm for manipulating public emotions to foster compliant behavior grew out of this self-interest.

The Magazine Bureau

The propaganda strategies of the advertising industry were more blatant than those of the magazine industry, although the participation of writers, publishers, and editors in OWI campaigns was just as complete. As with advertisers, publishers and editors pressured government officials to organize the media after Pearl Harbor and requested that Washington give them accurate information about the war front while telling them what needed to be done at home. In the spring of 1942, a representative was sent to New York from the Office of Facts and Figures, predecessor to the Office of War Information, in order to get some idea of how magazine editors felt about the proposed establishment of a magazine division. She found that they all favored the plan and believed it "long overdue." Because most could not afford to send correspondents to Washington, they suggested that someone frequently meet with them in New York and that they be sent "a regular memo as to themes the government wants stressed."[50]

As a result of the spring meetings with editors, the Magazine Bureau was established with the reorganization of government information offices in June 1942. Bureau officials quickly grasped the utility of creating efficient lines of communication with the magazine industry, pressing for greater funds and authority to disseminate information for the purposes of influencing the public. The chief of the Magazine Bureau was Dorothy Ducas, a journalist and personal friend of Eleanor Roosevelt. She had discovered in her visits to editors that stories concerning war news were frequently held up by lack of government information while inadequate and sometimes conflicting directives from Washington were interfering with their aid to government programs. Concerned that they would give up trying to cooperate altogether, she asked Gardner Cowles to give her more power throughout the summer of 1942 and insisted that magazines were well suited for influencing large numbers of people.[51]

Ducas and her staff carried on a voluminous correspondence

with government officials while answering an average of six hundred letters a month from editors and writers requesting background material for stories. They took an active role in ascertaining the publicity needs of war agencies, information about which was then sent out as suggestions for specific stories to individual writers. To illustrate campaign goals and strategies, they sent photographs, pamphlets, posters, and guidebooks to editors. Ducas tried to further minimize public misunderstanding of government programs by arranging meetings between editors and heads of agencies. So that she could get accurate information out to writers, Ducas attended all such meetings and met regularly with the War Department, the Navy Department, and the War Manpower Commission.

Because so few publications had stationed correspondents in Washington, Ducas made frequent visits to their New York offices both to insure that stories were not working against policy goals and to suggest taking up subjects that were useful to the government. A typical visit occurred in March 1943 when she contacted editors of Fawcett Publications, *This Week* Home Institute, the Russian War Relief Committee, *McCall's*, *Click*, Dell Publishers, and *Ladies' Home Journal*. She arranged a meeting between a writer for the *Journal* and a member of the Russian War Relief Committee; smoothed the feathers of a pulp editor who was denied clearance for a story he saw in another magazine; obtained information for the WMC on a story it considered damaging to labor recruitment; met with a writer concerning an article on "combatting race hatred" while suggesting to *Click* that it publish the story; and encouraged the planned publication of an article on teenage war workers.[52] Later, these contacts were systematized by assigning staff members to specific magazine groups so that the special needs of each market could be incorporated into propaganda appeals.

The major activity of the bureau was publication of the bimonthly *Magazine War Guide*, which was the main avenue of communication between OWI and the magazine industry. It began publication in July 1942 and ran until April 1945. Published and circulated three months in advance of the desired publication date of stories, the *Guide* gave editors time to contact writers who would put together an appropriate piece. This wartime agenda was widely circulated, reaching four hundred to six hundred magazines with a combined readership of over 140 million people. By the end of 1943, the *Guide* was being sent to more than nine hundred people on magazine staffs and four hundred government information officers. One thousand copies were distributed to free-lance writers.[53]

According to OWI files, magazines were major supporters of the "womanpower" campaign, perhaps because their audience was primarily female. Their extensive involvement was early indicated in the summer of 1942, when editors asked Ducas for information about the employment of women; she in turn urged Elmer Davis to develop a coordinated policy on the subject— how many women were needed for what kinds of jobs and where they could go for training. She also mentioned that magazines were taking the lead in mobilizing women through anticipating the need for day care centers: "Magazine editors have been convinced that nurseries are necessary before the full womanpower of the country can be tapped." They had complained that there was no central source to consult for a list of centers and for procedures to get them established in war production areas.[54]

The bureau reacted quickly to these requests, taking credit for a number of stories on womanpower and labor needs that appeared in national magazines in the fall of 1942. In addition to providing information through pamphlets on how to get women into the work force, many of Ducas's activities in New York concerned this subject. She encouraged several magazines to print stories on nursing, for example, because the bureau made nurse recruitment one of its major efforts. She provided *Harper's Bazaar* and all the Sunday supplements with a picture spread and suggested stories to *Cosmopolitan* and *Life*. Similarly, to recruit clerical workers, Ducas agreed to help *Woman's Day* with a story on housing for government workers, congratulated *Redbook* for serializing a novel in support of the campaign, and provided a suggestion to Fawcett Publications that a story be written about a worker who "sacrificed for her country and was rewarded." She also discussed pieces with *Mademoiselle* that glorified working in Washington and finally succeeded in placing material on the subject in several magazines.[55]

These reports indicate that the recruitment campaign was of prime concern to the bureau and to magazines; they worked closely together in developing stories that would encourage placement of women in jobs where they were needed. Ducas took an active role in making suggestions to magazines with certain audiences for stories suited to those markets, in answering requests from editors and writers for background information, and in seeing that magazines were moving in the right direction. A New York liaison office, set up in August 1943, provided editors with freer access to government information although the visits from bureau officials to writers and magazine editors continued until it folded in August 1945.

The Magazine Bureau played key roles in two major efforts to get women into the work force, an awareness of which helps us determine to what extent magazines cooperated with OWI. I have already described one of these—the "Women in the War" campaign, which occurred in the spring of 1944. This propaganda blitz was aimed at recruiting women into the military, getting more workers into labor-short local economies, and keeping women already working on the job. While the peak of war production had passed, the WMC wanted to retain a large supply of female workers to ease the transition from war to peace. It informed OWI that if women filled civilian production jobs that opened up as the war drew to a close, men would not be as likely to leave their war jobs to seek more permanent work in consumer goods industries; women would be easier to displace when veterans returned.[56] Though the Bureau of Campaigns and advertisers handled the bulk of this campaign, the Magazine Bureau contributed to it by advertising the continuing need for women workers and servicewomen in several 1944 issues of the *Magazine War Guide*.

Ducas's office handled the other major campaign, entitled "Women in Necessary Services." It was conducted in the fall of 1943 in response to serious labor shortages in service, trade, and supply industries. These were fields that had been drained of female labor by the exodus of women from poorly paying jobs in laundries and restaurants to war factories and of male labor in transportation by the draft. The simultaneous increase in demand for public services, including restaurants and laundries, exerted stress of critical proportions on war-boom communities. In addition, the low salaries and monotony of many of these occupations made it difficult to fill them when workers found better opportunities in manufacturing plants. Because market forces were inadequate to the task of filling the enormous vacancy in nonmanufacturing work, the Magazine Bureau shouldered the responsibility for luring women into such fields through patriotic appeals.

The major goal of the campaign was to inform women that work not directly related to manufacture of war material was vital national service and just as important as the more glamorous jobs receiving so much attention. Women were desperately needed as conductors, telegraph operators, laundresses, grocery and drugstore clerks, saleswomen, waitresses, stenographers, teachers, truck/bus/taxi drivers, and agricultural workers. The Magazine Bureau phrased the problem this way to editors and writers: "By and large, women do not view work of this kind as war work. Many who could do it are still standing by. . . . The time has come for them to realize how urgently they are needed—to keep the wheels of our civilian economy turning during the war period." The primary aim of the media, therefore, was to persuade the unemployed woman that taking any kind of job was patriotic and necessary: "stress the unglamorized, strenuous, often overlooked civilian jobs . . . which go begging because they are not recognized as war jobs."[57]

For a 1943 Labor Day drive, the Museum of Modern Art sponsored a cover competition complete with prizes for those that combined good design with effective communication. As further incentive to participate, the Magazine Bureau provided a detailed list of occupations that could be featured in the illustrations. The campaign brochures stressed that the Labor Day covers for September 1943 were merely the centerpiece of what OWI hoped would be a major fall offensive in which magazine content would address the issue too. Fiction writers, for example, were asked to write stories about women who found a new sense of fulfillment in jobs "behind counters in food or other vitally necessary stores, in banks or telegraph offices, driving buses or trolleys, or perhaps acting as community leaders in solving local problems."[58]

Though the high-paying, skilled work in war manufacturing industries offered compensations for the woman newly entering the labor force, OWI pointed out that menial jobs would need to be associated with a noble cause in order to make them look attractive and that the image problem was so severe that wholehearted support was required: "These jobs will have to be glorified as patriotic war service if American women are to be persuaded to take them and stick to them."[59]

The bureau was delighted to discover that 146 magazines with a total circulation of more than eighty-seven million had elected to participate in the fall promotion by August 1943.[60] It later noted that 2,135 stories and articles on topics mentioned in the *Guide* or suggested by the staff had been published between September 1942 and May 1943.[61] These figures led Ducas and her group to believe that their efforts were bringing results, a feeling that was reinforced by the responses they received to a questionnaire sent out in October 1943 asking editors to what use they put the *Magazine War Guide*. Out of 348 replies, 163 editors said they read the *Guide* thoroughly and 166 others said they found it at least helpful in selecting material for publication.[62] The extent to which editorial decisions were influenced by the campaign timetables and thematic directions requested by OWI is not fully revealed by this questionnaire, but bureau officials were pleased to find that editors were at least taking them seriously. They were also satisfied that their efforts were producing results after making monthly spot checks of two hundred magazines from March 1943 through August 1945 identifying stories, articles, and editorials that conformed to government guidelines.[63] All indications are that the magazine industry was at least aware of propaganda needs and tried to cooperate within the restrictions of editorial policies.

Popular Fiction and Propaganda

The Magazine Bureau made special efforts to involve fiction writers with OWI campaigns. In fact, Dorothy Ducas's central argument in her ultimately successful appeal to enlarge her staff was that magazines were ideal vehicles for shaping public opinion because they published fiction, which could subtly generate desirable attitudes. She made a point of contacting fiction writers and asked them to write stories that would make war work sound attractive to women readers while making a special request to the bureau's Magazine Advisory Committee, which consisted of representatives from ten major publications, that editors publish fiction designed to combat prejudice against working women.[64]

Ducas's attempts to bring fiction into line with government campaign goals were systematized in the *Magazine War Guide*, which recommended ways fiction writers could weave appeals into their plots. It suggested that characters be portrayed buying war bonds, conserving scarce resources, renting rooms to boomtown migrants, planting victory gardens, and in general maintaining a stoic, optimistic, patriotic attitude. To discourage use of strained telephone and transportation lines, for instance, the *Guide* asked that characters not be portrayed calling loved ones long distance for "trivial" conversations: "If possible, don't set the example in fiction of lovesick heroes calling heroines on the telephone to say 'Goodnight' or lonesome wives phoning soldier-husbands to say 'Merry Xmas.'"[65]

OWI saw no problem with fiction writers weaving home-front campaigns into romances and adventure stories, suggesting that even the most mundane government regulation could be the premise of a popular story plot. For example, the government's plan to conserve rubber through gasoline rationing could be supported by developing fantasies around characters who used a car pool: "The young man down the block, hitherto utterly ignorant of our heroine's existence, may now drive her or be driven by her and the meeting thus brought about by war conditions may lead to romance."[66] Similarly, the unromantic topic of price and rent control was not without its dramatic possibilities: "A typical treatment in fiction might be one in which the young lover solves for the girl some pressing financial predicament through clever use of the penalty provisions of the price control act."[67] The Magazine Bureau wanted to drive home the point that no aspect of life in wartime was to be overlooked as writers cast about for new themes and that they had a vital role to play in securing victory: to raise the public's awareness of how all the directives being issued from Washington and the inconveniences it was suffering were connected to a winning battle plan. By creating characters who served as models of good behavior and spirited cooperation, writers could foster appropriate attitudes toward domestic conditions.

The Magazine Bureau understood that people of different classes read different publications and that it was important to reach the blue-collar audience upon whose labor victory depended.[68] It therefore proposed that special efforts be made to work with the pulp industry whose audience was primarily working-class. Dorothy Ducas saw here a golden opportunity to marshal support for home-front campaigns and stated how important it was that pulp stories present, "emotionally, the story of democracy's fight, the attitudes of good Americans, the stakes of all of us in the war." Understanding the key role workers would play in the wartime economy, she argued that propagandists could not afford to ignore the vast pulp audience: "persons of inferior education on the lowest economic level are most in need of understanding of the true issues of the war." Leo Rosten, deputy director of OWI, expressed similar sentiments when he addressed a meeting of pulp editors: "Pulp magazines reach one of the largest and most important audiences in America. Propaganda is aimed to hit the readers of pulp magazines more than any other group."[69] As Ducas emphasized to Gardner Cowles, it was "in the pulp field where 15 million readers [would] get their war messages disguised in fiction."[70]

Ducas was aided in her efforts by the willingness of pulp publishers to help. They were afraid that the pulps would be forced to fold because they were considered peripheral to the war economy and had complained to OWI that the War Production Board and WMC followed discriminatory policies toward them in allotments of paper, labor power regulations, and access to transportation.[71] Consequently, the publishers at Fawcett Publications and Standard Magazines—which handled a total of ninety-three pulp magazines—were eager to provide service to the government. When Ducas made her early visits to editors before the formation of OWI, she found the most enthusiastic responses were from this group, which was willing to slant material for propaganda purposes but was hampered by neglect from Washington. Pulp editors wanted clear direction on what attitudes they should be encouraging in their readers.[72]

A good reflection of the pulp industry's willingness to disseminate propaganda is the role assumed by an editor at the first meeting of the Magazine Advisory Committee, a group set up to facilitate communication between the bureau and the magazine industry. It was at this meeting that the only objec-

tions were raised to the government's using magazines as propaganda. An editor from *McCall's* expressed reservations about
the *Magazine War Guide*, drawing parallels between its directives and the propaganda operation in Germany. He insisted
that such activities were appropriate for advertisers but not for
objective news media: "if this country is to continue to have a
free press, the editor must have complete scope to make his
own decisions as to what thing to do and at what time." He also
considered illegitimate any attempt by OWI to "originate, or
edit, or color" information from war agencies. An editor from
Standard Magazines took it upon himself to defend the bureau,
asserting that his readers would have heard nothing about
home-front campaigns had it not been for the *Magazine War
Guide*. He stated that he welcomed OWI guidelines because
they gave him an accurate and realistic view of how the war
was proceeding and gave him a way to involve his readers in
the war effort.[73]

To effectively communicate propaganda goals to pulp writers, the bureau established a New York office where a supplement was put together by a staff familiar with mass market
formulas. Pulp writers were put in charge of writing the supplement, which provided sample plots illustrating ways popular
fiction could support campaign goals. The special supplements
developed for major story formulas were printed only in the
fall of 1942; by spring of 1943 the explicit plot suggestions were
dropped entirely in favor of general guidelines. As will be seen
later, some of these early plot adaptations were used in published stories, but most served the purpose of merely encouraging writers to slant their normal formulas in directions that the
government felt would promote the best attitudes toward wartime conditions. They were intended to reassure all those who
wrote formula fiction that propaganda need not destroy the essential features of story types carefully crafted for entertainment, which followed tried and true patterns. Stereotypes of
heroes and villains, conventional settings, standard dramas
could all be adapted to propaganda needs without damaging
their appeal to the reader.

Some of these sample plots were rather far-fetched, such as
the suggested racist treatment of the enemy in sports pulps:
"the adventures of a professional baseball team touring Japan

would be an excellent vehicle in which to show Japanese slyness, ruthlessness, and inability to comprehend the spirit of sportsmanship"; or the recommendation that westerns feature Axis agents in traditional antagonist roles—the old rustler, the sheepman, the cattle baron.[74] Others, however, skillfully wove campaigns into formulas quite divorced from the world of patriotic service to one's country. For example, confessions writers were presented with the following two ways to support nurse recruitment while using the standard story line of seduction and betrayal: "A story . . . might show a seduced and despondent girl regenerated through observation of the good done by a nurse, and her self-sacrifice." "A seduced girl throws herself into [war work], say physiotherapy, to forget. Working side by side with a crippled doctor, learns to love him. After crisis in their task which she helps him meet, she discovers that although he knows all about her past, he loves her."[75]

It was hoped that such stories would subtly encourage readers to take war jobs, conserve rationed goods, plant victory gardens, and take other constructive steps by featuring patriotic characters with whom the reader could identify and by lacing escapist, privatized fantasies with references to the real world of national struggle. In this way, entertainment media could be mobilized to do something useful without sacrificing the essential elements of their success with the public.

OWI's campaign to reach the working class through the pulps and a more general audience in fiction of the slicks was made easier by the existence of a group of popular writers who worked closely with the Magazine Bureau. The Writers' War Board was formed in January of 1942 to put the talents of novelists, short story specialists, newspaper and magazine writers at the service of the government. The group was organized by mystery writer Rex Stout. A formidable manager, Stout compiled a file of four thousand writers and classified them by field of expertise, writing forte, and geographical region. He and his advisory board also established more than a dozen committees to handle special propaganda needs.[76]

It was due to the controversial nature of writers creating propaganda that the Authors' League, which had been approached by Stout originally, asked him to set up the group as a separate organization. The board saw itself as an important tool for shap ing public opinion. Its first annual report stated its intention to help the government in this way: "[Members of the board] are of differing political views, but are united in the belief that the Board should furnish whole-hearted support of any measures which the government considers necessary to a speedy and complete victory over the Axis."[77] As writer Robert Landry later said: "I think we broke through a lot of taboos, did many things the government wanted done and could not itself do. . . . The government was slow; we were fast. . . . World War II was strangely unemotional and needed a Writers' War Board to stir things up." Another writer of popular fiction, Clifton Fadiman, agreed, characterizing the board as "an arm of the government." Stout's group worked so closely with OWI that it was frequently mistaken for a government agency and, indeed, it received subsidies from both OWI and the Office of Civil Defense, though Stout insisted that the government money accounted for only 25 percent of his budget.[78]

The board dealt with many home-front campaigns, but most of its energies went into the recruitment of women. Even before the War Manpower Commission launched its intensive drive to mobilize the female population in March 1943, for instance, the board had been busy creating stories to use during the emergency. Dorothy Ducas was Stout's principal correspondent with OWI, and her office's emphasis on the womanpower campaign resulted in his giving the subject a great deal of attention. In addition to the close personal contact between Ducas and Stout, the board insured that writers understood recruitment policy through distributing to them the *Magazine War Guide* with its supplement along with its own monthly report.[79]

It is important to keep in mind that groups like the Writers' War Board were never coerced into cooperating with the government although some magazine publishers and advertisers were clearly operating under the threat of government regulation and loss of revenue. These groups were composed of individuals whose self-interest combined with a sincerely felt belief that their work was nonmanipulative because they were helping the nation survive. Their desire to help the government came from, in their minds, a noble, patriotic, and practical motive. They also insisted on maintaining a degree of autonomy;

in at least one instance, for example, the Writers' War Board de-
fied OWI requests to halt recruitment propaganda.[80]

The Womanpower Campaign

What was the image of war workers that Washington wished
magazine writers to create? The initial goal was to draw as
many women into the work force as possible, especially into industries that normally relied on male workers and that desperately needed them to manufacture war supplies. The campaign
concentrated on two things: providing women with encouragement for entering the labor force, especially in male jobs, and
convincing the public that traditional prejudices against working women were inaccurate and destructive to the nation's welfare. To these ends, the Magazine Bureau provided publishers
with photographs of and detailed reports on women who had
entered nontraditional fields in order not only to publicize
those occupations but to saturate the media with new portrayals
of women, images more appropriate to wartime demands.

Dorothy Ducas's early activities were largely devoted to these
aspects of the campaign, asking magazines to do feature articles
on women in men's jobs and to concentrate on subjects that
would facilitate their proper placement. In the fall of 1942, she
published a booklet entitled *War Jobs for Women*, which was in
part a response to complaints by the WMC that treatment in
magazines of employed women was not properly balanced.
They were giving too much attention to nonessential fields,
such as modeling, and not enough to the industries that needed
workers. This booklet listed the kinds of jobs for which women
were being hired, how to get training for them, and what the
range of pay was for factory work. Ducas distributed seven hundred copies, and by November the demand had become so great
that she ordered another edition of fifty thousand. Magazines
printed sections of the text, reviewed it favorably, and used it as
a reference for articles. This was the first of several publications
that were sent out to editors in supplementation of the *Magazine War Guide*. These included reports on how to meet the demand for skilled workers, housing for war workers, day care facilities, and a series of memos on occupations short of people.

Typical of Ducas's other efforts to create a better climate for hiring unprecedented numbers of women were the feature she negotiated in *Parade* lauding a female executive and one she persuaded the *Saturday Evening Post* to do on women in factories along with one on day care centers. She also tried to discourage stories that fostered a negative attitude. In one instance, the War Manpower Commission asked her to chastise the persons responsible for an article entitled "Fired Because They Were Women," which claimed that women workers had been let go from a metalworking plant because they suffered from hyperacidity.[81] Editors were asked to select fiction whose theme concerned acceptance of women in new roles while the writers were urged to make war work look attractive to female readers.[82]

Some of the suggestions to pulp writers reflect this part of the government's strategy. The following plots, for example, were recommended as devices for increasing acceptance among male workers of women in blue-collar fields: "The men in these fields must be prepared to receive women as co-workers. This can be done through stories showing the advent of women in the logging camps, on the railroads, riding the ranges, and showing them *not* as weak sisters but as coming through in manly style." For westerns, it offered the model of pioneer women: "Women fought rustlers, highwaymen, and bandits beside their men. Women helped to carve out an empire; it is only fitting that they help in the fight to preserve it." Even science fiction pulps had a role to play: "An Amazonian economy might trace its inception to this war-enforced change in our mores. A story of the supernatural might be woven around a woman locomotive engineer, for instance, or a feminine bus driver meeting with eerie adventure in lonely streets. . . . [There might even be] stories of utopias in which public health setups [are] administered by the descendents of nurses of our day."[83]

Messages fashioned for a female audience attempted to create new models of romantic fantasy that would point the reader in the direction of socially useful jobs and expand her notions of those for which she was suited. OWI provided, for example, a revised version of what single women should dream about: "[the young woman] does not regard marriage as her only career in wartime. She stays in business circulation, knowing that the war program and her country need her brains and skills.

She does not retire to the attic to become the 'world's greatest painter.' She wants to make some concrete use of her talents— become a draftsman or take up commercial art. . . . She knows this is not the time for a concert career. . . . The world of entertainment certainly plays its part in building morale, but the modern . . . girl knows that there are plenty of actresses, dancers, and singers."[84] To rely on the traditional heroines of romantic fantasy would encourage an unrealistic view of and selfish disregard for wartime conditions. Writers could perform a great service by reorienting the young reader from a dream of creative self-expression to one of practical service to a common dream. Enamored of glamorous performers and the trappings of superficial sophistication, the nation's female youth needed different role models of seriousness and dedication: "Short stories are suggested utilizing some of the many character-types now in the industrial army—former artists, pianists, beauticians, models."[85]

In addition to defining a new image of women that focused on the competence and intelligence they could bring to a challenging career they had not previously considered to be within their scope, OWI asked magazines to highlight the occupations to which women should be drawn: clerical work, shipping, aircraft, nursing, heavy transport, service and trade. If these jobs could be linked with adventure, glamor, and romance, women might be more likely to seek employment where they were needed rather than to set their sights on marriage or to take a noncommital attitude toward their work. More importantly, placing war jobs at the heart of popular stories and magazine articles would give the impression that women, as well as men, were expected to be engaged in paid employment and to assess their talents in the light of national service. By implication, the woman who did not enter the labor force had to assume the burden of proof that what she was doing was socially useful. She could, of course, justify her failure to take a job, but the image was designed to make her evaluate her home role from the standpoint of good citizenship and personal fulfillment. In other words, OWI wanted to reverse the idea that the employed woman was an aberration in American life by placing her at the forefront of the public mind.

Magazines were asked to broaden their treatment of women,

not only be featuring them in nontraditional roles, but by including older women, especially mothers of children over the age of fourteen. This was a significant departure from the normal practice of the media, which spotlighted young women as figures of beauty and desirability. Since the government expected that mothers of young children would stay at home and knew that young single women were already in the labor force for the most part, it aimed for older women whose maternal responsibilities were not so heavy as to preclude their taking on added work hours. While the subject might require some extra effort on the part of fiction writers, it was still presented as an important element in propaganda for the recruitment campaign:

> Fictional treatment is difficult, because the women to be appealed to have passed the age of romantic love, but perhaps such a woman could furnish a sub-plot. . . . For instance, the love affair of a young girl might be tangled by her mother returning to nursing, herself being required to take up home duties. A typical plot might run like this: A young doctor is struggling to maintain medical service in a town whose physicians are depleted. The girl tries to help, not being trained is inefficient. At a critical juncture she visits an ex-nurse, persuades her to help—giving writer a chance to put over message—thus saves the situation—and wins the doctor.[86]

Married and older women were also addressed by OWI propaganda requests for magazines to portray child care centers in a favorable light and to suggest ways that housekeeping chores could be kept to four hours a day.

The issue of breaking down prejudice against black women in new areas of employment was also addressed although it received very little attention in the bureau's instructions to magazines. Ducas's office made a gesture toward eliminating racial discrimination by calling for stories that "combatted race hatred" through highlighting the achievements of black people in order to further their acceptance into the wartime economy. An article entitled "Negro Women in Skilled Defense Jobs," for instance, was arranged as part of the campaign to counter racism among the public.[87] Though racist portrayals of the Japanese were considered legitimate, OWI wished to foster home-front solidarity and employment of minorities by showing that black and white Americans should work together for victory. Racism was a divisive force that weakened the nation at a time when all hands were needed to guide the country to safety.

The progressive idea that women could perform all kinds of work in society was accompanied, however, by a shrill patriotic appeal that undermined its potential as a feminist reordering of national values. The recruitment campaign was subsumed and shaped by a larger propaganda goal that exerted a reactionary influence on the concept that women deserved an equal place in the work world. This was the campaign to instill a sense of patriotic self-sacrifice in the population and to discourage individualistic attitudes so that civilians would connect their daily lives, which in peacetime carried no larger social implication, with victory overseas. OWI tried temporarily to suppress the materialistic self-interest and ambition normally engendered by American ideals of individual freedom in order to garner collective cooperation in home-front campaigns. The war worker, as the most visible manifestation of wartime changes, became a powerful symbol of this collective spirit—national purpose, civilian dedication, and home-front support for soldiers. The emphasis was not on women's right to be treated fairly and judged as individual workers but on their heroic service to the nation, a duty that required self-sacrifice and putting the welfare of soldiers above one's own desires.

The *Magazine War Guide* emphasized two themes in this regard. One of these was to make explicit connections among the safety of soldiers, the securing of victory, and the activities of civilians. What OWI was trying to do was encourage citizens to view their role with as much seriousness as they did the role of soldiers in combat. It asked fiction writers, for example, to glorify war workers as "soldiers of industry" in order to attract people to the understaffed lumber mills and mines of the northwest: "Fiction stories of any kind, set in these industries [steel, coal, copper, lead, zinc, lumber] help considerably in showing their importance to the war, *the interdependence of the armed forces and the workmen and workwomen who make the weapons.*"[88] It also recommended that popular writers try to mobilize civilian support and develop feelings of responsibility for the nation by dramatizing work on the home front as a great collective struggle for survival: "Fiction should bring out the . . . spiritual satisfaction of serving the common cause."[89]

The key theme struck in this regard was national unity and the awareness of community danger. Rather than assume that the military was going to carry the burden of defense alone, citizens should understand their importance as a home-front team, pulling together to meet a national emergency, one that required the wholehearted support of every person: "Today, Government cannot succeed in its programs of sharing unless it is supported, actively and implacably, by the whole people." "In this total war a nation's army is the whole nation."[90] The normal personal boundaries of peacetime, which allowed people to pursue their own livelihoods, were seen by OWI as an impediment to winning the production battle: "it should be easy to weave stories bringing out the many ways in which, *by united efforts*, all the wide range of things that need to be done if we are to win this war can be done more efficiently."[91]

Fiction writers could bring this point home to civilians, even though they were far removed from combat, by fashioning home-front heroes who willingly gave of themselves to help their country and set an example of subordinating personal wishes for the good of the whole. Villains should be characters who selfishly thought only of their own troubles and failed to share their skills, resources, and energies with others: "[The] most powerful weapon of all that the people can use against those who . . . fail to share with other civilians, our fighting men and our allies, is public condemnation. This psychology should be built up by its reflection in . . . fiction." Those who set aside their ambitions and losses to fight for a worthy cause, on the other hand, could be shown finding a new sense of comradeship and fulfillment: "the fraternity of young women and young men engaged in a common endeavor will furnish an inspiration for romantic treatment."[92]

In addition to encouraging an attitude of collective responsibility, OWI also wished to foster tolerance of wartime dislocations, such as crowded transportation, rationed gasoline and food staples, inadequate housing, and unavailability of consumer goods. The campaign to engender stoic acceptance of such inconveniences was called "Toughening Up for War," and

magazines were asked to feature "war-minded" citizens in articles and stories: "Occasional articles showing the way in which
typical American families have adjusted to the toughening-up
process would be helpful. But chiefly we call it to your attention as the basic philosophy for stories dealing with present-
day American life." "Fiction stories which are written *war-
mindedly*, even when dealing with non-war subjects, stories
that accept the changed standards of living that war creates as
part of the 'color' and 'background' of the stories, are particularly valuable, as many magazines have already proved."[93]

The government wanted civilians not only to view themselves as part of a collectivity upon which their individual fates
depended but to take the initiative in salvaging tin/paper/fat, re-
fraining from travel unless absolutely necessary, finding ways
to stay within rationing guidelines for food and gasoline, and
buying war bonds. These campaigns were portrayed as a challenge to the toughness of the home front, a litmus test for determining who was willing to stand up to the enemy and who was
not: "The challenge that Hitler has flung in the face of free Americans is that precisely because we are a free people we will not
submit to the restrictions on our traditional ways of living without which victory in a total war cannot be won. . . . This makes
crystal-clear the part . . . magazines can play in answering this
challenge. To bring home to [their] readers the reason for rationing, for control of prices and of rents, for whatever disruption of
our traditional customs civilian logistics makes needful."[94]

These emergency measures were no doubt necessary for successful prosecution of the war, but they received far more emphasis than they objectively deserved, being characterized as
the difference between victory and defeat. The propaganda urging people to look out for enemy agents and to not talk about
their war jobs is an especially good example of OWI's over-
dramatization of conditions on the home front. Yet the com-
mands to take an active role in helping defeat the enemy through
carefully observing government requests did serve a purpose:
they gave people the message that a war of such magnitude required the mobilization of noncombatants and that what happened on the production front was the key to victory on the
battlefield. Such a message not only gave the civilian a way to
strengthen symbolically his or her ties to loved ones far away

from home and to feel useful but raised the public's awareness of how dependent military strategy was on the economy. Without the required planes, ships, ammunition, medical supplies, and necessary equipment, Allied forces would suffer heavy casualties and ultimately, perhaps, defeat.

As will be evident from an examination of the magazines themselves, war workers became the chief representatives of these two attitudes—dedication to the welfare of the nation and its fighting men, accompanied by stoic endurance of wartime conditions: "It is for the women of America to say whether America shall live slave or free."[95] They were used as inspirational figures and models of what all citizens ought to be doing. The Amazonian image of women as leaders of the home front certainly carried with it the positive notion that women are strong, competent workers. However, its simultaneous use as a mobilizing tool for the public created an inaccurate impression of the women who were staffing war plants and reinforced traditional ideas about women as a group. For instance, the concept of war work as heroic national service, equivalent to male service overseas, fed into the belief that this was a temporary disruption of peacetime routines, that women's "real" place was in the home just as soldiers' "real" place was as breadwinner for the family.

In addition, the use of war workers as a model of home-front patriotism with its blend of martyrdom and subordination of personal concerns masked the very real benefits women enjoyed from their employment in lucrative industries and the occupations normally closed to them. For professional women, the war provided a chance to become newspaper editors, personnel managers, pilots, engineers, and to enter other occupational fields offering creativity, power, and status. For working-class women, it lowered barriers against employment in high-wage industries with chances for advancement. The emergency opened new vistas for black women too as many left domestic service and farm work to take jobs previously performed by whites. The proportion of black females in industrial occupations rose from 6.5 percent to 18 percent from 1940 to 1944, although they were confined to the lowest paying sectors of manufacturing. They were also employed as white-collar workers in federal agencies for the first time, gained increased access to the nursing profession, and expanded their numbers in the apparel industry by 350 percent.[96] Most of these gains made by women were later lost, but the labor shortage temporarily provided job opportunities usually denied to them.

The propaganda emphasis on collective welfare overshadowed these benefits and, moreover, underplayed the whole concept of women's rights. OWI's efforts to weld the home front into a disciplined army willing to observe government regulations took the form of discouraging individual self-regard. Though it might be tempting to hoard rationed goods, for example, propaganda urged that people resist such selfish impulses for the good of the country. The vision was survival of the nation rather than advancement of any individual or group of individuals. Such a perspective conflicted with the idea that women had a right to better themselves, even though this theme was touched on in the recruitment campaign. The more forceful view was that women took war jobs out of duty, not because they would benefit from them personally.

As early as the spring of 1943, magazine editors and writers were asking the government for a "blueprint" of postwar American society "as the U.S. would like to see it," and OWI addressed itself to the issue of what would happen to the new female army of industrial workers.[97] In handling reconversion of the economy to peacetime production, the *Magazine War Guide* and the guidebooks issued by the Bureau of Campaigns reinforced the recruitment message that women's new role was temporary, although they did not directly advise writers and advertisers to encourage women to leave their jobs. This latter failure was due in part to the slowdown of OWI activities in late 1944 when the War Manpower Commission asked that the womanpower campaign be ended. OWI was also hampered during reconversion by congressional budget cuts resulting from Republican attacks on the propaganda operation as a tool of the Democratic party.[98] After the "Women in the War" campaign of early 1944, OWI failed to launch any other major drives. With adequate funding, it is conceivable that it would have provided the media with more detailed instructions for dealing with reconversion, in particular for handling demobilization of the wartime labor force.

In the absence of congressional support, however, the Bureau of Campaigns completely dropped the issue of womanpower, and the Magazine Bureau limped along until the summer of 1945 when it finally folded. Publication of the *Magazine War Guide* was the bureau's only activity from June 1944 to August 1945, although the Writers' War Board remained active through the spring of 1946, determined to carry on despite OWI's enfeeblement. Though it never tackled the issue of reconversion in a clear and comprehensive way, the *Guide* did inform magazines that, according to the Women's Bureau, the best fields for women in the postwar market would be in traditional female areas: teaching, nursing, and clerical work. In addition, the *Guide* dropped the campaigns to generate positive attitudes toward child care centers and to develop ways for women workers to cut down their hours of housework. These items were replaced by suggestions that magazines concentrate on the "new national problem" of juvenile delinquency, one of the social ills blamed on working mothers.

More importantly, however, the close connection between propaganda groups and the magazine industry throughout the war made unnecessary specific instructions to encourage the movement of women back to the home and to female fields in the labor force during demobilization. As will later be demonstrated, fiction and advertisements during this period portrayed war workers leaving their jobs for domesticity, office work, and unskilled jobs in manufacturing. This largely resulted from information writers had received from the government for two and a half years—information based on the assumption that new women workers would not remain in "male" occupations once veterans returned and the dominant perspective of which highlighted the needs of the country. Propaganda appeals sometimes mentioned the career advantages women might find in war jobs, but the assumption was that women's role was to help out in an emergency, which led naturally to the conclusion that they would leave once it was over. In the absence of clear government directions during reconversion, those who had written recruitment propaganda continued to use an ideological framework that emphasized female patriotic service over self-advancement.

The campaign to recruit women into war jobs did not work perfectly. It gave insufficient attention to skilled jobs, especially

in the metal trades which numbered one third of the new open-
ings, nor did it give adequate publicity to executive and supervisory positions. The need for clerical workers throughout the
war far outstripped the space given to it while the specific demands of local production economies were left up to individual communities ill equipped to deal with the problem.

These deficiencies can be partially attributed to an assumption that market forces alone would take care of some labor requirements. However, many of the errors can be attributed to
the government's failure fully to coordinate labor mobilization
with propaganda. If the government had wanted to make full
use of the magazine industry to recruit women, it should have
begun its propaganda drives in early 1942 to get women into
training programs and into geographical areas where they were
needed. The economy needed two million extra women workers in 1942, while aircraft production and shipbuilding reached
their peak in early 1943—when the Magazine Bureau and the
Bureau of Campaigns were just beginning their activities. Likewise, the strain on community services began well before the
fall of 1943 when the campaign for women in necessary civilian
services was launched. Finally, propaganda only partially addressed the need to have women in civilian production during
1944 and 1945. This lack of coordination is illustrated by a
memo from the WAC concerning the spring campaign of 1944
and complaining that it was impossible to get accurate labor
forecasts from the War Manpower Commission. By the fall of
that year the WMC had ended its recruitment drives.[99]

This does not mean, however, that propaganda groups were
ineffective. OWI filled the gap left by the failure of the War
Manpower Commission to centralize information on labor needs
and was the major source of information for magazines on wartime policies concerning women workers. It performed a service for editors that they would have had difficulty in providing
for themselves since so few publishers had contact with government officials. We can assume, then, that without a centralized information agency magazine treatment of women
workers would not have been so closely allied with labor needs
and economic policies to employ women as a wartime labor reserve. One lesson we can draw from the events that led up to
the setting up of OWI is that the absence of government direc-

tion in a national emergency makes it likely that the media will in some ways work against policy goals. Having recognized the confusion that prevailed from 1939 to 1942, the Roosevelt administration bowed to pressure to rationalize the mass media so that they more closely conformed to government needs.

It is also clear that the media desired government direction and took steps to organize even before OWI was established. The primary reason for this willingness to disseminate propaganda was economic survival. Advertisers and magazine publishers were faced with the possible loss of most of their business with the shift from consumer to military production, and all the media were threatened by nationalization and government regulation. By convincing the government that they could be of great strategic value in the battle to produce war material, the entertainment and advertising industries created a way to survive and even prosper during the war years.[100] Thus, the interests of both government and media were served by the propaganda operation. OWI coordinated information disseminated to magazines with labor campaigns so that stories would have maximum impact on the public. All the propaganda groups provided exceptionally good communication channels between government agencies and the magazine industry, an important medium of mass communication.

It is important to recognize the essential features of OWI's recruitment campaign and its other attempts to mobilize the home front, not as examples of government manipulation of the media but as a partial explanation of their failure to challenge traditional ideas about women and work more radically. From examining OWI records, we get a clearer picture of why the public image of war workers took the shape it did, influenced as it was by general propaganda goals. We are also provided with a description of a process that is normally left invisible by creators of popular entertainment and advertising: how social changes are incorporated into formulas with mass appeal. The use of such formulas as propaganda makes explicit the kinds of decisions that artists must make in maintaining their products' appeal while reflecting contemporary issues and realities. In this case, we see some of the reasoning behind choices popular artists made in their portrayal of war workers, and OWI records present us with a microcosm of the attitudes displayed toward women workers in the media as a whole. Wartime propaganda was, then, a conscious interweaving of widespread values for specific ends rather than an imposition of alien views. As will be evident from the following two case studies of mass-circulation periodicals, the requests for portraying the home front made by OWI were fashioned into elaborate fantasies that drew upon deeply rooted myths in American culture.

2 Middle-Class Images of Women in Wartime

IT is clear from OWI records that magazine advertisers, editors, and writers were provided with information that war agencies wished the public to have and with general guidelines for treatment of new wartime conditions. We see that the recruitment of women received special attention from propaganda groups as they made specific campaign goals for staffing labor-short industries and tried to create a favorable climate for the hiring of women in nontraditional occupations along with acceptance of married women as wage workers. To what extent did magazines cooperate with such groups? How were the general aims of the propaganda operation translated into specific story plots and advertising techniques? We know, for instance, that the Magazine Bureau asked fiction writers to glamorize war jobs and to break down prejudice against working women but, aside from a few plot samples, it avoided overly specific instructions. Were writers able or willing to take on tasks like these and, if so, what methods did they choose for doing so?

Through looking at fiction and advertising in the *Saturday Evening Post*, we can find some answers to these questions. The *Post* is a good representative of middle-class family slicks. Its handling of the recruitment campaign suggests the ways magazines of its kind were dealing with the subject, and since it had a subscriber circulation of over three million during the war years, we can see what image of war workers many Americans were given. Because popular writers and advertisers had to appeal to a mass audience, the strategies they followed for mobilizing the female labor force tell us a great deal about what the audience, particularly women, valued and how those values were meshed with themes the government wanted stressed. The beliefs and attitudes reflected in a magazine like the *Post* are especially important because they were part of the dominant middle-class American ethic. As such, they indicate what some of the prevailing myths have been in our culture and how those myths relate to conceptions of women.

The image of women in magazine stories and advertising resulted from a number of factors: imagined needs and attitudes of the audience, experiences and values of the artists, marketing decisions by editors, business interest of companies, and propaganda requests from the government. It is difficult, if not impossible, to sort all these out and state which factor produced which part of the picture. It is possible to establish, however, that *Post* editors and writers participated extensively in the recruitment campaign, which makes it likely that portrayals of war workers were greatly influenced by OWI plans. For instance, the editors met regularly with government officials concerning home-front campaigns, and the *Post* was a member of the Magazine Advisory Committee to the Magazine Bureau. It also carried advertisements from major companies that bear the stamp of the War Advertising Council. In addition, it had long employed writers who became members of the Writers' War Board, including WWB organizer Rex Stout, whose popular Nero Wolfe mysteries had appeared there for many years.[1]

The congruence of war-related stories in the *Post* with campaigns and suggestions of the Magazine Bureau—as well as the communication links between it, OWI, and the WWB—suggests that magazines were working closely with the government and that much of wartime fiction was shaped by propaganda imperatives. Stories of the *Post* with persuasive messages regarding factory work, for instance, were printed largely between March 1943 and June 1944, when the recruitment campaign was at its peak. Twenty-five out of forty-four lead stories with female characters in war work appeared during this period of sixteen months. Twenty were printed in 1943, the year designated by the Magazine Bureau as one in which magazines should make womanpower their primary issue. These figures may at first glance seem low considering that the *Post* was a weekly. However, the incidence of stories with "womanpower" characters during the most active period of the recruitment campaign is higher if one considers that many stories were westerns, sea adventure tales, combat dramas, and murder mysteries, formulas that did not lend themselves to this subject. In addition, not all lead stories featured female characters. Out of a total of 266 stories from January 1941 through March 1946 (6 were missing), 147 contained prominent female characters, or 55 percent of the total. From March 1943 through June 1944, however, 50 of the 74 lead stories contained prominent female characters, or 68 percent, while the proportion of the latter with women in war work was 50 percent. Those stories with female characters during the intensive months of the recruitment campaign that did not concern women war workers generally focused upon characters for whom war work was inappropriate, such as young girls, women past the age of fifty, or homesteaders on the frontier.[2] (See table 2.)

The *Post* also participated in the two major drives conducted by OWI. To support the "Women in Necessary Services" campaign in the fall of 1943, it asked its foremost illustrator, Norman Rockwell, to create an appropriate Labor Day cover. His illustration was featured on the 4 September issue, which showed a woman dressed in red, white, and blue coveralls, rolling up her sleeve and striding purposefully toward a distant goal while loaded down with the bric-a-brac of defense work—air raid warning equipment, a wrench, and a service hat. Rockwell's figure reflects the campaign's emphasis on service jobs with her milk bottles, railroad lantern, farming tools, conductor's change carrier, oilcan, and mop. Six stories (out of eight) that month concerned women in defense work, and five lead stories on the subject appeared from September through December 1943. Similarly, in apparent response to the "Women in the War" campaign of 1944, the *Post* ran ten lead stories concerning women in war work; six of them appeared in the spring when the campaign was officially launched. An additional ten pieces during this period focused on women in military service, a significant increase over 1943 when only two concerned the services, thus reflecting the campaign's emphasis on the armed forces.

It is clear that some of these pieces were a result of the womanpower drive. In an OWI progress memo concerning the 1944 campaign, for instance, two of these *Post* stories were mentioned as examples of the kind of support the government desired from the media.[3] Other evidence is provided in the Magazine Bureau's tabulation of magazine articles and fiction that supported campaigns advertised in the *Magazine War Guide*. It

Table 2　Lead Stories from the *Saturday Evening Post*
with Prominent Female Characters and with
Female Characters in War Work

Year	Stories with prominent female characters	% of lead stories with prominent female characters	Stories with female characters in war work[a]	% of stories with prominent female characters that concerned war workers	Total lead stories
1941	26	52	0	0	50
1942	28	54	5	18	52
1943	35	67	20	57	52
Mar. 1943– June 1944	50	68	25	50	74
1944	28	56	10	36	50
1945	23	46	8	35	50
1946 (Jan.–Mar.)	7	58	1	14	12
Total	147	55	44	31	266

[a]Factory worker, shipyard worker, Red Cross and other volunteer, nurse, office worker, waitress, gas station attendant, taxi driver, policewoman, journalist, WAC or WAVE, pilot.

identifies as propaganda twenty-six *Post* articles and fiction on labor needs from March 1943 to July 1945. Six of these dealt with women in war production, two were on child care centers, ten concerned servicewomen, and the rest publicized nursing and farm work.[4] Considering that the *Post* was issued weekly, with an average of six fiction pieces and eight articles per issue, the number of stories cited by OWI seems rather small. However, the fiction listed as propaganda provides a starting point for identifying the kinds of themes and characterizations OWI was looking for. The recommendations of the *Magazine War Guide* provide another standard for determining whether stories incorporated propaganda themes. Using these additional guidelines, I found that much more fiction appeared supporting the recruitment effort than OWI noted.[5] Given that the *Post* was only one of two hundred magazines of which the bureau tried to keep track and that the womanpower campaign was one of several issues it noted, it is understandable that a small staff would not have had time to do a thorough job of perusing all the periodicals.

Fiction before Pearl Harbor

One method for beginning to determine the impact of propaganda and the conditions of wartime on images of women is to examine prewar stories with prominent female characters. What were the formulas that had been established by the time the recruitment campaign began? Which ones survived the war period, and which were dropped? What kind of heroine did writers inherit from the 1930s, and how amenable was she to the new kind of image shaping that they undertook? The answers to these questions lead us to insights about two issues. One of these is the interface between formula art as entertainment and as propaganda. To tease out even partially the story characteristics that appear to have resulted from writer cooperation with the government from those that reflected reader desires for satisfying fantasies, we need to establish a framework for analyzing fiction of the war years. It is the mixture of these elements that makes World War II fiction a fascinating study in the capacity of popular art to instruct and entertain. Second, it is useful to examine a spectrum of stories broader than a wartime sample in order to draw conclusions about the war's impact on portrayals of women in the postwar period. Cultural images can change very rapidly, but there has to be a degree of continuity as those changes do not emerge from a void nor do they inexplicably disappear. One of the tasks of this study is to articulate and clarify the complex configuration of ideas about women that alternately allowed for expansion and contraction of their sphere within a short period of time.

The following passage from a 1931 story describes very well the kind of figure Betty Friedan found to be so inspiring in women's fiction of the 1930s. It concerns a woman pilot who daringly enters a race to fly from the United States to France, a race she wins:

A young woman opened the car door and got out, pulling off her heavy driving gloves. She was pretty nice, if you get it. Clean sweeping lines and a cool air of knowing what the score was. No tickling strands of hair loose under her tight little hat; stockings straight and tight, with the seams dead center; and a pair of shoes that looked as if she could walk a mile or two if she had to. But her eyes were the best—pale china blue—with a straight keen light in them and no nonsense; and a mouth that looked as if it could say what it meant the first time and stick to it afterward. [James Warner Bellah, "She Eagle," 13 June 1931]

The straightforward, confident demeanor of this character is typical of an important heroine popular during the Depression. She was witty, athletic, self-possessed, urbane, appearing in the roles of competent secretary, aggressive businesswoman, ambitious college graduate, or adventurous aviator. These independent, autonomous heroines caught up in the drama of achieving high goals were the stars of one major category of stories featuring women: work adventure romances.[6] Such dramas concerned young single women who had set their sights on a career filled with challenge, one which demanded quick-wittedness, dedication, courage, and self-assertion. This might be a career in journalism, show business, undercover work, or aviation, and the heroine's drive for success was portrayed as a healthy desire to participate without prejudice in the world of men.

Many of these stories have at their base a conflict between the heroine, who is trying to break into a male world, and a man who initially resents her intrusion but gradually comes to admire, accept, and even love her. For example, in "She Eagle," a pilot is initially hostile when he is approached by the heroine, who wants to fly the Atlantic with him: "Women give me a pain in the neck, and these flying dames are the worst of the lot." Through her clever manipulation, however, he finds himself co-piloting her plane in a transatlantic race. As the heroine coolly handles all the tasks for which she is responsible and deals calmly with the crises they encounter, he comes to trust her judgment completely, relying on her as an equal, and realizes that his first impression sprang from irrational prejudice.

Though they do not qualify as romances, a series of stories about a female ship captain have at the core of their appeal the winning of such battles through the heroine's determination to do a job for which she is qualified and illustrate the degree to which women were portrayed as men's equals. Tugboat Annie Brennan, captain of the Secoma Deep-Sea Towing and Salvage Company, is large-framed, solidly built, with rugged features and shrewd, quick blue eyes: "Her movements had an elephantine energy that galvanized everyone with whom she came in contact. When she passed through a room, dust and odd bits of paper danced in her wake" (Norman Reilly Raine, "Tugboat Annie," 11 July 1931). With her antiquated bonnet and salty language, she rules the line authoritatively while beating out all competitors through her superior knowledge of law and sea. Every episode involves Annie's pitting her wit and skill against seamen who assume she is unqualified for her post because of her sex. In "Tugboat Annie" she is fired because a wealthy client does not think a woman can manage a fleet of ships: "Her influence, in what essentially is a man's sphere, is bound to have undesirable results." As evidence, he points to her ships' names—*Daffodil, Asphodel, Pansy*, and *Narcissus*. Annie is not one to let such things get her down and competently salvages a ship against his orders: "If I'd left him piled up on the rocks, the *Barracuda* would have been pounded to pieces in the gale. But bein' just a stupid, mutton-headed female, I yanked her home. So instead of a lousy towin' fee of $240, we'll get a salvage award of about one third the value of the ship and cargo." Again, in "If the Cap Fits—" (25 January 1936), she wins a bid on a towing job, but the owner balks when he sees Annie is a woman. She performs superbly, however, and reminds him that women are just as competent as men: "Don't you forget, me fine-feathered-friend . . . that it was a woman what l'arned you to eat, and talk, and walk, and blow yer nose, and put yer little britches on!"

In stories like these, the heroine pursues her own goals confidently, undeterred by prejudice and, for the most part, unconcerned with marriage. Though she may fall in love with the male protagonist, she does not usually scheme to ensnare him, nor does she worry very much about whether he loves her since her attention is focused on the task at hand. She does not hesitate to lock horns with the man she loves, who eventually sees things her way. They are equally matched in their aggression, ambition, and wit. Frequently, indeed, the man pursues the hero-

ine, thinking of ways to win her love as he finds himself competing with another man or with her career ambitions. As Friedan
notes in her analysis of middle-class magazine fiction, " [The
heroines of women's magazine stories] were young in the same
way that the American hero has always been young: they were
New Women, creating with a gay determined spirit a new identity for women—a life of their own. There was an aura about
them of becoming, of moving with a future that was going to be
different from the past. The majority of heroines . . . were career
women—happily, proudly, adventurously, attractively career
women—who loved and were loved by men. And the spirit,
courage, independence, determination—the strength of character they showed in their work . . . were part of their charm."[7]

Indeed, a prominent feature of work adventure romances
is that the heroine is stronger than the male protagonist. She
knows more about the world than he does and better understands how to protect herself. Therefore, she guides him through
the battles he must win in order to realize his dreams. It is only
through reliance on the heroine's superior knowledge of life
that the hero is able to succeed in his goals. Jean Arthur played
roles like this in *Mr. Smith Goes to Washington* and *Mr. Deeds
Goes to Town* wherein she guides idealistic, naive young men
through a confusing urban maze to their moments of ultimate
victory over corruption.[8]

A prewar *Post* story that illustrates this theme well is Clarence Budington Kelland's "Silver Spoon" (14 June 1941). The
protagonist is an upper-class college graduate, Ogden Pieter
Van Stoel, who wagers that he can make his own way in life
without the benefit of his class privileges. Having had no experience with hardship or even in holding a job, he sets out to
prove to his friends that he can take care of himself. He quickly
runs into trouble as he discovers that he has no marketable
skills and that he is physically too weak for most blue-collar
jobs. His problems are aggravated when he is robbed of all his
money. The heroine, on the other hand, is a nightclub entertainer who has survived a childhood marked by penury. She
knows how dangerous the world is and has toughened herself
to get through it. She is a fighter whose strength has been suffi-
cient to take care of people less well equipped to defend themselves: "Her worries had not been for herself, but for others who

had made themselves dependent upon her." Luckily, Ogden accidentally encounters this heroine, who immediately impresses him: "She seemed so amazingly self-reliant." It is from her that he learns how to survive the assaults he has suffered upon his dignity, how to find the courage he needs to overcome his weaknesses.

Given the unemployment crisis of the Depression years, it is surprising to find stories like these which feature heroines involved in exciting careers. Moreover, they are rewarded for their skills in negotiating their way through a male-dominated world. One would expect that the media would have discouraged women from entering the work force at a time when the economy was unable to provide enough jobs for men, who ordinarily were provided with the best work available. In addition, the feminist movement had been moribund since the early 1920s. How, then, can we account for the positive image of ambitious, capable women in work adventure romances?

One explanation for the proliferation of strong, assertive heroines during the prewar years may lie in the demoralization of men thrown out of work by the Depression or threatened by loss of their jobs. It is possible that male characters' reliance on a strong woman reflected male feelings of vulnerability and inadequacy. Stories in which men depended on women may have reflected men's loss of confidence in their ability to be masters of their fate. Feeling that self-actualization was problematic for them, perhaps men found it easier to accept an adventurous, competent woman and indeed needed such a figure on which to rely for support.

Another explanation for the existence of this heroine is that female independence was acceptable and even attractive to men, but only as a prelude to marriage. While men in these stories were taken by her intelligence and self-sufficiency, they insisted that the ambitious heroine give up her career for love. For instance, in "Bright Danger" (Hugh MacNair Kahler, 15 November 1941), the protagonist falls in love with the daughter of an oil rig owner when she directs a fire-fighting operation for her father: " [Jan] was alive and real and awake; she fitted into the world he lived in, was herself a part of it." However, after the danger is over, he concludes: "What Jan needed was to get away from ships. It wasn't a woman's game." Jan then relinquishes her post of authority in a way that makes it clear that she will be a traditional wife. She insists that the protagonist take over the wheel of the car she is driving, saying: "'You're driving now.' [Dusty] was thinking that this was a better way of saying it than any of the things a woman had to say when she was getting married." Similarly, in "Heads, You Win" (Zachary Gold, 30 August 1941), a couple undergoes a painful separation because the wife is tempted to sign a Hollywood contract she is offered. They reconcile only after she agrees to turn it down. Single women and widows were the only characters in prewar fiction who were portrayed positively in public roles, and generally stories about them ended in engagement with the understanding that they would quit their jobs. Independence was fine, but only as a way to fill a woman's life before she assumed her "real" job, homemaking: "Henry . . . was all for women being themselves, and he approved of girls having jobs until they met some man" (Struthers Burt, "Tomorrow and Tomorrow," 28 March 1931).

Women who persisted in following their ambitions after marriage were arch villains during this period. The career-oriented wife was a selfish, exploitative neurotic who callously neglected her home for fame and wealth. An excellent example of this character is provided in "The Rising Star" (Alice Duer Miller, 23 May 1936). The protagonist is a loving, responsible husband who suffers from the ambition of his cold, self-centered wife to be a movie star. He raises their child with the aid of a sensitive, self-effacing nurse while his wife establishes herself in Hollywood. Typically, the wife is punished for her destructive pursuit of a career. When husband, child, and nurse move to Hollywood, the nurse attains stardom while the wife fails. Moreover, she loses her family to her rival, who promptly gives up her success to be a homemaker. Similarly, in "Men Are Such Fools" by Faith Baldwin (21 March 1936), a beautiful businesswoman freely acknowledges the fact that she uses men to get ahead. She marries a man who tolerates her job, but only on the condition that she quit when he gets his first promotion. However, she is more concerned about her career than his and, when the promotion comes, reneges on her promise.

Foreshadowing the feminine mystique with its "devil career" theme, "Sarah Bane's Husband" and "I Refused A Career" (anonymous, 20 June and 26 September 1931) similarly warn women of the pitfalls involved in trying to combine a career with home-making. In the former, Sarah Bane is a successful author. Her husband is pleased at first until he realizes she is making more money than he is. Frantically, he seeks another job but resigns himself to playing second fiddle while becoming his wife's agent. Their children grow up hating their mother for not pay-ing more attention to them and for being famous, thereby not allowing them to shine. Son Jack leaves his fiancée when she states her admiration for his mother, then marries an Italian woman who cannot speak English. The daughter is studying medicine to overcome her inferiority complex but decides never to marry because, in her words, "I'd never be enough of a cheat to try to combine a job with a family." Likewise, the au-thor of "I Refused a Career" recalls her temptation to pursue a writing career after some initial publishing successes. After ob-serving that her high salary was ruining her marriage, she gives it up, leaving it to her husband to "cut the channel of life." She warns the reader: "For years . . . the persistent urge to write was to struggle to annihilate my decision in favor of domesticity. I am grateful that I did not fully realize the seriousness of the condition until after I was cured." She ends by saying she would much rather change baby diapers than typewriter ribbons.

Though female characters with ambitions larger than that of housewife were loved for their courage, it is equally clear that men perceived them as threatening if they carried their dreams too far. Any woman who made work an important part of her life for more than a few years came under attack as a cold-hearted, power-hungry machine. This stereotype of the hard-bitten career woman appears in "Thirty Days Hath September" (Dorothy Cameron Disney, 8 February 1941). The protagonist is upset when his wife expresses an interest in working for a busi-nesswoman acquaintance, characterizing her as a steely, hollow shell of a woman: "She was a natural member of that well-corseted, firm-jawed little band of determined females who have climbed from oblivion to well-publicized successes with-out the help of husband or children or other awkward connec-tions." Similarly, in "Prescription for Murder" (Hannah Lees, 6 September 1941), the director of nurses at a major hospital is a man-hating, arrogant, sadistic, domineering older woman who values work only because it grants her power over people. As the murder victim of this mystery, she meets with the usual horrible fate of the selfish, ambitious female.

The beautiful, courageous woman of action whose ability to take care of herself so enchanted men when she was single was transformed into a menacing monster if she retained her powers beyond her early twenties. Though men valued women for their strength at a time when life was uncertain, they admired female ambition only as a stage that prepared women to be strong partners. Once women had proven themselves to be trustworthy and capable, men wanted them to focus their energies totally on the family. The stereotype of the cold, selfish career woman, then, warned women not to get too caught up in their quest for self-actualization or to expect that they could combine work with love.

The Impact of Propaganda on Romances of the War Years

Perhaps because recruiting efforts had not yet been coordinated by the War Manpower Commission, fiction appearing in the year after Pearl Harbor did not take up the issue of women in war production. Stories dealing with war focused on the Allied effort in Europe, on the glamorous figure of the combat pilot, and occasionally on women doing volunteer work. By January of 1943, writers began responding to the suggestions of the *Magazine War Guide*, although it was not until March that significant numbers of stories appeared dealing with women in war work.

The risk-taking, courageous, competent heroine of the 1930s was an excellent model for creating a heroic image of women compatible with wartime—a figure that dominated fiction of the war years. A poised female spy helps crack a sabotage ring in "The Saboteurs" (John and Ward Hawkings, 10 April 1943); a policewoman captures a Nazi in "The Bride and Delehenty" (Thomas Walsh, 11 September 1943); and a resistance fighter battles Germans in the mountains of France in "Avalanche" (Kay Boyle, 23 October 1943). Stories also emphasized the thoughtful reflectiveness and quick wit of the ideal woman on the home front. A common female character of the 1940s, one inherited from the previous decade, was the heroine who seemed to be a flighty chatterbox but who used this pose as a cover for her clever manipulation of men standing in her way. This character was adapted to military recruitment in a series of stories, written by Frank Bunce from 1944 through 1946, featuring a WAC named Dorrit Bly whose nonstop patter extricates her from humorous conflicts with the army. Her phenomenal memory enables her to cite army regulations and civil laws, which destroy her opponents' arguments even when she is clearly in the wrong. Never irrational, she is so adept at arguing a case that she earns the admiration of her puzzled antagonists.

Thus, wartime fiction continued to feature the competent, assertive heroine of work adventure romances, but propaganda imperatives produced some key alterations in this formula. As was true in the 1930s, women frequently encouraged men to find the courage and strength to realize their goals, but writers added elements suggested by OWI. One of these was to set stories in labor-short industries and to portray women as helping men defeat enemy forces. In "Black Jack" (Robert Pinkerton, 20 November 1943), for instance, the setting is a small lumber town of the northwest, which has been drained of labor power by the more lucrative jobs in shipyards and aircraft factories. Jack Meade is an idealistic young man who wants to save the town from dying by taking over management of the major plywood factory, which has suffered a production slowdown. He is often discouraged as his efforts meet with failure, but his spirits are renewed by the faith of Sandy Torrant, a newspaper editor who sees to it that Jack's venture receives favorable publicity. In working together to expose the saboteurs who are ruining the town, Jack falls in love with Sandy, in large part because he is grateful to her for all the help she provides.

Another example of the tough, supportive woman who guides a vulnerable man to success is the heroine of "A Pain in the Neck" (Lucian Cary, 18 September 1943). Connie Gage is a competent receptionist in an aircraft plant who becomes a lathe operator because she believes the job to be more vital to the war effort. Her skills as a worker attract the personnel manager, Hank Allison, who lacks self-discipline and is so overweight that the army will not take him. Connie spurns his advances, making it clear to him that she thinks he is not working up to

A lathe operator inspires her fellow worker to get in shape for the war effort. From "A Pain in the Neck," reprinted from *Saturday Evening Post*, 18 September 1943. © 1943 The Curtis Publishing Company.

"Why did you do this?" she asked. "You told me I was a heel if I didn't," he said.

A Pain in the Neck

By LUCIAN CARY

HANK ALLISON saw that it was two minutes of five and began to run. He wanted to get to the office before Connie Gage left. Douglas Avenue was jammed with men and women coming off the day shift at the airplane plants and he was a big man. Running through a crowd reminded him of something he'd once been good at. It was easier than carrying the ball through the other team, but the principle was the same. You found the holes. He ran up two flights of stairs rather than wait for an elevator, and opened the door of the Jefferson Johnson Oil Company and

thought the offices were empty. He stood a moment, puffing more than he liked, and then he heard her step.

"Hello, Connie," he said as she came in.

Just seeing her again gave him a lift, even though he knew she had no use for him. She was an exceptionally pretty girl, with thick chestnut hair waving almost to her shoulders and the bluest eyes he'd ever seen. He'd fallen for her when she came in answer to a want ad, and hired her to sit at the receptionist's desk and run the switchboard. In the year and a half since then she'd become the responsible person in the office, the one everybody turned to. But he'd never got anywhere at all with her. When he'd persisted in trying to make a date with her, she'd taken to saying

impudent and disrespectful things to him about his shortcomings, with an air of bland innocence, as if she didn't know they were the kind of things a girl doesn't say to her boss even if they are true. He felt she rubbed it in by calling him "Mr. Allison" when everybody in the Southwest called him "Hank."

"You're later than usual, Mr. Allison," she said. "You were due at your draft board at half past six this morning."

"I was there. It took all day to get examined."

He'd have liked to tell her how he got there. Jeff Johnson had been on a binge, and when J. J. got drunk he still looked for trouble, forgetting that he was no longer as tough as he had been. Hank had rescued him after one of those fights he was so used to, and cajoled the police into forgetting about it, and put the old man to bed in Ponca City. He'd caught a bus after midnight that got him into Wichita at half past five in the morning. He'd had time to take a shower and change his clothes and get a cup of coffee. But he knew Connie wouldn't be impressed. She'd never been impressed by anything he did.

his potential or doing his part for the country. To gain her respect, Hank takes a more difficult job in the machine shop, increases production by a factor of three, and loses his extra weight. Connie's admiration for him grows, and she finally confesses that, while she liked him from the beginning, she feigned disinterest in order to motivate him to have confidence in himself and to change.

Thus, supportive heroines from the prewar years who aided men with their superior knowledge of the world similarly served to inspire male protagonists in wartime settings. Due to the pressing need for women in the labor force, however, the strong, assertive woman of the 1930s was shown to be so worthy of trust that she could responsibly fill positions of great authority. A common formula used during the war years featured women as managers of war production industries or businesses that OWI had identified as needing workers. Typically, the only child—a daughter—of the supervisor or owner of a vital enterprise takes over when he is temporarily disabled by enemy agents. "Dangerous Ways" (Robert Pinkerton, 2 January 1943) uses this story line to propel the heroine into managing a shipyard when the owner, who has adopted his orphaned employee, meets with a bad accident. Previously the shipyard secretary, she has a vast technical knowledge of shipbuilding and a good head for business, which enable her to handle the operation despite the presence of saboteurs. The formula is used again in "Heart on Her Sleeve" (Clarence Budington Kelland, 29 March 1943), another serial in which the daughter of a plywood company owner takes over the plant when her father is incapacitated. She also must single-handedly ferret out saboteurs and does so while ignoring the hostility of her male employees. Similarly, in "Taxi! Taxi!" (Clarence Budington Kelland, 14 April 1945), the shrewd, sardonic sister of a taxi fleet owner manages the business when he is drafted, hires brawny female drivers who have no trouble subduing rowdy fares, and not only defeats an international spy ring but makes the business more efficient.

Such stories promoted confidence in female ability to keep things going at home while the men were gone and also legitimized female authority in a male occupation. Most importantly, showing a woman taking over the reins of power from a temporarily disabled man symbolized the substitution of female workers for males in the wartime economy. These stories emphasized the temporary nature of this state of affairs by implying that while women were capable of shouldering male responsibilities it was desirable that they do so only when a man was not available for the job.

Another element of work adventure romances that was adapted to wartime conditions was the heroine's battle to win acceptance in a man's world. Prewar stories showed women trying to succeed as individuals, whereas wartime pieces emphasized the need to overcome barriers against women as a group. Writers had been asked by the Magazine Bureau as early as 1942 to counter prejudice against women in male-dominated blue-collar or supervisory occupations, especially in the skilled work needed in aircraft, machine shops, and shipping.[9] In apparent response to this request, stories were published showing how male resistance to women entering these fields could be overcome and that prejudice against women in them was wrong. In "Rough Turn" (Ray Millholland, 7 August 1943), the manager of a steam engine factory, now manufacturing guns for the navy, has been forced to hire women as machinists by the War Manpower Commission. Within two weeks, he is at his wits' end because two male workers have quit and a superintendent is threatening to leave as a result of friction with the new workers. In desperation, he puts one of the women in charge of the others. She informs him that the women are uncooperative because they are angry that men have been assigned the most skilled work and "get to have all the fun." She convinces him not only that women are capable of performing such jobs but that they desire them. After giving the women more interesting and difficult jobs, the problems come to an end.

Similarly, the heroine of "The Wall Between" (Margaret Craven, 25 September 1943) is hired to supervise the insurance department of a war plant that employs many female assembly workers. She has confidence in herself but is discouraged by the negative attitudes of her male colleagues. After several hostile encounters with men in the office, she understands the bitterness of women trying to find acceptance in a male world: "Ann knew that when working women got together and talked shop, they spoke frequently of the prejudice which men held against their sex in those top jobs where women compete with men." She finds herself in an office whose view is obstructed by a brick wall. It symbolizes for her the wall of prejudice she has encountered in the office. Ann manages to win the respect of most of her colleagues in spite of their initial hostility, however, and the story ends with the hiring of two more women in managerial positions. Such stories attempted both to persuade men that women could work with them as competent equals and to encourage women to stay on the job even if they were subjected to sexual harassment, which OWI knew was causing many women to leave war jobs.

Calculating that romantic entanglements could be used to highlight the war worker's virtue, OWI recommended that writers both emphasize her attractiveness and portray her patriotic service as the essential element in success at romance: "The poor girl, meeting conditions with courage and ingenuity, showing her community, perhaps, how to cooperate in lessening common sacrifice, demonstrates to the rich young man her superiority to the gals of his own milieu."[10] Such a strategy could simultaneously inspire war service in women and transmit the message that love of country was stronger than class barriers. We see this theme of the working-class heroine moving up in the world in "The Winning of Wentworth Jones, Jr." (Richard Thruelsen, 11 November 1944). Lois Neeley is from a working-class background (her father is a night watchman). Though she is not particularly beautiful, she has ambition and the cleverness necessary to achieve her goals. She has set her sights on a Princeton graduate, Wentworth Jones, Jr., who works in the local bank. He is from a wealthy family, which makes Lois's chances of marrying him very slim. She gets caught up in the patriotic spirit that follows Pearl Harbor, however, enlists in the Women's Army Corps, performs heroically in Italy, and becomes the town's most famous person. As a result of her newfound fame, Wentworth falls in love with her.

The major way writers supported labor recruitment in fiction was to reward war-minded heroines with male approval. Women who took war jobs in order to meet their obligations as patriotic citizens found romance whereas those who did not respond to government entreaties lost the respect of men. OWI's primary goal in all its home-front campaigns was to convince civilians that their cooperation was vital to help bring soldiers home alive; this goal was translated into romantic terms for women as fictional soldiers fell in love with "female soldiers" on the home front.

The preference of soldiers and civilians for women who put the country's interests over their own resulted in war workers being described as more sexually attractive than those who dressed alluringly but failed to understand that prewar femininity was inappropriate at a time when women were required to enter male roles. As one male character says, "Styles in beauty change . . . a blank baby stare will frighten even a college boy in 1943" (George Bradshaw, "An Afternoon Some Weeks Later," 4 September 1943). Because the country needed women to fill in for men overseas, they were valued for their physical strength, intellectual acuity, courage, and ability to competently perform challenging tasks. Hence, writers explicitly rejected "do-nothing" femininity in order to reassure women that they would continue attracting men even though they were assuming male responsibilities: "In days of peace, the really attractive numbers were to be found at senior proms, night clubs, beaches and even, occasionally, garden parties. War changed all that. The beautiful things are now discovered often wearing khaki or coveralls, driving recon cars at airfields, fitting gaskets in a war plant or piloting a packed bus on a downtown street" (Robert Carson, "Parting Is a Pain in the Neck," 25 March 1944).

One of the most dramatic changes brought about by the war was the positive image of married women workers that appeared during the recruitment campaign. A tabulation of the married female characters in lead stories featuring women engaged in wage labor shows that in 1941 no married women were portrayed in occupations other than housework. In 1943, however, 18 percent of the female characters in the *Post* engaged in wage labor were married, and half of these were in male work roles. The proportion of women workers who were married increased to 30 percent in 1944. In stories of the postwar transition period, there were more married women shown working than in 1941, but the proportion dropped to 11 percent (see table 3). The increase in married female characters who worked outside the home can be partially attributed to the rise in the number of married women in the labor force, but this increase is too

Table 3   Married Female Characters Portrayed in Wage Labor in Lead
Stories Featuring Women in the *Saturday Evening Post*

Year	% of females in wage labor who were married	% of all females in wage labor
1941	0	40
1943	18	57
1944	30	51
1945 (Jan.–July)	12	53
Aug. 1945–Mar. 1946	11	38

great to have resulted solely from actual labor force patterns, in
which the proportion of women workers who were married increased from 36 percent in 1940 to 44 percent in 1944.[11] It appears that writers were also responding to government directives, which asked that they not portray marriage as a full-time
career and that they make special efforts to encourage married
women to enter the work force: "It is high time that the housewife . . . begins to understand that the invitation to women
to work outside their homes means the woman who has not
worked in a paying job before. (And time her husband begins to
understand it too!)"[12]

Although the destructive career wife was a common figure in
prewar fiction, wartime stories portrayed working wives as able
to handle their home responsibilities without harming their
families. For example, a story cited by the Magazine Bureau
as supportive of the womanpower campaign features a WAVE
lieutenant who is the mother of the heroine's boyfriend. A dynamic speaker who lectures on the vital need for women in the
military, she is at the same time a warm and responsible family
woman. She fills a motherly role for the heroine, who accom-
panies her on the lecture tour, and serves as a role model for
her. When the heroine accepts her boyfriend's proposal of marriage, she decides that she will remain a WAVE largely because
her future mother-in-law has demonstrated that it is possible to
combine work with love.[13]

Another story that illustrates the efforts writers made to recruit married women into the labor force is "The Belittling Parent" (Isabella Holt, 11 September 1943). Appearing as part of the
fall campaign in 1943, it tries to reassure housewives both that

they could handle a job and that husbands, whose resistance OWI recognized to be a key factor in women not taking a job, could be convinced to support their employment.[14] The story features a middle-aged housewife named Mildred who is the mother of two teenagers. Her sister, Dr. Augusta Milgate, is a dean of women at a university, and she tries to convince Mildred to take a war job: "People with your capabilities are so much needed!" Mildred's children, however, think she is incapable of handling anything more challenging than housework. "Aunt Gus" reminds them that their mother graduated from high school with honors in chemistry; moreover, she completed one year of college. In a sharp reversal of prewar attitudes toward women giving up careers for marriage, the story makes it clear that Mildred has suffered from her choice to be a full-time homemaker: "'Then,' said Aunt Gus with intentional flatness, 'she married and took to wangling butter out of the grocer.' We [the children] stared at each other. Our mother a chemical prodigy! 'It's the skeleton in my closet,' [Mildred] said, 'It's dead and buried.' . . . 'I sometimes wonder,' said Aunt Gus, 'why we bother about educating women.'" Having won the support of her niece and nephew, Aunt Gus then counters the objections of Mildred's husband that the family needs her at home: "But this is wartime . . . the Government wants everyone to use his highest skills." Though initially dubious about their mother's qualifications for seeking work at a munitions plant, the children join forces against their resistant father, asserting that it is appropriate for women to shoulder other responsibilities in wartime: "Look at the Russian women. Most of them are generals." He eventually comes around to their point of view, and Mildred, bolstered by their encouragement, signs up for a training course at the university.

The stories that portrayed working wives show them as a normal feature of wartime living, and romances ending with engagement frequently make clear that the heroine will continue her career after marriage. The narcissistic career woman driven by ambition who ends up lonely and unloved disappeared from wartime romances. The closest figure to her is the beautiful goldbricker who fails to take a job and who thereby loses her sweetheart to a hardworking riveter or welder. Writers thus altered long-standing formulas wherein marriage marked the end of legitimate female participation in the world outside the home.

Other evidence that writers supported government pleas to draw homemakers into the labor force is provided by romances which depicted day care centers as a healthy environment for children. The *Magazine War Guide* carried detailed information about the Lanham Act to encourage magazines to publicize the child care program. Responding to reports from the Federal Works Agency, which showed that mothers were missing work and even quitting war jobs because they could not find adequate care for their children, OWI asked writers to create a favorable image of day care centers: "Mothers need to be convinced of the advantages of community services for their children. . . . Magazines have done much, may care to do more, in interpreting what steady, reliable care for children of war working parents means. The advantages to the child in health, nutrition, training, and play, and the dangers of neglect due to haphazard arrangements for supervision may be shown through magazine articles describing actual situations in communities all over the country."[15]

Fiction writers supported the campaign to increase public acceptance of institutionalized child care by setting romances and comedies against the backdrop of a day care center. In "Sea Change" (Phyliss Duganne, 20 November 1943), for example, a romance develops between a shell-shocked veteran and the head of a child care center where he helps her with her duties while recovering from his wounds. A story by Paul Gallico, one of the members of the Writers' War Board, similarly puts a day care center at the center of the action. "Parties Are Out" (20 February 1943) concerns two fun-loving debutantes who take jobs in the welfare department of an aircraft factory to help the war effort. They are charged with seeing to it that the women workers are productive and happy. After raising money for this purpose, they decide to establish a nursery at the factory. The project is so successful that they are swamped with requests from defense plants all across the country for information on how to set up similar facilities. Coupling humor and love with the concept of public child care helped make such a radical change in child-rearing practices seem normal and safe.

Although these elements of the recruitment campaign produced positive images of employed white women in the *Post* and expanded definitions of their roles, they did not have a like impact on treatments of black women. A mere thirteen stories in my sample contained black characters and most of these were placed in background roles as domestic servants, which was the way blacks had been incorporated into fiction before the war.[16] Only three of the stories featured black female characters in prominent roles, the nature of which indicates to what a great degree black women failed to benefit from the changes OWI tried to effect.

"Look Well on His Face" (J. J. DesOrmeaux, 27 February 1943) concerns the cook and chauffeur of a white doctor and his wife whose son has been killed in action. Comfy and Joe are about to marry but experience a crisis in their relationship when Joe is drafted. Joe is afraid to join the army because of a childhood trauma—his unbalanced father ax-murdered his mother and Joe was with him when the police made their arrest, having first fired numerous shots into their home. Ever since, Joe has been terrified of guns and cannot bring himself to defend his country. Comfy is filled with guilt and shame as Joe prepares to flee but also feels that he should not have to die for "white folks." In the midst of her confusion, she sees a statue of Abraham Lincoln in the town square and is reminded of her mother's admiration for him. She hears her mother's voice counseling her that black people could never repay what Lincoln had done to free the slaves, and Comfy proceeds to cure Joe of his fear, stating that she has made a soldier of her man "for Mister Lincoln." The story's main point is that blacks have a stake in victory as well as whites because America stands for freedom of all races.

The other two stories focus on a mammy figure who looks after Judith, a young service wife ("Lunny is So Helpless!" 13 May 1944, and "Admirals Ain't No Problem," 9 September 1944, both by Jan Fortune). Lunny is so devoted to her employer that she follows Judith, at her own expense, when she joins her new husband at a naval base near Baltimore. This is despite the fact that Lunny has been hired by another white woman at almost twice her former salary and that Judith cannot afford to pay her nor can she furnish board and room because blacks are not allowed to live on base. Undeterred by these circumstances,

Lunny proceeds to strike up a relationship with the black gar-
bageman, Dan, who services the navy officers, taking care of his
numerous children so that he can join the navy himself and
help out his country. She eschews Judith's suggestion that she
find a defense job in Baltimore because that would mean not
being around to run Judith's household. Besides, she claims,
she already supports the war effort by freeing Dan for military
service and taking care of his children; in fact she advises Judith to have a baby of her own so that she has a part to play too.

In all these stories, black women are shown as content to remain in their subservient relationships to whites, despite the
fact that, in reality, they left domestic service in large numbers
to seek better work in war production centers: between 1940
and 1944 black domestic service workers declined from 59.9
percent to 44.6 percent of all employed black women.[17] In addition, they perpetuate racist stereotypes of black men as cow-
ards, of black families as pathological, and of black women as
loyal to whites, putting aside their own opportunities for advancement in favor of those they serve.

Writers translated OWI's desire to eliminate racial prejudice
through stories that reassured whites that blacks were patriotic
people who would not step outside the boundaries of white su-
premacy and who accepted segregation. This assessment is
supported by a study of minority representation in magazine
fiction from the years 1937 to 1943 by Bernard Berelson and Patricia Salter, which concluded that blacks remained in prewar
marginal, low-status roles. In wartime stories, no blacks appeared as heroes or heroines, and they were cast in the lowest
occupational ratings of all groups surveyed. Furthermore, they
(along with Jews) were the only group to possess more disapproved than approved character traits. In short, the study concludes, the war had no positive impact on the fictional treatment of black people.[18]

Although images of white women were improved as a result
of the recruitment campaign, they were undercut by the overall
context of the drive to weaken traditional preconceptions about
women's roles. Propaganda for the home front was to inspire a
feeling of collective responsibility, selfless dedication to winning the war, and solid identification of civilian activity with
men overseas. The primary message writers were asked to con-

vey was that individuals should drop their normal routines and private dreams in order to pitch in wherever needed to help the community, whether that be a local problem or a national emergency. Fiction from the war years is infused with a sensibility of common struggle as families pooled their resources, neighbors volunteered to help each other out, and small towns embarked on civic projects.

In "My Kind of Guy" (Alice Lent Covert, 27 March 1943), for instance, a small town is disrupted by the arrival of hundreds of workers for an ammunition plant. The provincial suspicion of outsiders is compounded by the fact that the migrants have settled in makeshift trailer camps, which the townspeople consider an eyesore and evidence of the inhabitants' shiftless attitudes. The story focuses on the mayor's daughter, who works in the plant and comes to love one of the migrants. Her father violently disapproves of the match, saying that "his kind of people" are roughnecks and hoodlums. His opinion reflects the town's hostility, a factor of which the workers are keenly aware and one that lowers their morale. Clearly, the division is destructive to both sides and to the productivity of the plant. The conflict is resolved when a tornado hits the migrant camp and triggers the townsfolk's natural spirit of neighborly concern. In extending a helping hand, they discover that the outsiders are hardworking people struggling to put together a decent life under harsh conditions, and the workers see a warm, generous side of those who had hurt them. The young lovers' receipt of the mayor's blessing mirrors the reconciliation that occurs between the middle-class merchants, the long-time residents, and the working-class migrants.

The message of "My Kind of Guy" is that the hardships of wartime will be eased if people set aside their prejudices and recognize that the common welfare depends upon the cooperation and goodwill of every member of the community. Class divisions are not only inappropriate but destructive to the interests of the country. Writers found in class conflict a good premise for demonstrating the need for national unity and respect for the contributions of blue-collar workers; creating romances between lovers from different class backgrounds was an especially useful strategy for dramatizing the idea that all individuals shared a common goal, one which overrode the socioeconomic differences between them. The young lovers stood as an example of purehearted, enlightened souls whose selfless dedication to their love overcame the illegitimate authority of small-minded adults. Their modern idealism provided a stark contrast to the fearful prejudice of an outmoded narrow mentality.

The theme of class cooperation in easing community problems is struck again in "Parties Are Out" when two upper-class debutantes turned personnel supervisors of women on the line encourage a working-class assembler to heal her broken heart through raising money for a factory nursery. Similarly, "For Women Only" (Margaret Craven, 16 January 1943) concerns the successful efforts of a small town to raise money for war relief. Spurred on by the scoffing attitude of the men, women unite across class lines to fill their coffers with donations. These images of civic-minded volunteers from every walk of life both reinforced the notion that united effort was required to win the war and put forth a positive portrait of the working class.

OWI had asked writers not only to foster a spirit of national unity but to provide inspiring stories of people dealing well with hardship in order to emphasize the danger threatening the country and to stimulate individual initiative in coping with domestic inconvenience. The *Post* had for years published stories about the frontier and rural life, along with sparkling tales of urban glamor, because they represented the foundation of an idealized national character: hard work, independence, spiritual innocence, natural piety, and strong community values. These stories came to the forefront during the war years, as did images of pioneering in advertising, because they conveyed an image of ordinary people meeting the challenge of survival with ingenuity and dogged persistence. These were characters who did not need to be told to ration supplies or look out for each other or rely on themselves. They knew that the only thing that stood between themselves and disaster was their own energy and making the most of limited resources. Heartache, loss, and uncertainty were a normal part of life, to be gotten through with a minimum of self-pity or fear.

Because the family farm evoked images of an American rural tradition with its equal components of stoicism and tough-minded individualism, it became a favorite backdrop of *Post* writers for developing "war-mindedness." "Happy the Bride" (David Lamson, 3 July 1943) is a nostalgic look at rural living and the rewards of toughening up. Carol Vaughn is a middle-class, city-bred young woman earning her living as a bank clerk. She falls in love with the eldest of six farm boys who takes her to live with his parents and brothers after their marriage. Initially hampered by her lack of experience with farm work, Carol eventually strengthens her muscles and her mind as she learns to make butter, milk cows, bake bread, mold candles, and complete the daily chores. She comes to appreciate a strong family environment after her painful experience as the child of divorced parents and realizes that she can do without the luxuries on which she had come to depend.

Farm life is glorified too in a story about an office worker at a shipyard who lives with her aunt and best friend in a crowded apartment. Happy that she is making good money and helping her country, Florence Vail nevertheless longs to live on a farm and finds that her dreams will come true when she meets a sailor who owns a farm in Minnesota (Agnes Burke Hale, "Love Me, Love My Cow," 25 September 1943).

The connection between patriotism and farm life is made more explicit in "Yellow Is the Color of the Sun," a story by WWB member Phyliss Duganne that attempts to recruit cannery workers and farm laborers (12 June 1943). The protagonist, Milo Penney, has been deferred to help his parents run their farm while his three brothers become war heroes and his sister ferries bombers to England. Intensely patriotic, Milo stands proudly at attention in the local movie theater when the national anthem is played on the screen and feels ashamed that he is not fighting for his country. His fiancée does not help matters with her negative attitude toward farming. His unhappiness vanishes when he meets Emily Murdock who, though she comes from a wealthy family and does not have to work, has taken a menial job in her father's canning factory. Emily has a more complete understanding of the relationship between production on the home front and the battle lines abroad and so persuades him that he is performing heroic national service by growing food for the boys in uniform and the production fighters at home. Similarly, the mother of two male war workers in "Trust Mother" (Lucian Cary, 22 May 1943) runs her Kansas dairy farm by herself, rents out a room to a migrant who has come to work at a shell factory, is a hostess three nights a week at the local recreation center for the plant laborers, and refuses her sons' offers of help, saying that everyone needs to pull her own weight in wartime. Furthermore, she gives all the gifts they buy her with their high wages to needy people in the town.

The rural settings were good backdrops for characters with tough minds, strong bodies, and big hearts, people who were used to dealing with crisis and to doing without when they had to. They also reminded readers of their frontier heritage, the long, hard struggle the nation had come through to become a modern industrial giant. To protect those gains, Americans now had to revivify the qualities that had made their country great and realize that survival was once again at stake. Finally, the emphasis on agriculture and family farms served to link an army mobilized through advanced technology with the peaceful activities of people working at basic, mundane tasks. The home front was a giver of life, the sower of hope in a future victory, the backbone of and breadbasket for the soldier abroad.

One other characteristic of fiction from the recruitment period is that characters were sharply divided into two camps: those who put the needs of others at the forefront of their minds and hearts and those who had no social conscience. Compassionate women (and occasionally men) nursed invalid parents, adopted orphans, took in roomers desperate for housing, volunteered for community service work, entertained GIs far from home, and kept their worries and complaints hidden from the world. These were the heroines and heroes of wartime stories, people with wisdom, strength, intelligence, and a deep sense of connection to others. They were loved, admired, and considered special individuals by those who were most important to them, gifts made all the more precious by the fact that they were unsolicited. Once embarked on a path of service, heartaches healed and feelings of emptiness or resentment disappeared. Those who refused to contribute or give up their self-oriented desires, in contrast, were chided, rejected, or unmasked as enemy agents.

"Knoll Island" (George Agnew Chamberlain, 7 August 1943) contains characters with these qualities. It concerns a farm couple that have uncomplainingly sent their three boys to war. To help ease their loneliness, they adopt a sixteen-year-old orphan whose father has been killed in action. Karry is a tough survivor who has been taking care of herself for years as her mother died when she was just a baby. Determined to take the place of the sons, she learns to plow, works very hard, and refuses to cry when people tease her about looking like a boy. When the eldest son returns, severely wounded, Karry nurses him back to health and becomes his close companion. Exploring the coastline of Delaware, they stumble upon a wire spool stamped with a Nazi insignia and set out to capture the spies to whom it belongs. The boy veteran swears Karry to silence as she vows to do whatever is necessary to bring in the saboteurs. After many dangerous episodes, they corner the guilty party, a draft-dodging poacher with a reputation for shiftlessness. Not only has the adventure routed a traitor, but the young patriots heal their various wounds by falling in love.

In this story Karry's standing in for her adopted brothers symbolizes the replacement of men by women as the chief laborers who stepped into male roles. Though unsure of herself, she toughens up to do what is necessary on the farm. The prejudice she encounters does not deter her either; Karry is from strong stock and does not give up easily. Her resilience and toughness, however, do not "masculinize" Karry. She can be tender and nurturant when called upon to do so. She can also follow a man's leadership, as is demonstrated when one of the sons returns from battle to wage another kind of war at home.

The following piece produced by a member of the WWB also illustrates the interweaving of romantic fantasies with selfless behavior. "Don't Talk about Love" (Phil Strong, 29 April 1944) appeared as part of the spring "Women in the War" campaign in 1944.[19] It features a college student, Hepzi Bradford, who leaves school in order to help her father with the family farm when her mother dies. This aspect of the story reflects the many pleas made by the Magazine Bureau for magazines to recruit agricultural laborers.[20] Hepzi also learns to shoot an antiaircraft gun as part of her plane-spotting duties for the Office of Civil Defense and serves voluntarily as the town's fire warden. In addition, she is a qualified Red Cross worker and sells war bonds in her spare time. She and her good friend Evelyn Leslie, who is also a plane spotter and volunteer worker, are admired by two war heroes who fall in love with them. Contrasting with these hard-working, patriotic characters is Evelyn's widowed mother, who is selfish, lazy, and interested mainly in finding a husband. Mrs. Leslie has no idea how to use ration points, plants a victory garden only because she wants to win a prize, and pressures Evelyn not to join the WACs. The patriotic characters are clearly portrayed as more attractive people than the rather silly and pitiable slacker.

Female characters were the primary exemplars of these community-oriented, selfless attitudes. Perhaps writers found it easier to justify a woman's civilian status and so make of her a representative of the home-front spirit. Soldiers were such obvious glamorous figures that admirable men in stories were usually in uniform; their willingness to serve their country needed no further illustration. But women had the option of sitting out the war (at least this was the middle-class image that dominated the public mind). In addition, selflessness was a well-established element in the traditional role of women, so writers could easily include it in characterizations. Finally, of course, the propaganda goal of bringing women into the labor force meshed smoothly with the overall mobilization program in that war-worker heroines could be inspirational examples of people toughening up for war, tackling new jobs, giving up a life of ease for the good of the whole.

The war worker often served as an object lesson in how the proper citizen ought to be behaving. She should tolerate unpleasant conditions, gladly sacrifice her own comfort, and love her country unreservedly. "Have Fun, Kid" (Naomi Lane Babson, 31 July 1943) is typical in its disapproval of people who were not pulling their weight. The heroine is a young service wife who has quit her job at a tool factory because the hours were too long and the work too hard. She resists the idea of putting her nose to the grindstone and not having any fun so, despite the protestations of her husband overseas, she goes to work in a bar as a glamorous cigarette seller. Ralph, the bar owner, is a sleazy sort who has faked a case of ulcers to get out of the army: "[He had] a kind of softness . . . a talcum-powder-and-lotion look mighty different from the boys up at camp." Barby begins to feel uncomfortable with his sexual advances and with the underhanded way he conducts his business. Seeing that the bar attracts people of low character and realizing that her husband was right about the need for civilians to stick to their war jobs, she returns to her old position determined to grow up and help out her country.

A common story line designed to make readers critical of those who were not living up to their civic responsibilities concerned a wealthy young woman who initially resents wartime conditions but eventually reforms. Although it could have been developed independently, this plot was suggested by OWI in a memo to fiction writers: "The rich girl who has never lacked anything finds herself denied luxuries, is resentful and proclaims it, is shown the error of her ways by the handsome young soldier from the other side of the tracks, with whom of course she falls in love."[21]

The fun-loving, glamorous heroine of "No Orchids, Please" (Travis Mason, 7 April 1945) is typical of this character type. Lacey Thorne is a hard-boiled cynic who has turned her back on the concept of virtue after her hard climb to the top. She does not like the pressure put upon her by her soldier boyfriend and his friends to volunteer her time for war relief as she feels life is to be enjoyed at every moment possible. Altruism is to her a fake impulse, motivated by a desire for approval: "her skeptical looking brows were faintly mocking as she watched Fran and May Norris with their knitting, Kay Van Dyke feather-stitching white flannel for a Red Cross layette, and Sue Crane mending a coat for Russian Relief." Besides, she is too sophisticated for such homey, dull tasks. Lacey rationalizes her abstention from war service by saying that she does not go in for Hollywood patriotism and melodrama: "the dream of herself in a WAC uniform, sticking to her post while cannon thundered and Mike appeared at the door, picturesquely haggard, . . . well, that was adolescent movie stuff, gooey enough to make her shudder."

Her conscience starts to bother her, however, when she wonders what she will tell young people of the next generation when they ask her what she did in the war. The death of an elderly neighbor's grandson pushes her over the edge of her defenses, and she changes her attitude about pitching in: "I know how smug and dull I've always said [Fran] was. But, well, it's better to be smug about galloping around doing good deeds, than to be smug about not doing them." Having heard about her transformation, the soldier with whom she is in love comes home on furlough and asks her to marry him. Grateful for their reconciliation, Lacey drops her arrogant, hard-bitten facade and allows her newfound morality to come to the fore: "She bent her head and laid her lips humbly against his big bony hand. 'I won't be much fun either' she assured him in a small subdued voice. 'I'll just be good.'"

These stories try to demonstrate that old-fashioned virtue is not something at which to sneer; rather, urbane cynicism is out of place in the modern world. Perhaps the hedonistic stance of the modern generation used to be a glamorous aspect of liberated young women. Now, however, women were being called upon to perform their traditional role of putting others first and to adopt a wholesome attitude of tenderness and compassion. Declaring one's freedom from the Victorian virtues of earnestness and female self-abnegation was not only selfish but monstrously irresponsible.

The heroine of "Lady Bountiful," written by WWB member Robert Carson (6 March 1943), undergoes a similar metamorphosis as she is forced to shed her flirtatious, sardonic persona for a life of war service. Katy Ramsay is rich, beautiful, and spoiled. Though her mother sets a good example by working as a nurse's aide for the Red Cross, Katy can think of nothing but clothes, parties, and boys, complaining that "War was an insidious presence. It was picking off the boys right and left. Pretty soon life would be exclusively devoted to the weaker sex." To her great chagrin, she offends the soldiers at a USO dance by wearing flashy clothes and making cynical wisecracks about the war. Rejected by a handsome pilot who bluntly tells her she is a parasite, Katy decides to change her ways by accepting a job on an army base doing backbreaking work as a file clerk. When her brother is declared missing in action, it is all she needs to commit herself firmly to the war effort, to keep her troubles to herself, and to put others first, an attitude that wins her the love of the personnel manager. Such stories were in line with OWI guidelines, which stressed that patriotic characters should be integrated into romantic fantasies: "The girl might almost lose the boy because of her flippant, or perhaps resentful, attitude toward [home-front campaigns]."[22]

Recruitment propaganda put forward the liberating message that prejudice against women in nontraditional occupations was wrong and that women did not need to make a choice between employment and family. The simultaneous use of war workers and other women as models of home-front patriotism, however, reinforced values that circumscribed female behavior. Rather than fostering images of independence and power, wartime stories made it clear that women were to subordinate ego to a cause more important than the self, that the work they chose should not empower them personally; folding bandages was as valuable as operating a riveting gun. The paramount factors in war work were a desire to contribute and a generous heart. The humbling of arrogant, self-absorbed women was a major theme in fiction of the recruitment period, as was the softening of a hard protective exterior. While designed to motivate community effort, the image of women as paragons of virtue dovetailed with a reactionary ideology that counseled female service to the family, personal modesty, and self-forgetfulness.

As the war progressed, this reactionary aspect of home-front propaganda became more pronounced. A story appearing in May of 1944 illustrates the direction taken by writers in their treatment of women's new roles as the recruitment campaign came to a close. It features a young aircraft worker, Candy Sherwin, who lives with her lower-middle-class family in a modest bungalow. The story opens with Candy ending her shift and joyfully pocketing a big raise; it will allow her to buy a glamorous black evening gown with which she will greet her high school sweetheart home on furlough. Most of the dialogue centers on her hefty salary, which is almost as much as that of her bookkeeper father, and the feeling of independence it brings her: "[She felt] like somebody new and important." A conflict develops over the dress because Mrs. Sherwin feels it is too grown-up for a seventeen-year-old, but Candy believes it is an appropriate symbol of her newfound adulthood: "I am not a little girl dressing up. I am not a child to be spoiled or not spoiled. I am full grown. I am working, helping to build planes that will win the war, doing an important job." Chafing at the attempts of her parents to control her, she threatens to find an apartment of her own, something she can now afford.

The climax of the story occurs when her boyfriend arrives for their date. Eager to make a dramatic entrance, Candy waits upstairs while he greets the family and overhears him sigh with relief: "This is swell. Everything's just the same. . . . This is what soldiers dream of—a nice soft sofa, a warm room, a family, lemon cake—" When he sees her, however, his face falls and he becomes distant and cold. It is only after Mrs. Sherwin describes Candy's war job that his mood changes:

> "She works terribly hard, eight and ten hours every day. She's got a real important job, making parts for airplanes, and it takes a lot out of her. When she's through, she's good and tired, and she enjoys a quiet evening, don't you, Candy?" "Yes," Candy said weakly. "Yes, I do." She looked at Jack and she saw his eyes change. "I didn't know you made airplane parts. You never—I should say that is an important job. You must be pretty good." His voice was warm and alive and interested, and he put down the plate and grabbed her hand. It was the first time he had touched her. . . . He was looking at her in a different way now. He was looking at her as though she were somebody special.

After he informs her that he just wants "to do all the things I used to do," Candy changes into bobby-socks and sneakers before they set out for a movie and a soda. The next day she returns the dress, appreciating the wisdom of her mother's words: "You don't always get good out of money" (Gertrude Schweitzer, "My Own Money," 6 May 1944).

The heroine's delight in the power granted to her by a high salary is shown here to be selfish and immature. The soldier is alienated by her new image and responds positively only when he learns that she is performing a key job in war production. Not only does the story discourage war workers from spending their money (to discourage consumption of scarce material), but it conveys the idea that they should view their role as one of duty to the men overseas, not as an opportunity for exercising personal power. In addition, Candy's retreat from her stubborn insistence on the privileges of adult power delivers the message that war workers should accrue not individual authority as a result of their new experiences but rather a moral authority that flows from realizing they are working for an abstract principle.

By late 1944 the theme of nostalgia for an imagined prewar

gentleness and calm dominated fictional representation of the home front. Returning soldiers were shown longing for the days before they put on a uniform, for the time when they were still young at heart and carefree. In "Home Coming" (Dorothy M. Johnson, 1 July 1944), for example, Bud Winslow tries to adjust to civilian life after losing a hand and finds that home just does not seem the same. He feels burdened with the maturity the war has brought him and wishes people would stop treating him like someone special. When friends and family begin to see the boy inside, his world finally takes the shape it had before he left. Likewise, in "Nothing Must Change" (George Carousso, 29 July 1944) the younger brother of a veteran comes to understand his need for life on the home front to remain unchanged because it was that for which he was fighting.

The traditional family unit became the focal point of stories dealing with soldiers, both as a comforting shelter from the storm of combat and as the way of life they were defending. The protagonist of "Just a Few People" (Eric March, 18 November 1944) articulates this perspective to a family he has adopted as replacement for the one he never had: "I found out that nothing made a damned bit of difference to any of those guys [soldiers in the Sahara] but people, a few people that they knew were thinking of them at night. America was those few people. It was worth fighting for those few people."

Part of this romanticized vision of normal stability and safety was the sweetheart who made sure the home remained comfortable and familiar, who represented a wholesome blend of old-fashioned sweetness and gentle caretaking. The primary role of women in homecoming stories was to help the veteran adjust while healing the wounds of war. Susan Hartmann believes that the literature on returning veterans was a major factor in re-establishing traditional roles because women were counseled to focus themselves completely on the needs of men and to curb their independence: "Underlying such advice [for women to quit their jobs] was the assumption that masculine status deriving from productivity was critical to family stability and took precedence over women's needs for self-expression."[23]

Post fiction supports Hartmann's conclusion as soldiers grew misty-eyed over quiet, shy young women who symbolized to them the best of American womanhood. In "A Faint North

Wind" (Edwin A. Peeples, 28 October 1944), for instance, two sisters work in an aircraft factory. Opal Porter is plain and demure, preferring to fix up the house and bake rather than go to parties like her vivacious sister. Used to being upstaged, she is surprised to find that a soldier on leave whom she meets at a USO dance thinks she is far superior to the sister, who has stolen many a beau: "these jitterbugs take a girl—you know, a girl like we're fighting for, so we can come back and make a home for her, and they sling her around like she was a mop or a dishrag." Declaring that she is different, he asks Opal to marry him. The soldier of "The Lady Said 'Please'" (William Barrett, 21 October 1944) is also enamored of an innocent teenager he meets on furlough. Though she feels like a parasite because both parents and a sister are working while she is not allowed to, he assures her that she symbolizes everything for which he is fighting.

Hartmann goes on to say that the instructions to women for soothing veterans through putting a damper on their own ambitions flowed naturally from a belief that they were responsible for social morality: " [It was] part of a larger trend in the popular psychology of the period which saw women as the cause and/or potential redeemers of a deteriorating society."[24] In addition to idealizing retiring, old-fashioned women, fiction thrust women into the spotlight as guardians of morality by chronicling the horrendous consequences of female irresponsibility. Cruel and selfish mothers were so busy with their own lives that they neglected their children; wives of servicemen who were unfaithful to their husbands ruined perfectly good marriages. In "Honor Bright" (Doris Hume, 23 September 1944), a teenager gets mixed up with a juvenile delinquent who kills a soldier in a hit-and-run accident because her mother is hanging out in bars flirting with other men while her father is in boot camp. A veteran is stunned to learn that his divorced wife (who works in an aircraft plant) has given away their baby son in "Too Young to Know" (Harlan Ware, 16 December 1944). A mother of two soldiers mentally abuses the son left at home because she is jealous of her husband's success and so needs a scapegoat in "Whipping Boy" (Phyliss Duganne, 8 July 1944).

The refashioning of images to attract women into new occupations carried with it a rethinking of the direction in which modern women had been moving. The liberated, glamorous ideal of the 1930s was reassessed as well as the old notion that married women had no place in the world of paid employment. The previous decade was filled with sexist stereotypes of career women, but it idolized the woman who could make her way in the urban scene. She was exciting because her self-confidence and curiosity led her into great adventures. Her independence from family responsibilities freed her to investigate areas of modern life about which the public was intensely curious and marked her as a special person.

The setting for this figure was a fast-paced, glittering city pulsing with energy, exuding an almost frenetic aura as its inhabitants jostled for room in which to spread their wings. Survival meant thinking quickly, cutting through red tape, taking advantage of unexpected opportunities, and rolling with the punches. Being too sensitive to others or failing to protect one's own interests aggressively were guaranteed to set one back in the race for success.

The modern heroine, therefore, was applauded for her shrewd insight into the realities of life, her street-wise disregard for rules formulated by someone else standing in her way, and her unabashed pursuit of a personal dream. Sarcastic rejoinders were appropriate weapons in a society of individuals competing for status, and a healthy amount of cynicism was useful for dealing with complex, powerful people. The baubles of city life were treasures to possess, but they were meant only for those bold, wise, ambitious, and sophisticated enough to reach them. Women, as well as men in popular culture, were admired for their ability to rise to the top of the urban jungle without losing their sense of humor, their class, or their passion for life.

As popular artists changed entertainment formulas to deal with the war, however, this fantasy was replaced by the serious theme of national struggle and images of rural traditionalism coupled with a longing for a womblike world in which nothing changed or challenged. The sparkling achiever with her keen appetite for adventure and endearing iconoclasm began to be perceived as a threat to the nation's survival. She needed to curb her individualistic impulses in order to take care of the urgent business at hand: propping up soldier morale and keeping the home front stable and productive. It was paramount that she stop making waves so that a sorely needed calm would not be shattered. Female hedonism, disregard for tradition, and personal ambition were all luxuries a besieged nation could no longer afford.

Conceiving of national strength as a solid family unit, fiction writers drove home the message that women were to be especially vigilant in carrying out their social responsibilities. They could not flirt with playfulness or with stepping outside the boundaries of the family circle in this vulnerable time. Female risk taking and self-assertion were dangerous by-products of modernization for they threatened to dilute the collective will, sap the moral strength of a populace dependent upon feminine virtue and maternal altruism. It was crucial that people give up their adolescent dreams of carefree adventure and assume the sober mantle of citizenship. For men, this meant endangering their lives; for women, it entailed putting husband, children, and community first. For all, it required an earnest dedication to shoring up a world that could no longer be taken for granted, one in which the placidity of home was carefully protected.

Reconversion

The message that the work women were doing during the war was temporary became a major theme of the reconversion period as writers portrayed war workers leaving the labor force or returning to traditional female occupations. From August 1945 to March 1946, those heroines who worked outside the home were generally portrayed in nursing, teaching, or clerical work, reflecting the channeling of women into traditional employment areas that was occurring in reality. Some stories featured former war workers who took postwar female jobs. A pilot becomes a stewardess in "Diapers for Flight Six" (Win Brooks, 30 March 1946), for example; a WAC takes an unskilled factory job in "The Reconversion of Johnny" (James Lynch, 14 July 1945); and Dorrit Bly leaves the Women's Army Corps to resume her secretarial career in "Dorrit Remembers a Riddle" (Frank Bunce, 23 February 1946). The tabulation of occupations in which female characters are found in stories featuring women shows that the proportion of females in male jobs declined dramatically during the reconversion period to approximately prewar levels. The proportion of female characters in all wage work similarly declined (see table 4).

Just as writers had found in the woman worker a convenient symbol of collective strength during the mobilization of civilians, so now did they find in that figure the embodiment of peace: a tender, nurturant family woman. The domestication of the war-working heroine was most marked in stories wherein women who had performed competently in challenging war jobs were shown yearning for domesticity. A common figure was the stoic, tough-minded worker who gladly turned in her factory overalls or blue-collar shirt for a "normal" life that revolved around a family. For example, a female aeronautical engineer and pilot in "Mission for Henry" (Robert Carson, 21 July 1945) is pleased when the soldier protagonist anticipates her transformation into a homemaker: "I keep visualizing you in a rose-covered back yard, wearing simple coveralls and designing a baby carriage with retractable wheels." Another characteristic of fiction of this period is that stories concerning war workers portrayed them not as performing in their war jobs but as taking on maternal tasks. One piece that typifies this approach is "The Reconversion of Johnny," which concerns an aircraft worker and former WAC who is an expert in bomber instruments. However, we do not see her performing mechanical, skilled operations; instead, she is caring for her deceased sister's baby whom she has been forced to bring with her to the plant. Similarly, in "Diapers for Flight Six," the heroine is a pilot and former poster model for military recruitment now employed as a stewardess. The story concerns her efforts to care for an abandoned baby on board, and the pilot's reaction indicates the postwar shift in attitudes toward female employment: "Hanscomb looked good holding the baby, dim-eyed and sweet and motherly. . . . Ladies should be having babies, not flying all around the country. . . . Hanscomb wasn't a Career Girl, after all."

What at first glance seems to be a dramatic change in ideology, one which initially glorified women as workers, then as homemakers, was in actuality at least partially consistent with the portrayal of women's roles throughout the war years. The normative image of the full-time homemaker did not disappear during the recruitment period; it was modified through a mini-

Table 4   Occupations of Female Characters in Lead Stories Featuring Women in the *Saturday Evening Post*

Year	% in atypical female occupations[a]	% in typical female occupations[b]	% in no occupation[c]	% in occupations of neither category[d]
1941	16	44	30	10
1943	28	33	29	10
1944	28	21	33	18
1945 (Jan.–July)	47	20	33	0
Aug. 1945– Mar. 1946	13	17	58	12

[a] Business executive, journalist, servicewoman, psychologist, factory worker, pilot, policewoman, commercial artist, farm owner, college teacher, taxi driver, engineer, shipyard worker, gas station attendant.

[b] Nurse, nurse's aide, housewife, teacher, office worker, clerk, waitress, maid, housekeeper, stewardess, cashier.

[c] No occupation mentioned, volunteer war work, student, adolescent, retiree.

[d] Entertainer, detective, spy, writer, resistance fighter, Red Cross Motor Corps, work not specified.

mization of the marriage-career conflict, by emphasizing women in wage-work roles (especially male ones), and by featuring married women workers. Indications that this modification was temporary appear in many of the stories that encouraged women to enter the labor force.

The following three stories illustrate the way writers created themes that simultaneously encouraged increased acceptance of women in male roles and conveyed the message that war workers were homemakers at heart. They are also good examples of how romance adventure formulas were used to attract female readers to war work. "Heart on Her Sleeve" (Kelland, 29 March 1943) is a serial that appeared the month the recruitment campaign began. It spoke to three issues the *Magazine War Guide* repeatedly asked writers to stress: combating sabotage, setting stories in labor-short industries, and womanpower. The heroine is Andrée Senlac, daughter of a plywood company owner who has graduated from college with a degree in chemistry. Her father insists that she memorize his secret formula for treating wood in case anything happens to him. The company has converted to production of bomb noses, and he realizes

War workers are mothers at heart. From "The Reconversion of Johnny," reprinted from *Saturday Evening Post*, 14 July 1945. © 1945 The Curtis Publishing Company.

It isn't long before Sally is sprinkling milk on her wrist and saying it is just right. That girl knows everything.

The Reconversion of Johnny

By JAMES C. LYNCH

INSTEAD of being production manager for Sonegard Aircraft Appliances, I wish I had taken on a softer job, like wiping out the Japanese Empire singlehanded or something. You would think I was the only guy around the plant who knew anything. The hired help even ask my advice about marriage, when they know I hate women. And the married ones tell me about kids, and I hate kids. All such things interfere with production. So they call me Hard-Boiled Johnny Ramsey behind my back. And right now, two of them have me cornered.

Trent Albuzzi, the machine-shop boss, is pawing at my right arm, and a redheaded girl from the assembly line is plucking at my other sleeve and acting all ready to shed tears. And Herb King, assembly-line boss, is standing down the shop, looking at me as much as to say, "You side with that redhead and I'm through, brother."

"Johnny," Trent says, "we got a shortage on turbo vanes and the bed on Number Two mill is sprung and all the other mills are set up and —"

On Monday he was a confirmed bachelor; on Tuesday he met Miss Sally Jones; by Wednesday evening he had a beautiful sweetheart . . . and a baby.

And the redhead says, "Johnny, you will just have to make that awful Herb King stop scolding me because I can't remember the names of all those silly little parts."

Then the loud-speakers start squawking. "Mr. Ramsey! Telephone!"

"Switch mills!" I yell at Trent. "Put those slide rods on Two! It won't make any difference if the bed is sprung!" . . . And you," I tell the redhead, "don't bother Herb about parts. Ask Ray Valk, at the stock

ILLUSTRATED BY GEORGE GARLAND

room. He'll know what you want. The coming now."

I start her toward Ray and turn toward but Ray hails me. He waves a long white "It's come. My induction notice."

"Your what?" I almost scream. "Wh crazy! They can't do that!"

"The wife," says Ray, "will be glad to hea decision. But I better report in two weeks order reads."

"Give me that thing," I tell him, and envelope and run into my office and snatc phone and say, "Ramsey."

"Aren't those speakers working out in th says Mr. William Sonegard Aircraft Applia have been trying to get you for three minute my slippers and lounging robe when the n woke me up."

"O. K.," he laughs. "I just called to tell Treasury Department turned down my reque your pay. They claim you are making enough a forty-eight-hour week." *Continued on*

how important it is to the government. His concern is heightened when he discovers evidence of sabotage. Andrée is extremely bright but immature and flighty at the beginning of the story, thinking only of how she can capture the affections of a handsome commander who has been assigned to inspect the plant by the navy.

Andrée quickly develops "war-mindedness," however, when her father is suspiciously run off a mountain road, which forces her to take charge of the plant. She is immediately confronted with an accident that halts production, a crisis compounded by the resistance of male workers to taking orders from a woman. She rises to the occasion, following the advice her father gave her before the accident: "You must learn to decide, and to decide promptly. If your employees fail to have confidence in you, organization breaks down. It is essential to impress them with your ability to decide. . . . You must never show hesitation or nervousness." Because Andrée delivers her orders decisively and refuses to be intimidated by her workers, she wins their respect while handling the emergency with authority. The quick wit she demonstrates in this episode is a focal point of the story as is her refusal to bow to male domination. A scene that illustrates these qualities is one in which she encounters a saboteur. Mr. Batten is bragging to her about his handsome son in a way that sets him up as a representative of German authoritarianism: "I desired an heir of whose appearance I could be proud. I willed it." Andrée takes advantage of the opening he has provided by retorting that American women have the backbone to resist such treatment:

It must have been hard on Mrs. Batten to have you sit and glare at her, willing a Barrymore profile on the baby she was going to have, when she would much rather have played gin rummy with you to take her mind off things, and if my husband ever sits around and tries to . . . hypnotize me into having a matinee idol, I will double-cross him and have twins with cross eyes. . . . If anybody snipes at us [Senlacs] with will power, we blast right back at them with sales resistance. I mean, if you were hinting anything about like you want papa to give in to your foul desires about the plant, then you might as well bring your will power in out of the rain or it will get all water-soaked and warped."

Not only is Andrée sharp-tongued when she needs to be, but her courage enables her to fend off an attack by three men who try to break into her house, to disable the chillingly malevolent leader of the sabotage operation, and to hold a saboteur over a vat of boiling water in order to make him talk. There are several elements in this story that indicate that the writer was following OWI guidelines. I have earlier mentioned one of these—placing the story in a lumber mill, which the *Magazine War Guide* asked be done in January of 1943 in order to attract workers to this labor-short industry. Another is the focus on sabotage, which the *Guide* suggested as a way to dramatize the role of workers on the home front. A third is the reference to Andrée's chemistry degree, which reflects the *Guide's* instruction to encourage female students to take science and math courses since there was a shortage of labor in technical fields like engineering.[25] Related to this is the story's central message that women are capable of supervisory work. Andrée's filling in for her father, of course, adds to this message the image of women capably shouldering male responsibilities. Finally, the writer makes it clear that, though women should be accepted as strong leaders, their managerial positions are only temporary. After Andrée destroys the sabotage operation (thereby winning the love of the handsome commander), she realizes her father's return will mean giving up the business. Initially, she is chagrined at the thought of turning over the reins of power for "the affairs and interests of young womanhood." But she soon changes her mind as she considers how pleasant it will be to settle down with Commander O'Toole.

The message that women belong in male positions only for the duration of the war is made even more explicit in Phyliss Duganne's "When the Boys Come Home" (17 July 1943). Duganne was an active member of the Writers' War Board, and her stories take careful account of the propaganda needs requested by the Magazine Bureau. Here she deals with the resistance of men to women in heavy industry. Lt. Pete Verplank has left his managerial job at an iron foundry to enlist on the assurance that he will get his job back at the end of the war. While overseas, he receives a letter from his fiancée, who excitedly tells him about her training at defense school where women are learning to operate machines, rivet, and weld. Pete initially fails to take her seriously, but on his way home on leave he is upset by a man who complains that women entering male jobs will refuse to give them up when the soldiers return. When Pete sees how calloused and dirty Marilyn's hands are from welding, it is all he needs to set himself against the womanpower campaign. Gradually, however, he changes his mind as he realizes how wonderful Marilyn is to be able to do what her country needed. In addition, he comes to understand that beneath her welder's mask she is still the pretty and gentle girl he loved: "She was such a helpless, feminine girl. She was the ideal of what every man in the armed forces fought for—to preserve her world and return to her in it." He can accept Marilyn's wartime job because she will leave it when he comes home: "When he returned . . . she would be waiting, in a pretty dress, with flowers in her hair."

Duganne's attempt to reassure men that women would not supplant them or lose their femininity is echoed in a serial that grew out of the Magazine Bureau's "Women in Necessary Services" campaign, which tried to attract women into male jobs in transportation. "Taxi! Taxi!" (Kelland, 14 April 1945) stars a working-class heroine named Maggie McTigg who takes over her brother's taxi service and hires all female drivers when he enlists. Maggie is an astonishingly courageous character with the wit to handle herself in any situation: "she developed . . . a self-protective shrewdness [and] . . . a certain humorous detachment." However, her self-assertion is no threat to men, who feel at ease around her. The story quickly establishes Maggie's trustworthiness, which both reassures the reader that women can manage a male business and that their assumption of male roles is beneficial, not damaging, to men: "if she had one characteristic that stood out above all others, it was that she inspired confidence and trust. You knew that in human relations she would be reliable. Men liked to have her around, because they knew she never would take advantage or let them down." Like Andrée Senlac, Maggie finds herself embroiled in a dangerous case of foreign conspiracy to commit a major crime. Similarly, too, she keeps her head in a crisis, thereby thwarting the criminals.

The following scene reflects Maggie's strength of character and is representative of the heroism displayed by patriotic women in wartime romances. She and one of her drivers have been cornered by the crooks, who are trying to steal a trunk filled with money. Maggie refuses to give them the trunk even though they threaten to shoot her and set the house on fire. She calmly assesses the situation, finally deciding that she has the advantage: "If we just sit tight, you'll have to go away sometime. How long can you afford to sniff around the rathole? Nix, friend. You're stymied. We can stick it till hell's a skating rink." When she sees that help has arrived, Maggie makes a key move that results in capture of the criminals: "Toots pushed into her hand the handle of a suitcase. Maggie lifted it with both hands and threw it over the top of the trunk and down the stairs. . . . 'Heave!' she said shrilly to Toots, and the great wardrobe trunk went thundering, end over end, down the stairs. . . . Maggie leaped to her feet and stood recklessly at the head of the stairs, peering downward." Her physical and mental strength has insured her survival.

The story is typical of recruitment propaganda in four ways. First, Maggie is a sterling representative of the working class, which reflects the positive image of those from lower-class backgrounds generated by wartime dependence on blue-collar workers. Because workers played a vital role in procuring victory, popular artists featured them as home-front heroes. Second, she is shown as competently handling a job with much responsibility, which symbolizes the ability of women to take charge in an emergency. The story demonstrates that women can be trusted to do the things men have always done without usurping male prerogatives. Third, through her daring performance Maggie wins the love of an intelligence officer who is from the upper class thereby demonstrating that all classes should unite in the face of danger. Finally, she fantasizes about domesticity at the end of the serial as the story makes clear she will leave the taxi business for marriage. Though she has expanded the taxi operation and helped destroy an international spy ring, Maggie dreams of trading it all in for a home of her own in the last installment: "No taxicabs, no telephones. Just a home and a long, drooping, sleepy man coming to it each evening and leaving each morning. And maybe some dratted kids."

An Amherst graduate falls in love with a working-class manager of a taxi fleet. From "Taxi! Taxi!" reprinted from *Saturday Evening Post,* 14 April 1945. © 1945 The Curtis Publishing Company.

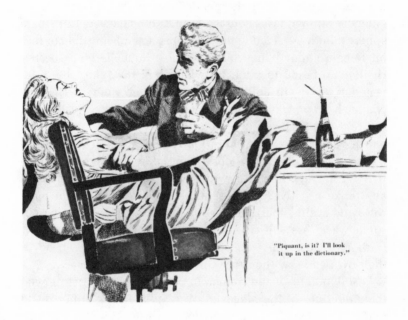

"Piquant, is it? I'll look it up in the dictionary."

All three stories exemplify many of the themes used in *Post* romances to recruit women into war work on a temporary basis. The major characteristic of such fiction is the transformation of an ordinary or a flippant young woman into a hardworking patriot who wins the love of a soldier through her steadfast dedication to the war effort. The war-working heroine shared with her prewar counterpart tremendous strength of character, resilience, shrewdness, courage, and competence within male spheres. Both attracted men who appreciated being able to rely on female strength in troubled times. Such heroines bested rivals who failed to pitch in, whereas in the 1930s these defeated rivals were coldly ambitious career women. Another change from prewar stories is that heroines were motivated by a desire to support soldiers rather than by desires to prove their worth. They were also more concerned about losing sweethearts as a result of their jobs and far more focused on domesticity. Ironically, however, while wartime propaganda tried to neutralize negative public sentiment against women in male roles and against married workers, heroic war workers were in some ways less self-actualizing than characters before Pearl Harbor because they placed the country's interests ahead of their own and saw their true role as being in the home.

Post fiction featuring women in war work generally followed the guidelines of the *Magazine War Guide* in that it portrayed married women favorably in defense roles, showed college graduates devoting themselves to defense work, featured females in blue-collar male occupations, refrained from using mothers with young children as heroines, favorably portrayed child care centers, and encouraged the employment of married women. The timing of stories also tended to follow campaign timetables. In some respects, however, recruitment goals set by the government were ignored. For example, the 1943 September campaign concerned service, trade, and transportation work, but the fiction that month was about business managers, factory workers, WACs, and office workers. If writers had followed precisely OWI guidelines, they should have written about truck drivers, waitresses, cooks, telegraph operators, ticket takers, and the like. Conversely, in 1945 two stories appeared that would have supported that campaign as they featured a taxi driver and a gas station attendant. The desire of the War Manpower Commission to relieve strains on community services was not reflected very much, and the call for clerical workers in government agencies was given scant attention. Most stories focused on skilled assembly-line workers, nurses in combat, and supervisors of defense plants. Finally, the heroines of defense-related stories were primarily young and single, even though the most plentiful source of workers was married older women.

Some of these discrepancies can be accounted for by the small staff and meager budget of the Magazine Bureau. Particularly after a large budget cut in 1943, it had few resources for implementing policies. In addition, the commissioning of fiction may have involved a greater time lag than the three-month period allowed by the *Guide*. Another problem that may have interfered was perhaps inadequate understanding on the part of writers of just exactly what labor needs were. Since the bulk of persuasive stories concerned factory workers, it may have been that writers failed to perceive the importance of recruiting women into other areas of the economy.

A more likely reason for ignoring some aspects of the campaign, however, stems from the nature of popular fiction and from the use of war workers as symbols of home-front militancy. Though writers cooperated with the recruitment effort, they were constrained by the entertainment function of their medium, the conventions of their craft, and the other general goals of the propaganda operation. Romances generally feature female characters, and since courtship is the province of the young and unattached the heroines of such stories naturally fell into that category. Furthermore, it was easier to create an inspiring example of female heroism through a young woman breaking new ground in dangerous, authoritative male occupations than to create a romantic heroic adventure around a middle-aged married office worker, waitress, laundry worker, or mail carrier. As John Cawelti says of the cultural limitations placed on popular writers: "One cannot write a successful adventure story about a social character type that the culture cannot conceive in heroic terms."[26] Using as heroines the group of women designated as a war labor reserve and featuring them in low-level service jobs would have made it extremely difficult to satisfy the reader's desire to identify with someone to whom exciting and romantic things happened.

Writers wove OWI requests into work adventure romance formulas from the 1930s, attempting to provide readers with attractive figures appropriate for their own personal dreams and compatible with the economic and social needs of wartime. The
reward for enthusiastic performance of war production work
was the love of an upstanding soldier or patriotic civilian whose
talents were needed at home. This choice seems to have been
governed by a number of factors. One is that the connection between civilian labor and soldier welfare could be underscored
by portraying romances between hardworking women and admiring men in uniform. Another is that the support of a vulnerable man by a resourceful, tough, working woman was available as a model from fiction of the previous decade and lent
itself easily to the campaign for mobilizing support of the female population for endangered soldiers abroad. A third stems
from attempts to make war work look exciting and glamorous to
women while keeping the new roles women were being asked
to assume from being threatening to men or offensive to women's
sensibilities. Wartime stories showed that married women who
entered the labor force could remain loving wives and that
those who stepped into male occupations did not lose their capacity to attract a man; indeed, they enhanced it.

Finally, of course, the stories reflected what writers considered to be audience entertainment needs and ideals: romantic
affairs with national heroes, dangerous encounters with vicious
enemies of the country, and soothing dreams of safe, happy
homes. All were blended to meet the double function of encouraging collective identification with the nation's welfare
and providing escapist fantasies. Certainly, they were not intended to mislead the public or manipulate women in an exploitative way. Writers merely tried to meet a number of needs,
including those of women readers, and used for their guide-
posts the requests of the government, successful plot conventions from the past, and what they sensed to be the national
mood. In doing this, they inadvertently reinforced inaccurate
beliefs about the true war worker and her plans while failing
fully to develop the feminist dimension of changes wrought by
the emergency.

Images of Women in Advertising

Unlike fiction, the war had an immediate and dramatic impact on advertising, presumably because the War Advertising Council organized earlier and was able to produce results more quickly than the Writers' War Board. Even before Pearl Harbor, advertisements frequently depicted battle scenes and informed readers what companies were doing to defeat the Axis powers. Once the country was fully engaged in war production, such ads multiplied as advertisers switched from selling consumer goods to producing war material. To fill the vacuum left by conversion to war production, many advertisers supported OWI campaigns. Between 1943 and 1945 the *Post* ran many advertisements that made no product pitch and devoted the entire copy to recruitment messages.

Advertisements that were designed specifically to attract women to war work comprised 16 percent of the total number appearing during this three-year period. The impact of the campaign is not accurately indicated by this figure, however, because such ads received prime space in the magazine as full- or half-page copy, a position occupied by a minority of the advertisements. The proportion of recruitment ads in this category was 55 percent. (See Appendix A for coding procedure.)

Companies that devoted 75 to 100 percent of their advertising space at various times during the war to the campaign were generally those that no longer produced consumer goods, especially household appliances, or that were directed to a female audience. Eureka vacuum cleaners ran a series celebrating all aspects of women's war work. Crosley and Servel refrigerators and Easy washers featured war workers manufacturing or using their products. Wayne gas and Kelly tires devoted much space to women performing male jobs in service and trade. Food product ads, such as those for Maxwell House coffee, Canada Dry ginger ale, and 7-Up, also glorified women in war work, while the paper shortage freed Kleenex to play a major part in the "Women at War" campaign.[27]

Companies that needed female workers (with the exception of the national railroads) generally stayed out of the recruitment campaign, preferring instead to celebrate the weapons of war they were manufacturing and postwar products. Advertisements for De Soto, Pontiac, and Nash-Kelvinator, for example, featured battle scenes rather than pleas for women workers. Likewise, the aircraft companies were more likely to feature strides made in aviation than female riveters. Companies with a female market carried the bulk of recruitment copy, perhaps because their advertisers were more familiar with female images and because their audience was the group that needed to be reached.

The images of war workers in advertising during the recruitment campaign had the major purpose of attracting women into fields drained by the enlistment of men and encouraging public acceptance of women in new roles. This was accomplished by demonstrating that women were capable of nondomestic work and in fact had been engaged in arduous labor outside the home throughout American history. As was true of fictional glorification of patriotic war workers, one of the dominant characteristics of wartime advertising is that it praises them for their stoicism, dedication to the cause, and capacity for hard work. The prevailing image of war workers—and indeed all women—was that they were reliable, tough, efficient guardians of the home front, seeing to it that society functioned smoothly in the absence of men. One of the major sources of this treatment was the War Advertising Council's strategy for enlisting civilian support of government programs. It suggested to OWI that civilians who planted victory gardens, salvaged tin, paper, and fat, stayed within rationed allocations of scarce resources, and took war jobs should be apotheosized in order to encourage compliance with economic and social goals: " [OWI must encourage] the development of a militant spirit—a desire to excel on the Home Front. We want more than just favorable compliance. We want zeal, enthusiasm, and individual initiative that will raise the standard of the whole effort. We Need Home Front Heroes."[28]

Presumably because the role of women was so vital, they became the symbol of this militant spirit and the model for proper civilian attitudes. An advertisement by Kraft is representative of the way women were featured. It shows a mother pitching hay while her daughter drives a tractor with the caption: "Heroines . . . U.S.A." The text reads: "Always on our dairy farms, women and girls have had plenty of chores to do. . . . But what

they are doing *now* would amaze you" (1 July 1944, p. 87). This
ad is designed to attract women into farm work, one of OWI's
major campaigns in the summers of 1943 and 1944, but at the
same time it glorifies women's work as heroic service to the nation. Other tributes to women praised them for their efficiency,
intelligence, and uncomplaining performance of their job. Bell
Telephone, for instance, labeled its operators "Soldiers of Service"; Crosley refrigerators applauded the "resourcefulness and
ingenuity of American women" (12 February 1944, p. 75); and
Eureka proclaimed, "You're a Good Soldier, Mrs. America"
(9 January 1943, p. 50). Bibb Manufacturing pictured women
and men marching with determination toward victory (27 March
1943, p. 95); Arvin Manufacturing declared that "Women are
doing their part to help win the war . . . working shoulder to
shoulder with men" (5 June 1943, p. 93); and an optical company praised women who "fight beside their men" (27 May
1944, p. 91).

It was due to advertiser emphasis on women as militant partners in the struggle to defeat the enemy that many ads placed war
workers in a long tradition of heroines who helped their men in
wartime. The Pennsylvania Railroad, for instance, informed
readers that women were filling jobs that required strength and
coolness and had "proved they can fill these roles most capably" (13 May 1944, p. 64) while at the same time it linked them
to patriotic heroines of the past by referring to a larger-than-life
railroad worker as "Molly Pitcher, 1944" (21 October 1944,
p. 90). Similarly, an Armco ad referred to a female truck driver
as "a 'covered wagon' girl": "'I got a job driving a truck when
Paul went across. I'm hauling the stuff they fight with.' . . . Hers
is the spirit of the women who reloaded the long rifles as their
men fought off the Indians . . . the courage that helped build the
kind of America we have today" (15 April 1944, p. 103). The
strategy to develop a militant spirit in civilians also explains
the observation made by Leila Rupp that "Magazine illustrations and advertisements pictured women in uniform to an extent out of all proportion to their actual numbers."[29] Rupp concludes that the overrepresentation of servicewomen resulted
from public fascination with them as an exotic wartime phenomenon. However, the emphasis on women in uniform grew
largely out of the War Advertising Council's plan to equate ci-

American women have always been strong. Advertisement: "Molly Pitcher, 1944," Pennsylvania Railroad, *Saturday Evening Post*, 21 October 1944. Reprinted by permission of The Penn Central Corporation.

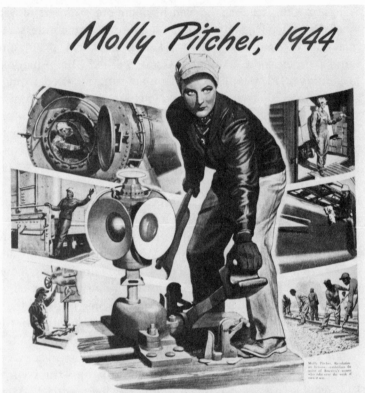

Women are doing a big job on the Pennsylvania Railroad

More than 48,000 experienced Pennsylvania Railroad men have entered our armed forces. Yet, wartime's unusual needs for railroad service are being met . . . thanks in great part to more than 23,000 women who have rallied to the emergency. From colleges, high schools and homes, these women—after intensive training—are winning the wholehearted applause of the traveling public.

You see them working as trainmen, in ticket and station masters' offices and information bureaus, as platform ushers and train passenger representatives, in dining car service. Yes, even in baggage rooms, train dispatchers' offices, in shops and yards and as section hands. The Pennsylvania Railroad proudly salutes these "Molly Pitchers" who so gallantly fill the breach left by their fighting brothers-in-arms.

 **Pennsylvania Railroad**
Serving the Nation

BUY UNITED STATES
WAR BONDS AND STAMPS

vilian support of home-front campaigns with the brave and loyal actions of soldiers in the thick of battle. Since women were the major representatives of home-front militancy, it makes sense that female military imagery abounded during the war.

The woman in a nontraditional job was portrayed as valiantly leading the nation to victory. Women were provided with positive role models for entering male occupations, and the public was given a standard-bearer of home-front solidarity and protection. Other ads promoted confidence in women's ability to do a man-size job by emphasizing that femininity was not incompatible with arduous high-pressure work, a theme that simultaneously assured the public that inhabiting masculine roles did not destroy female sexuality or "womanliness." The following ad, for example, pictures a diminutive female worker operating a huge machine and describes her as follows: "Five feet one from her 4A slippers to her spun-gold hair. She loves flower-hats, veils, smooth orchestras—and being kissed by a boy who's now in North Africa. . . . How can 110 pounds of beauty boss 147,000 pounds of steel? . . . through the modern magic of electric power. The magic that makes it possible for a girl's slim fingers to lift mountains of metal" (Electric Companies, 12 June 1943, p. 55).

There was an especially marked concern about femininity in advertisements recruiting women into the armed forces. A memo from the Office of Emergency Management concerning WAVES and SPAR recruitment indicates the conflict between military service and conventional notions of femininity: "There is an unwholesomely large number of girls who refrain from even contemplating enlistment because of male opinion. An educative program needs to be done among the male population to overcome this problem. Men—both civilian and military personnel—should be more specifically informed that it is fitting for girls to be in service. This would call for copy . . . which shows that the services increase, rather than detract from, desirable feminine characteristics."[30] OWI concluded that military recruitment would have to be heavily laced with references to servicewomen's sexual attractiveness. A good example of its suggested treatment is a sample one-minute announcement advertising WAVES intended for radio stations as part of the "Women in the War" campaign. The male announcer assures listeners that servicewomen are not masculine: "The girls in the WAVES are real American women—the kind who love parties and pretty clothes, and who are good at cooking and sewing too. They're very feminine, and proud of it."[31]

Both fiction writers and advertisers responded to this government concern by showing women in uniform as glamorous sirens who could turn on their sex appeal after working hours or excite male lust despite their formidable demeanor. Two *Post* stories cited by OWI as aiding the recruitment effort are good examples of this highlighting of servicewomen's sexuality. In "A WAVE for Mac" (Sidney Herschel Small, 11 March 1944), the heroine is so gorgeous that a soldier falls in love with her at first sight while both are on a train to California. Similarly, the blonde flight nurse in a later story "invariably drew whistles of admiration from lines of stretchers bearing soldiers."[32] Advertisers spoke to this imagined problem by picturing servicewomen in the company of attractive men in uniform and emphasized the beauty of the women themselves. Camel cigarettes ran a series on women in the armed forces that showed women in fatigues in one part of the ad and off duty in evening gowns with officers in another part. Canada Dry made a similar attempt to maintain feminine identities of servicewomen; the company participated extensively in military recruitment and frequently ran advertisements saluting women in uniform. One of its 1944 ads illustrates the way feminine desirability was paired with military roles. It shows soldiers raising a toast to photos of women in various branches of the armed services with the caption "To the Ladies" (11 November 1944, p. 76). A Whitman's ad used a similar technique by showing a beautiful WAC receiving the traditional gift a suitor brings to his sweetheart—a box of chocolates (9 January 1943, p. 8). Though the economy required that women assume male roles, don functional clothing, and engage in physically demanding dirty work, the emphasis on female sexuality gave the message that these new roles did not signify fundamental changes in the sexual orientation of women themselves or in their customary image as sexual objects. As Leila Rupp has observed: "Perhaps the glamorizing of war work signified an attempt to ease the transition from the apron-clad housewife of the prewar image to the woman worker in pants."[33]

Military recruitment propaganda also tried to reassure par-

Servicewomen are glamorous and feminine. "The Seventh WAVE,"
reprinted from *Saturday Evening Post*, 4 March 1944. © 1944 The
Curtis Publishing Company.

ents that enlistment in the armed forces would not lessen the femininity of their daughters. This in part developed out of OWI's belief that women were reluctant to join the armed forces because their families did not want them to enlist.[34] An advertisement sponsored by the Women's Army Auxiliary Corps indicates how the government attempted to neutralize parental disapproval. It consists of a letter written by a father to his daughter who has asked him how he feels about her joining the WAAC. He begins by admitting that her plans have given him "a queer mixture of feelings" but adds that her right to make her own decisions is "one of the things we're fighting for." After reminding her how proud the family was when her brother enlisted in the army, he finally reconciles his conflicts over having a daughter do the same thing: "You know I like *womanly* women. . . . And watching you grow up in that pattern has been a delight to me. I am firm in the belief that whatever your decision is, it won't make you any *less* of a woman—just a wiser, steadier, stronger one" (3 April 1943, p. 32). Fiction writers also tried to convince parents that female enlistment in no way would coarsen their daughters. I have already described one writer's attempt to infuse positive images of servicewomen as family members into *Post* stories.[35] Another example of how this message was incorporated into fiction is one of Frank Bunce's pieces about WAC Dorrit Bly. In "Three-Day Pass" (8 April 1944), Dorrit gets involved with a lieutenant whose niece has applied for the Women's Army Corps against the wishes of her aunt and boyfriend who do not believe she is mature enough to handle military service. When the niece becomes embroiled in a court case resulting from her quarreling with the boyfriend over this issue, the judge ends the dispute by supporting her right to serve her country: "It may be that you think she's too young or even incapable, but isn't it true that we've all been inclined to underestimate our youth—its strength and intelligence and fine courage in a cause? . . . [Military service] is a fine, decent occupation for a woman in wartime." Thus, writers and advertisers tried to give the impression that family fears about their daughters being masculinized by the service were unfounded.

The feminization of women in the military also reflects an unstated concern in the armed forces about lesbianism and military life. An institution that segregated large numbers of women into domestic quarters and encouraged them to develop strengths formerly reserved only for men provided opportunities for female camaraderie and affectional ties. There was, in fact, a campaign on the part of the military to discourage lesbian and gay relationships during the war. Allan Bérubé has documented the homophobic crackdown on gay life in the armed forces which resulted in dishonorable discharges and even hospitalization of known lesbians and gay men.[36] OWI directives do not allude to this campaign but the overriding emphasis of those engaged in WAC, WAVE, and SPAR recruitment on servicewomen as feminine heterosexuals reflects the antilesbian perspective of the military.

Finally, advertisers conveyed the message that employed women would not disrupt the family. Such ads praised homemakers who had found employment for fulfilling their obligations both at home and on the job. A Westinghouse ad, for example, congratulated a married aircraft worker for both building planes and running a home (16 January 1943, p. 41). Likewise, a Eureka advertisement described a soldier's mother making gas masks as "a two-job woman, running a house for Dad O'Rourke of a morning, and making gas masks on Eureka's 4–12 shift" (29 November 1943, p. 94). War workers were often shown in housewife/mother roles—working with or taking care of children or doing housework in factory coveralls. Children pictured in these scenes cheerfully helped their mothers with household tasks, especially young daughters who were frequently dressed in coveralls and kerchiefs themselves.

Not only did such advertisements try to encourage women to stick by their posts even though the demands of a two-job life style were considerable, but they implied that children and husbands would be well cared for. Maxwell House coffee recruitment ads portrayed war workers in warm domestic scenes to attract middle-class women into the labor force. Yet the subliminal message was that pulling women out of the home would not damage family life. A representative ad from this series appeared in March 1944. A war worker in her twenties or early thirties is resting after a hard day's work at the factory, still wearing her coveralls and identification badge; her lunch bucket is prominently displayed on the dining room table. She is flanked by an older couple, probably her parents, and a little

Women workers do not disrupt the family. Advertisement: "When you've done your bit for Uncle Sam," Maxwell House, *Saturday Evening Post*, 25 March 1944. *Maxwell House* and *Good to the Last Drop* are registered trademarks of General Foods Corporation. Advertisement reproduced with permission of General Foods Corporation.

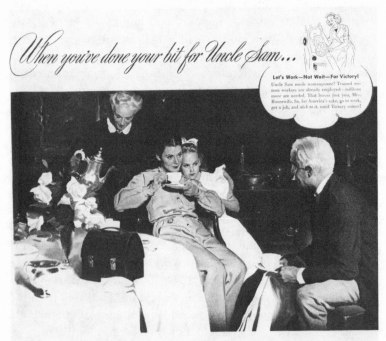

girl, her daughter, hugs her closely while she sips the coffee that her mother has just poured. All three are eagerly listening to her working-day tales and clearly full of respect for what she is doing (Maxwell House, 25 March 1944, p. 51).

In much the same vein, a Greyhound advertisement shows a young woman, lunch box in hand, dressed for work. She stands for those who have left home to find employment in war industries and is surrounded by photos intended for her family, which portray her in various aspects of war work, all with captions that point to how proud such women are of the work they are doing: "I helped build this ship! . . . I'm helping pour hot steel. . . . You should see me handle this tractor" (24 June 1944, p. 65). While publicizing work in labor-short fields, the ad delivers the message that war workers come from respectable families and that their wartime duties will not interfere with close family ties. Similarly, a Kellogg advertisement shows a WAVE serving breakfast to her parents (20 November 1943, p. 60), while the manufacturers of Pontiac feature a fresh-faced WAC described as "your daughter, sister, sweetheart, or wife" (30 September 1944, p. 33). These ads reflect advertisers' attempts to enlist women without economic need into the struggle, to pair positive images with nontraditional work, and to counter long-standing beliefs that proper, stable homes required a woman at the helm, undistracted by the outside responsibilities of a job.

As was true of the fiction, however, black women were not included in advertising's reassessment of female roles. Astonishingly, no black women were pictured in advertisements during the war. They had been occasionally featured in prewar advertising as maids and mammies, but these images disappeared in the 1940s. This may have been due to the emphasis on white women as sturdy workers who could maintain their responsibilities in the home while holding a war job. Their reliance on domestic help would have weakened the message that they could do two jobs at once. In addition, women were cast in heroic roles, as symbols of American strength and American values. Racial prejudice precluded using blacks in such a capacity because they were perceived by a racist culture as inferior to whites and therefore inappropriate figures of inspiration or national pride.

By the second half of 1944, advertisers had begun to reverse the direction of social change they had tried to effect in the recruitment campaign. As it became clear that the tide had turned against the Axis powers, attention turned to what the postwar world would look like. In fact, OWI had received numerous requests from magazines asking how they should approach the transition from war to peace, wanting it to be as smooth as possible.[37] One issue OWI was careful to emphasize was the return of battle-scarred veterans, who would need care and understanding in their readjustment to civilian life. Concerned especially about job placement, it asked that publicity be given to the Selective Service requirement specifying that servicemen be guaranteed their former jobs.[38] It also focused attention on the need of some veterans for retraining and help with finding appropriate work: "A large percentage of veterans are eager and capable of working in war industries. . . . Some of the men cannot be absorbed without retraining and rehabilitation; but many skills acquired in the armed forces can be put to use. An incapacitated soldier who has become familiar with the use of guns is given further training and makes an excellent gun inspector. A soldier who has had his arm amputated with training may become an expert welder."[39] Ads reflected this orientation by assuring soldiers that their rightful place was reserved and that employers eagerly awaited their return. Mobil, for instance, trumpeted this message: "Yes—your job is waiting for you, Soldier!" (23 September 1944, p. 41), while an advertisement for Greyhound pictured a soldier writing home about the good news he had just received: "My old dispatcher at Greyhound writes me that they're planning the finest passenger buses the U.S.A. has ever seen—and he says they'll want me back there to pilot one of 'em" (12 August 1944, p. 78).

Believing that wartime employment patterns for women were a temporary, stopgap measure, necessary only while the men were gone, advertisers assumed war workers would either go home or seek jobs in female areas. Taking advantage of this presumably automatic shift and eager to facilitate the changeover to peacetime production, typewriter companies encouraged working women to enter clerical work, one of the areas, along with teaching and nursing, that OWI had indicated would need large numbers of women in the postwar period.[40] A Smith-Corona ad, for instance, pictures a metal assembly worker con-

War workers are channeled into female fields. Advertisement: "When it becomes a souvenir," Smith-Corona, *Saturday Evening Post*, 4 November 1944. Reprinted by permission.

When it becomes a souvenir...

What then? Stay home . . . do nothing? You *know* you won't! Like our fighting men, you've earned the right to choose work you enjoy. And the time to prepare is . . . now!

A surprising number of war workers are going to learn to type . . . a skill easy for them to acquire.

For women who want careers, typing is the opening wedge to the world's most fascinating professions. For women who plan marriage, typing brings contacts with the world outside . . . keeps distant friends in touch, leads to club, business, and social activities that less accomplished women miss.

So *do* think about learning to type. Even today, some Smith-Corona typewriters, under certain conditions, are available for civilian use—or you can "beg, borrow, or rent" for practise purposes. It's a wise move for post-war planners. L C Smith & Corona Typewriters Inc Syracuse 1 New York.

SMITH-CORONA
Typewriters   *Groton Plant*

MORE L C SMITHS FOR CIVILIANS!
Note to Industry: W.P.B. has increased our fourth quarter allotment of new typewriters to be made for necessary civilian use. If you can qualify under "W. P. R.— 1319," we may be able to supply you; in any event, talk with our local branch office or L C Smith dealer.

templating her factory badge and asks: "When it becomes a souvenir, what then? . . . Like our fighting men, you've earned the right to choose the work you enjoy" (4 November 1944, p. 92). The message supports the notion that one may work where one pleases, but it also advises women to learn to type and suggests that women eschew factory for office work.

Another Smith-Corona ad shows several hands and asks the reader the question, "Are yours ready for that post-war job?" while urging her "to learn to type today and get ahead tomorrow" (16 September 1944, p. 108). Others made it clear that the future for women workers lay in clerical fields by focusing on little girls. An ad for Underwood typewriters, for instance, featured a child who was designated as a "Young Lady with a Future" because "she loves to type" (9 September 1944, p. 74) while entitling her "Future Secretary of America." This ad tells the reader how lucky this girl will be to grow up in the new world: "Whether she becomes secretary to the President of the United States or to the president of some one-man business, her mind and her hands will help speed and influence whatever projects cross her desk" (27 May 1944, p. 84). By 1945, advertisers had completely dropped recruitment themes of the previous two years, and women in ads were all, with the exception of servicewomen, in traditional fields or had no occupational role.[41]

Most ads implied, however, that currently employed women would have no outside job but would instead take up full-time homemaking at the first opportunity. Two themes used throughout the recruitment campaign led naturally into this portrayal. One was the praise of war workers for their remarkable achievements as double-duty workers—taking a war job and maintaining the home. Though the initial effect of this message was to foster positive attitudes toward employed wives and mothers and to reassure women that they could handle home responsibilities even if they entered the labor force, its implication was that the exhausting load could not be borne indefinitely. This idea was later brought out in ads that showed war workers eager to rest at home after victory and to use their high wages for purchasing a domestic paradise wherein work was kept to a minimum. A Briggs home appliance ad, for example, featured a woman in factory coveralls motivating herself to go to work every day by looking at a picture of the modern kitchen she would some day have (6 May 1944, p. 94), while a Monsanto ad proclaimed: "There'll come a day . . . when a lot of the good new things of peacetime will become important to Rosie the Housewife" (27 November 1943, p. 113). Similarly, Thermos Bottle advertised its product by showing a war worker pouring coffee for herself at the factory in one picture and serving coffee to her husband and friends as a housewife in another as she says: "This is what I'm working for—the carefree home parties we used to have" (8 July 1944, p. 88). Leaving her war job in favor of the home was shown as the woman worker's reward for a job well done.

Of course there was an element of truth in what advertisers were saying about wartime work. It frequently *was* exhausting, and there is evidence that many women could not cope well with the demands of families and enormous work loads at the factory. Reports of the Women's Bureau showed that one half of married workers bore full responsibility for housework and were in desperate need of increased community services. To support its request for more government funding of such services in 1943, it cited cases like the following: "A 45 year old woman, living on a farm fifteen miles from the plants, gets up at four, packs lunches for herself and two sons in high school, gets the family breakfast, and leaves home at six o'clock. For her ride home she has to wait for men who work longer hours, so regardless of the hours worked it is after six when she reaches home. Then she has dinner to get, dishes to wash, and the whole round of household work to do. . . . It is eleven p.m. when she retires, allowing only five hours for rest."[42]

Drained by factory work weeks averaging forty-four to forty-eight hours, pressured by husbands to continue their roles as homemakers, hampered by inadequate transportation, and forced to shop in crowded stores, women workers were often faced with intolerable work loads, a situation that the bureau noted led to high absenteeism and dropout rates. Undoubtedly, many women gladly left war work for a less rigorous work schedule. Most, however, were willing to tolerate having two jobs, because they needed an income either for survival or to improve their family's living standard—50 percent of the women in war production areas who described themselves as former homemakers voiced a desire to keep their jobs.[43] More importantly, the media's proposed solution to this problem changed from recommending ways women workers could cut down on housework during the recruiting effort to implying wage work was so distasteful that they would drop out when things were back to normal.[44]

In addition, the initial idea that working mothers could raise happy children was replaced by tragic portraits of families breaking under the strain of mother being away. By the spring of 1944, ads began dramatizing the unhappiness of children with war-working mothers. An Armco ad, for instance, featured a little boy in tears being comforted by his mother as she leaves for the factory: "Chin up soldier . . . just like Daddy said" (4 March 1944, p. 103). Another company that manufactured war material used the same idea when it showed a mother in coveralls and factory badge stopping on her way to work to answer her daughter's plaintive question: "Mother, when will you stay home again?" The text provides an answer for her: "Some jubilant day mother *will* stay home again, doing the job she likes best—making a home for you and daddy, when he gets back." The ad goes on to discuss the company's plan to convert to peacetime production in a way that illustrates advertisers' postwar focus on women as consumers rather than producers: "She's learning the vital importance of precision in equipment made by Adel. In her post-war home she'll want appliances with the same high degree of precision and she will get them when Adel converts its famous Design Simplicity to products of equal dependability for home and industry" (Adel Manufacturing Company, 6 May 1944, p. 99).

As manufacturers began to convert to production of consumer goods, advertisers intensified the attack on working mothers. A factory worker has to plead before a judge for her teenage son, who is labeled a "Victory Vandal" (Yale and Towne, 17 June 1944, p. 91), and a hysterical girl is carted away to a foster home because her mother has to work (State Farm Insurance, 17 March 1945, p. 93). These tragic scenes contrasted dramatically with ads showing mothers at home with their children playing happily nearby.

The other recruitment theme that laid a basis for the myth that women planned to return home was the idea that wives and sweethearts energetically toiled at their new jobs because

Working mothers hurt their children. Advertisement: "Mother, when will you stay home again?" Adel Manufacturing Company, *Saturday Evening Post*, 6 May 1944. Reprinted by permission of Transamerica Delaval, Inc.

Mother, when will you stay home again?

Some jubilant day mother *will* stay home again, doing the job she likes best—making a home for you and daddy, when he gets back. She knows that all the hydraulic valves, line support clips and blocks and electric anti-icing equipment that ADEL turns out for airplanes are helping bring that day closer.

Meanwhile she's learning the vital importance of precision in equipment made by ADEL. In her post-war home she'll want appliances with the same high degree of precision and she will get them when ADEL converts its famous *Design Simplicity* to products of equal dependability for home and industry.

ADEL

ADEL PRECISION PRODUCTS CORP.
BURBANK, CALIFORNIA, HUNTINGTON, WEST VIRGINIA
SERVICE OFFICES: DETROIT, HAGERSTOWN, SEATTLE

FOR WAR (AND PEACE) BUY BONDS

ADEL EQUIPMENT SERVES UNITED NATIONS' AIR FORCES ON EVERY BATTLE FRONT

they were spurred by the prospect of bringing their loved ones back. Once they returned, of course, there would be no reason to go on doing so. A riveter completes her task with determination and mentally signs the plane she is working on "From Alice to Eddie to Adolf" (Texaco, 20 March 1943, p. 36). An electrical worker in aircraft extends her hand aloft to a vision of a combat plane as the text characterizes the diamonds she is holding as follows: "Small things perhaps, these jewels a woman gives a man—but in war, as in love, there are no little things" (General Electric, 26 February 1944, p. 33). A drill press operator gazes wistfully into the future as she contemplates her sweetheart's return: "She's not so very tall . . . just as high as a man's heart. But there's nothing helpless about her hands on a press. You should see her assembling parts for the starter motor that whirls the props of the plane Jimmy flies. . . . she works to the rhythm of a little tuneless song. . . . she hears it in the great war plant's thud and hum. . . . This is bringing Jimmy back . . . bringing Jimmy back" (Eureka, 30 October 1943, p. 67).

This approach appears to have in part been based on Chester La Roche's idea to induce a public response to government appeals through threatening people with the loss of what they held most dear and arousing guilt in those not doing their part: "The citizen must be convinced that, unless he [or she] cooperates, he personally will pay a penalty, either through loss of the war or through loss of something precious to him—his son in the armed forces, his political rights and social privileges, his future freedom."[45] In recruitment appeals to women, this strategy took the form of making women feel guilty for not taking a job and causing them to fear loss of a loved one, through either death or alienation. To personalize this appeal, the War Advertising Council advised that soldiers be characterized as a brother or son or husband—a man intimately connected with the reader.

To relay the message that women owed it to men to join the armed services or enter the work force, mock ads designed for advertising agencies drew upon one of the primary aspects of female socialization: their responsibility for others' welfare, especially that of husbands. They did this by portraying soldiers as utterly dependent on women's work in the labor force. One of these shows a young unemployed woman troubled by her thoughts after reading a letter from overseas; the caption reads,

"When Johnny wrote 'we need you' . . ." Another reminds the reader that her words of love and support to departing soldiers mean nothing unless they are backed up with action; in this case, she is urged to join the Women's Army Corps. More dramatic suggestions were to place servicewomen in combat situations and thereby emphasize how vital women are to the men overseas. A navy recruitment sample ad, for instance, portrays a WAVE air traffic controller tensely guiding a pilot in for a landing. The suggested text contains maternal images and reinforces the idea that women's role is to support men: " 'Jim's life was in my hands!' Serve him and serve your country in the WAVES."[46]

The War Advertising Council created model ads that combined themes such as these, which were based on guilt over not meeting female responsibilities to men, with those arousing fear of male disapproval and alienation. Such copy assumed that the reader's world had been shattered by the departure of her sweetheart or husband and threatened her with permanent loss of the male love she depended on: "You know how it feels when someone you love says good-bye. You're lonely and lost and scared. Wondering when you'll see him again. Frantic at the idea of sitting home, waiting till it's over." Not only did the council aim to heighten women's fear of loss by death, but it pointed out that love could end through the couple's growing apart: "Remember the last time you saw him? He was still the boy you could always talk to—when nobody else understood. Next time you see him? He may be a stranger. . . . Perhaps the things you both used to laugh at won't amuse *him* any more. When they play your 'theme song,' maybe he won't still reach for your hand."[47]

The solution offered to the worried and abandoned reader was to join the armed forces or find a war job. By doing her part to win the war, she could meet her responsibilities as a supportive partner and guarantee that she would remain in touch with her lover's needs: "It takes a girl in uniform to understand a service man. . . . Do you want a chance to share his life today— and speak his language tomorrow? It's a chance . . . to share his life, as much as any woman can. And when it's all over, you'll have the same interests, the same viewpoint."[48] A Eureka ad that appeared in 1943 illustrates the use of this theme: "When Jimmy joined the Air Corps, she thought the end of her world

had come. But he set her straight . . . as always. 'This is something we can do together, kid. You make 'em. I'll fly 'em. It's still
the firm of Us, Incorporated'" (13 October 1943, p. 47).

Emphasizing painful feelings of abandonment and fear of losing love both played on the normal anxieties all people felt in
wartime and implied that women were not capable of function-
ing without having a man at the center of their life; they could
not find meaning outside of their role as confidante and nur-
turer. In addition, advertisers used war workers as a way to
dramatize or personalize home-front support through connect-
ing them romantically to soldiers, a technique also used by fiction writers. The image of a dedicated, devoted woman expend-
ing superhuman energy to safeguard the man she loved was an
emotional appeal for civilians to protect their own loved ones
by tightening belts, putting up with inconveniences, and working long, hard hours. The simultaneous campaign to recruit
women from the home made it easy for advertisers to strike a
familiar chord: wives do all they can to help husbands perform
front-line duties in the outside world to insure the couple's survival. In wartime, this support took the form of women making
tanks, bombs, ships, and fighter planes.

A strategy developed by the WAC for encouraging housewives to enter war production factories reinforced the image of
war workers as dutiful wives performing the same function in
the factory that they had at home. It drew a parallel between
housework and factory work to assure women that they were
adequately prepared for nontraditional jobs: "Many war factory
jobs are very similar to running a sewing machine or vacuum
cleaner, assembling a meat grinder, sewing by hand, and other
familiar household tasks."[49] Two examples illustrate this approach quite well. In a gasoline ad, Wayne featured a woman
gas station attendant with the caption, "The Missus Takes Over."
She is described as "Giving your car the same care she used
in keeping house and not a bit afraid of soiling her pretty
hands" (29 April 1944, p. 70). In another ad encouraging both the
womanpower and the victory mail campaigns, a factory worker
on her break writes a letter to her husband overseas and compares
the plant to her kitchen: "Here's a picture of me in my uniform.
Remember how you used to wipe the flour smudges off my nose?
Well, you ought to see me now—I'm a regular grease monkey. . . .

The plant's as bright and cheery as my own kitchen" (Mazda Electric Company, 30 January 1943, p. 7).

Leila Rupp points out that such imagery gave the impression that women were primarily suited for household tasks and, in addition, ignored the extensive factory experience of many women in society.[50] The government aimed its recruitment efforts at women envisioned as totally unfamiliar with the world of wage labor, especially with work in blue-collar fields. Rupp speculates that this approach may have been based on assumptions that women accustomed to outside employment would likely have sought war jobs out of economic necessity and therefore did not need to be addressed by propaganda.[51] Assuming, however, that housewives would not also enter the labor force for economic reasons or be prepared to perform anything but simple household chores reflects ignorance of the working histories most women shared: employment outside the home was a normal, if irregular, feature of the average woman's life, and many families required two incomes to achieve a middle-class standard of living. By casting nontraditional work into domestic images, propaganda implied that war workers had experience with nothing except homemaking and subtly undermined the idea that women and men could do the same work. As Karen Anderson perceptively observed when discussing this aspect of the recruitment campaign: "The demonstration by women that they could perform jobs hitherto assigned primarily or solely to men caused a reassessment not of the nature of women, but rather of the nature of the jobs they were doing so that they more nearly conformed to traditional preconceptions regarding women."[52]

Some appeals suggested by the WAC were progressive in nature, based as they were on female self-interest and egalitarianism. The desire for high wages, getting involved in a world outside the home, the excitement of performing a task usually denied to women, and the chance to acquire skills that would lead to a better postwar job—all these were mentioned in wartime advertising. Other appeals of an egalitarian nature were the ideal of partnership between women and men, the contributions of women to American history, and the reprehensibility of Nazi ideology regarding woman's place. These appeals, which had the potential to alter beliefs about women significantly, illustrate both the willingness of government planners to increase role options for women when the economy needed workers and the pressure brought to bear on traditional notions by the need for women to do work they had not done before.

At the same time, propagandists instructed advertisers that recruitment messages were never to focus solely on financial or personal gain but had to include some reference to patriotism and "desire to help our fighting men," an approach that followed recommendations of the British in their advice to Americans searching for a way to recruit female workers: "While fixing the 'will to win' spirit . . . that spirit must be translated into a sense of individual responsibility. The obvious baits of high wages or the security of the job were not used [in our own propaganda]. Wisely, the campaign was kept clear of the material appeal which is much less effective than that of service to the country in wartime."[53]

The emphasis on self-sacrifice, patriotism, and soldier welfare became the chief method for portraying war workers in popular fiction as well and was an important element in mobilizing the population as a whole. Advertisers thus tried to foster acceptance of women in nontraditional work, channel citizen anxiety over the safety of men overseas into productive activity, and draw on familiar cultural values to make campaign goals immediate and real. At the same time, through emphasizing that women's primary duty was to the men in their lives, advertisers avoided showing war work as leading to new roles for women in American life.

There were other propaganda strategies that contributed to a reactionary view of women at the war's end. One of these was that advertisers translated the complex issues over which the war was being fought into mythic symbols of national identity and meaning. The most profound of these was the home sheltering and nurturing an institution that came to be equated with the core of American values—the family. The War Advertising Council, in searching for ways to bring the issues of the war down to a personal level, had recommended that it be portrayed as threatening people with the loss of something vital to their well-being in order to, in La Roche's words, "create a burning desire in every citizen to cooperate in the war effort to the limit of his [or her] ability."[54] The primary image upon which advertisers settled for this purpose was the home. Typical of the way it was used in this capacity is a Servel refrigerator ad that shows a middle-aged woman stating emphatically to the reader: "My home is at war! Enemies of ours are striking at the roots of everything that has meant security and peace and dignity in human relationships—everything we sum up in that precious word HOME" (3 April 1943, p. 79).

The full-time homemaker was an integral part of this picture, which meant that two conflicting images of women existed during the war: the strong, dependable patriot who could run a machine and the innocent, vulnerable mother, outside the realm of technology, who was depending on soldiers to protect her way of life. Advertisers made homemakers into the living embodiment of every value Americans safeguarded; they thus became symbolic of the besieged nation. A good example of this representation is an Adel Manufacturing ad that shows a young mother and a little girl gently playing with kittens in a field of flowers. The pastoral scene conveys the beauty, peace, and innocence that war has temporarily obliterated. The ad makes clear that this is the way of life America is trying to preserve: "It's to keep that world and to bring back the birthright of millions of children elsewhere that American men and machines are fighting on every battle front" (10 June 1944, p. 101). This ad reflects the vulnerable image of women that resulted from focusing on the family as the key element of endangered American beliefs, as does the following advertisement, which pictures a young mother and baby surrounded by the violence of warfare: "Now, as in the past—the home is the bulwark of the nation" (American Radiator and Standard Sanitary Corporation, 3 January 1942, p. 1). This simultaneous glorification of women as symbols of the nation under attack and of soldiers as their champions strengthened traditional gender roles wherein men protected women from a harsh and brutal world.

The same identification of women with the country under fire had appeared in World War I propaganda posters, a phenomenon that Michele Shover suggests was due to cultural beliefs that women are ill equipped to protect themselves: "War was being fought to preserve women and children from the degradation of a brutish enemy. . . . Women, who are traditionally regarded as vulnerable, are the perfectly recognizable symbols of suffering."[55] Personifying the nation as a young homemaker also evoked a long-standing ideal of women as spiritually pure, innocent nurturers whose gentle, loving nature would be destroyed by entry into the corrupt sphere of men and machines. This ideal was deeply embedded in American culture by the nineteenth century when mothers served as sentimental models of spirituality and humanity in a society grown increasingly mechanized and materialistic.[56] The home, which was woman's domain, became enshrined as a haven from the cold, competitive marketplace. The sentimental vision of women as valuable primarily for their moral superiority, a quality that depended on their exclusion from the world of men, had in the twentieth century come under steady attack from feminists and the social forces pulling women into the labor force, though it had never disappeared. The symbolic portrayal of the nation at war, however, revivified this early idea by viewing women as repositories of decent, humane values.

An important related function served by images of women during the war was their role as guardians of a way of life temporarily disrupted by uncertainty, violence, and prolonged separation from loved ones. The desire for something stable to hold onto is evident in wartime popular culture. A 1943 ad, for instance, features a soldier in a combat zone wistfully daydreaming about the peaceful world he has left behind and yearning for the familiarity of home: "I want my girl back, just as she is, and that bungalow on Maple Avenue" (Nash-Kelvinator Corporation, 27 February 1943, p. 7). Fiction too reflects nostalgia for a secure, settled family life: "Things they had missed—permanent companionship, homes of their own, children—seemed suddenly important to young men going to war" (Phyliss Duganne, "When the Boys Come Home," 17 July 1943).

Melva Baker, in her insightful analysis of wartime films, states that Hollywood too focused on personalized realms in which women played a dramatic role as targets of fascism. These included "romantic love, an unfettered choice of mate, the freedom to have children when wife and husband willed, the sanctity of marriage and family, the privacy of home, and the license to experience uninterrupted time in which to strengthen a relationship, free of worldly demands."[57] Such a focus placed women at the center of a battle to preserve freedom through

staunchly defending the right of every person to develop relationships and establish homes, outside the purview of the state.
Baker concludes that, by defining freedom as the maintenance
of romantic love and family life, movies strengthened women's
traditional roles by casting them as defenders of marriage, home,
and church.

The task of women in wartime propaganda was to preserve
the integrity of family life and keep an orderly home to which
soldiers could return: "I'm glad you haven't turned the old
house into just a headquarters, Mom; I'm glad you're keeping it
our home, the way it was. That's the way I feel about it out here,
that is also part of a woman's war job—keeping up the home,
the homes we're fighting for, that some day we want to come
back to" (soldier in OWI propaganda film).[58] As the embodiment of safety and tenderness, the mother or wife stood for the
survival of the country's humane values and served as the guardian of its spirit through holding her family together.

A Eureka ad captures this aspect of women's symbolic function quite well. A young mother is holding her baby and both
are looking into the distance, metaphorically calling on the
young father overseas to protect them from harm. While she
looks vulnerable, the text praises her for carrying on without
her husband and bravely keeping her home secure even though
the fabric of her life has been rended: "Face to face with you,
my little son . . . I know there will be bright tomorrows. . . .
[Your father] may never see you now . . . but we must live in
hope, always. That makes you and me very special kind of partners. Building together the kind of life he would want for both
of us" (Eureka, 29 January 1944). The ad illustrates the double
function women served as faithful comrades trusting their men
to safeguard them from harm while courageously keeping their
home intact though it was without a leader and provider.[59] Both
concepts hearkened back to the Victorian model of women as
the gentle sex, specially suited for maintaining a domestic retreat for husbands who needed soothing after their battles in the
outside world.

An image that combined the contradictory concepts of women
as home-front fighters taking on male qualities to combat the
enemy and women as gentle caretakers of the family was that of
the pioneer woman who valiantly defended her loved ones

Women are relying on men to protect them and are preserving the family in their absence. Advertisement: "Courage, Feminine Gender," Eureka, *Saturday Evening Post*, 29 January 1944. Reprinted by permission of The Eureka Company.

from danger, a common figure in ads of the war years. Frontier wives were lauded as appropriate role models for contemporary women trying to manage without men. The National Life Insurance Company, for instance, ran a series entitled "Protecting the American Home," which stressed the bravery and strength of women of the Old West. Pillsbury also ran a series of pioneer ads emphasizing women's ability to withstand deprivation and to care for their families in the midst of danger. Eureka featured a welder who urged readers to "Keep the home fires blazing" (26 June 1943, p. 77). Using the image of the pioneer woman was one way to increase the acceptability of women in important, demanding roles since it established the idea of female strength and toughness as a vital part of American history. At the same time, it mitigated the potential threat of war work to traditional norms by evoking an image of strong women who nonetheless stayed within the homemaker role. The pioneer represented a capable, supportive, and stoic partner who could keep the home going single-handed until things returned to normal.

Housewives too were portrayed as vital defenders of the nation's homes. The work women did in the home was glorified as essential to victory because homemakers were providing a stable environment for soldiers, defense workers, and the country as a whole. An ad that illustrates this theme features three figures with identical faces, representative of the female soldiers of wartime—a servicewoman, a factory worker, and a housewife. The caption reads "Uniform, Slacks, Kitchen Apron" and praises all three for the valuable work they are doing to hasten victory (Eureka, 10 April 1943, p. 93). While glorifying housework may seem counterproductive at a time when women were needed in the labor force, it makes sense when viewed in the context of an ideology that placed the home at the center of American values. Just as the servicewoman represented civilian patriotism, so did the housewife stand for what made America strong: the family.

One of the most important lessons of the war period is that, in this time of militaristic aggression and conflict, the ideal of the family served as a national unifier, becoming a symbol of what the American system was all about. It was the vision of family members struggling to build a decent home, a wholesome community, that was used to inspire patriotic fervor in the population. By personalizing the goal of military conflict in this way, propagandists were able to tap deeply felt needs for security and continuity while making use of strong affectional bonds and key components of individual identity. Through identifying the interests of the nation with the survival of the family, it was possible to waken the most profoundly rooted impulses toward protection of what civilians hold most dear: the primary relationships established during childhood.

As the war drew to a close, the home continued to play a central role in visions of postwar life as advertisers began offering consumer products which, they said, would make it a domestic paradise. Both themes, of course, reflected genuine longings for prosperity, safety, and the familiarity of one's family roots at a time when lives were in danger and memories of widespread unemployment were still fresh.[60]

The central role played by the family in wartime ideology, in turn, had a profound effect on the image of women who became symbolic of the home-centered life style soldiers were fighting to protect. This dynamic helps explain why the need for women in male roles during the massive removal of men abroad failed to result in a reordering of attitudes toward women. We would expect the demonstrable competence of women in male occupations and the reliance on them as strong home-front soldiers to destroy or at least seriously weaken an ideology that defines women as weak, nonmechanical, incapable of leadership, and unsuited for the challenges of the public world. However, what should have encouraged a rethinking of gender roles instead produced reactionary views of women as loving homemakers who had no tools for or interest in taking on the adventures of the world outside the home. It was partially the use of women as symbols of the nation under siege and as representative of its most cherished institution—the family—that resulted in their enshrinement as wives and mothers in the postwar era. Because the need for women in male-identified roles coexisted with the need for the home as an emotional symbol of national unity and vulnerability, it did not make permanent changes in our notions of what constitutes suitable behavior for the sexes. Thus, propagandists infused new life into the very image that the glorification of Rosie the Riveter attacked: the vulnerable homemaker who depended on a man for her livelihood.

Finally, the idealization of women as mothers makes sense when one considers the need for hope in a violent conflict the magnitude of World War II. As givers of life, mothers were a logical locus of desires for a better world in which there was no want, deprivation, or uncertainty. The promise of renewal, sweetness, comfort lay behind the vision of women as bearers and nurturers of children that became so prevalent in the transition from war to peace. The impulse toward stability, as Friedan has pointed out, was apparently so strong that American society adopted a conservative, neo-Victorian model of the family and male-female relationships, one in which women devoted themselves to building a warm nest and left the realm of adventurous risk taking to men. Valued primarily as life givers in a society wealthy enough to promise miraculous new home products, women's previous contribution as dependable leaders of the production front became dwarfed by their special talent for healing the wounds of battle. They were needed no longer as models of autonomy and achievement who had overcome heavy odds against them but as figures of mercy, tenderness, and innocence who had remained unscathed by the brutal realities of combat.

3   The Working-Class Woman and
the Recruitment Campaign

THE audience for *True Story* has long been known to differ from that of big slicks like the *Saturday Evening Post*. From its inception in 1919, *True Story*, like other "confessions," has been aimed at the wife or daughter of the working-class male, and its readers generally have not read middle-class women's magazines: "the editorial formula [of confession magazines] attracted, from the beginning, persons who probably had never before read magazines, persons with little education or purchasing power, persons whom other publishers had neglected because they were not the sort that advertisers were especially interested in reaching."[1] With a subscriber circulation of over two million throughout the war, *True Story* led the confessions group in sales, and as part of the Macfadden publishing empire it is a good representative of reading matter for working-class women. Its audience was an important group, since it furnished many of the workers for war production who entered the labor force out of financial need and who were likely to continue working after the war.

Another feature of *True Story* that gives it significance for understanding working-class women's perception of war work is that its readers have seen it as mirroring their conflicts, as being realistic, and as providing them with solutions to their problems. Editors have billed its stories as truthful accounts of real people who are struggling with common problems. Bernarr Macfadden, the founder of the magazine, claimed that he printed only manuscripts that were sent in by readers and nonprofessionals and "patched up" by editors, but it is clear that most confessions have been written by people who have mastered the formula.[2] Muriel Cantor and Elizabeth Jones have found that *True Story* writers fall into two camps—amateurs and professionals—but that accepted stories are heavily edited by the editorial staff in order to appeal to the market at which they are aiming. Though some writers share the characteristics of the editors' perceptions of the audience for whom they write, their work is published because it follows a conventional formula that is relatively difficult to master.[3]

The formula has been so successful that the magazine has high credibility with working-class readers. Some typical comments from postwar subscribers to *True Story* indicate the degree to which blue-collar women have seen themselves reflected in its pages: "Well, the main thing is that the stories in *True Story* are stories that actually happened to people. They are true life experiences. I like to read *True Story* because I know they are true. . . . you can tell those stories are true, there are things like that just happen. . . . the stories seem real. They're interesting."[4] In addition, readers have turned to confessions for guidance in handling their problems: "I thought it taught a very good lesson [a story about a mother who causes juvenile delinquency] because it shows that you shouldn't be too strict, just as you should not be too lenient. . . . Those stories tell you about right and wrong. They show how what happens [*sic*] when people don't follow the straight and narrow."[5]

As we have seen, the Magazine Bureau enjoyed an extensive and cooperative association with all the pulps, including the confessions, in the early stages of the recruitment effort. Dorothy Ducas, chief of the Magazine Bureau, made several visits to the Macfadden Publishing Company and especially to *True Story* during her trips to New York in 1942 and 1943, while they in turn sent representatives to meetings set up by the bureau between magazine editors and government agencies. Esther Kimmel, editor of *True Story*'s "Victory Homemaker" column, was a frequent representative to these meetings, as was chief editor Henry Lieferant. Ducas boasted to the Bureau of Campaigns of having had "a great deal of success" in persuading confessions editors to support local recruitment and mentioned the pleasant relationship she had established with *True Story* in particular. The general manager of Macfadden, in turn, praised Ducas highly for the way she was doing her job.[6] This correspondence indicates that *True Story* editors, along with the confessions group as a whole, wanted to support OWI campaigns and took their role as propagandists seriously. Formula writers were sent the *Magazine War Guide* and supplement, which suggested ways propaganda themes could be integrated into pulp romances while other avenues of communication between the government and writers were established through the Confessions Committee of the Writers' War Board, which was set up to coordinate magazines like *True Story* with government goals.[7]

The Magazine Bureau's staff identified thirteen confession magazines as having printed 136 articles, stories, editorials, and fillers recruiting women into war production from July 1943 to August 1945. Fifteen pieces of fiction were listed as well as twelve articles from *True Story*. While *True Story* was not identified as having published fiction, other Macfadden publications were, indicating that its editors and writers also produced fiction with propaganda themes. As with the *Post*, a close reading of *True Story* suggests that its contribution was underrepresented in government records.[8]

The Confession Formula

The formula of the confessions has been characterized as "sin-suffer-repent." The heroine is victimized or violates norms of behavior, suffers the consequences, learns a vital lesson about life, and vows to live by the lesson she has learned: "one simple formula underlies three-fourths of all published confessions stories—a simple, trustful human is faced with a complex, real and brutal world. . . . In fighting back against brutality surrounding her, the heroine first sins, then suffers, then repents."[9] The most common subject of confession stories has been the pursuit of love.[10] Something interferes with the course of true love—a rival, past hurt, ambition, desire for adventure—which the heroine must overcome to gain happiness. While grappling with whatever obstacle is causing her difficulties with romance, she untangles her conflicting emotions about men, her role in society, and her sexual identity, generally through blaming herself for her problems.

The two essential features of confession stories are that marriage is the solution to women's unhappiness and that the hero-

Female error in the confessions. From "Bad Wife," *True Story*, January 1940. Copyright © 1940 by *True Story*. Reprinted by permission.

ine is swept along in a vortex of confusion and pain toward the final realization of how her mistakes have interfered with achieving a stable, intimate relationship. She has no power to protect herself from the harshness of the world, nor can she act wisely to actualize her dreams: "because of [a] motivating character flaw, she'll see only one way out of her predicament—and, of course, her warped judgment will prompt the wrong decision."[11] The confessions heroine, therefore, passively suffers both the cruelty meted out to her by fate and the disastrous consequences of her own mistaken notions about how to find happiness.

The confessions' sleazy reputation has come from their dealing with sensationalistic topics such as incest, rape, adultery, and other forms of illicit sex. The confessional format itself reinforces this image since it is an invitation to read about the hidden secrets of the self, which are ordinarily kept from public view because they concern forbidden desires or transgressions. Despite this focus on the forbidden, the final goal of the confessions formula is adjustment of the heroine to conventional middle-class values: monogamy, marriage, motherhood, and domesticity. In the words of a contemporary writer: "The confessions . . . still firmly believe that a complete and happy home is the most solid foundation for a sound and mature life."[12] It is this essentially conservative vision that prompts readers to characterize confession stories as moral lessons that provide a positive solution to life's problems. A close-knit family, a love-filled marriage, hard work, honesty, and loyalty are all highly valued. Characters who spurn these values are punished and suffer from regrets over past indiscretions.

To understand how the confession formula was affected by the goals of the recruitment campaign, it is useful to look at the themes of stories in 1941 and 1942. Ordinarily, the heroine was an orphan who early had to cope with traumatic events in her struggle to earn a living. Frequently she came from a single-parent home and had to assume the burden of financial responsibility for an invalid mother or father while looking after younger siblings. Her already difficult life was further complicated by the heartaches, disappointments, and confusion of intimacy with a man as her sexual relationships failed to provide her with the emotional security she so desperately sought. In "My

Introduction to Love" (June 1941), for example, the thirteen-year-old heroine lives with her alcoholic father in a boarding house. One of the boarders lures her to a deserted spot and rapes her. While recovering in the hospital, she learns that her father, who has been her sole source of emotional and financial support, has killed himself. Without resources, she is forced to go to an orphanage where she is abused until rescued by a couple who exploit her labor in the laundry they operate. Eventually, she escapes to find work in a circus where she falls in love with a lion tamer. Her happiness is cut short, however, when he is mauled because he is worrying about another man whose heart she has broken. At the end of the story, the narrator performs the lowly chores of a wardrobe mistress as she waits for death to end her loneliness. The lesson she imparts to the reader is to enjoy the few happy moments life grants.

This story illustrates a number of things about confessions stories. It concerns the crises of a young woman entering adulthood who has to cope with important decisions about the direction of her life and with the uncertainties and traumas of love. Its heroine comes from a single-parent home that has known financial and emotional hardship. It also indicates the dark, threatening atmosphere characteristic of the stories. Divorce, alcoholism, death of a spouse, child, or parent, and traumatic catastrophes were common aspects of life with which heroines had to deal and for which they often felt responsible. Finally, we see in this story the helplessness of the narrator as she dazedly recounts the horrors she has endured.

Not surprisingly, the chief quality valued in such women is patient stoicism as they struggle to keep their dignity and hopes intact despite their disillusioning ordeal. Characters who were embittered by their experiences only made things worse for themselves as they refused to risk falling in love or as they warped their children through constant reminders of how cruel life had been to them. The woman who maintained her faith in people despite the hardships she had to suffer was frequently rewarded with a mature and lasting love. The patient, understanding heroine, for instance, was a common figure who gently chastised or silently endured the abuses of an errant sweetheart or husband. Closely related to this emphasis on patience and forgiveness was the idealization of female self-sacrifice, kindness, and cheerfulness. Love was defined as selfless giving with no expectation of reward beyond that of the act itself. Selflessness and loyalty were accompanied by cheerfulness in the face of misery, and it was seen as the antidote to bitterness, a way to endure hardship until one's fortunes improved.

Women who disregarded the value of marriage, fidelity, and self-abnegation were punished and shown the error of their ways. An example of this kind of woman is the flirt, another common figure of these early romances and one who provided a dramatic contrast to the long-suffering good woman. "Too Many Beaux" (June 1941) illustrates the moral lesson she served for the reader. The narrator imitates her flirtatious, immature stepmother and, as a result of her imprudent behavior, gets pregnant during her senior year of high school. After an abortion, she further sullies her reputation by having an affair with a married man. His heartbroken invalid wife commits suicide, and they take up life together; however, her husband turns out to be a shiftless drunk who takes out his rage on her in violent attacks. She is eventually hospitalized as a result of his abuse, and a young engaged intern falls in love with her. At this point, the narrator is finally forced to change her ways when the intern's fiancée confronts her, angrily denouncing her as a cold-hearted home wrecker. Stunned by this personal attack, she learns that her husband has been committed to an insane asylum, her father is dying of a stroke, and her stepmother has gone to Reno to file for a divorce. Realizing that she has totally misunderstood the true route to happiness, the narrator vows to reform.

The high value placed on self-abnegation, meeting the needs of husband and children, and cheerful kindness placed the prerecruitment-period heroine in direct opposition to pursuit of a career. As was true of the *Post*, married career women in *True Story* lost the love of families through devotion to their work. The heroine of "Mrs. Medico" (February 1942), for example, is a doctor who attempts to combine family and work responsibilities. She is, however, a terrifically incompetent homemaker. Not only does the husband leave her, dissatisfied with the quality of her domestic skills, but her daughter becomes a delinquent, pronounces her mother's life a failure, and leaves home to join her father. The heroine admits her wrongdoing and rejoins her family after quitting the practice. She discourages her daughter from considering a career in medicine and repeating her mistakes: "Perhaps she'll be a happier woman than I have been if she learns to knit sweaters and make a strawberry shortcake, and lets the world of pain—of hospitals and sickbeds—take care of itself." Similarly, in "Never Do This to a Man" (May 1941) a young woman helps manage the family farm after her mother dies. Having no interest in marriage, she dreams of owning the farm herself one day and turning it into a financial success. Her plans are disrupted when she falls in love with an artist who tries to pursue his career after their marriage. She is so caught up in the business, however, that she fails to give him the moral support he needs and almost loses his love. By the time she realizes how wonderful he really is and how talented, he has given up painting entirely.

These career women were generally orphans or products of broken homes who devoted themselves to work and developed their ambitions in response to painful childhood experiences. Sometimes their mothers have pushed them toward a career out of bitterness toward a husband who deserted the family, or they have thrown themselves into their work to avoid the memory of a failed love affair. These are heroines who like their work and, unlike the egocentric career woman of prewar *Post* fiction, put a lot of energy into their marriages. However, their ambition interferes with their roles as wives and mothers, which forces them to choose between success in work and success in love. Thus, both magazines reflected the negative attitudes toward the working wife that prevailed in the 1930s, a time when many men were suffering from unemployment. More accurately, such images suggest that female self-actualization and independence were incompatible with harmonious family life.

Unlike the *Post*, however, which featured stories of successful, attractive single women who won the love of a man through dedication to a dream, *True Story* narratives showed that women who challenged themselves were punished. A common story type concerned a well-intentioned, likable young woman testing her powers and trying to realize a worthy goal. Her middle-class counterpart was the aviator, reporter, private secretary, or athlete who bravely thrust herself into demanding situations and triumphed, thereby endearing herself to a man who learned from her example how to be effective himself. In the confessions, such women found that their dreams were illusions and had been born of a warped desire to escape their true feminine destinies.

The coowner of a dressmaking shop in "He Was So Charming" (March 1941), for example, refuses to give up her job when her fiancé tells her he does not like career women. She breaks the engagement and visits some bohemian friends, who see no conflict between marriage and careers. She is nearly seduced by a married man who assures her he would never ask her to give up her shop. Realizing the disastrous nature of the course she has chosen, she remorsefully asks her fiancé for forgiveness, declares she wants nothing more to do with careers, and vows to be content with "a humdrum ordinary marriage."

A similar theme informs "Every Day Will Be a Miracle" (July 1942). In it, a self-sufficient wife who knows how to repair things around the house and whose adventurous spirit has led her to obtain a pilot's license is cursed with infertility. Though she desperately wants a child, she cannot conceive. It is only when she assumes responsibility for the child of an absent friend, thereby awakening her dormant femininity, that she becomes pregnant. Her doctor explains that it was her reluctance to give up the masculine interests generated by having been raised like a boy which kept her from maturing into an adult woman: "You had to grow first, psychologically; accept your true nature." The dream of independence, then, was revealed to be a false god, luring its innocent victim into soul-destroying debauchery or barren loneliness. Risk taking and competence in the world outside the home were equated with masculinity while female assertiveness was viewed as extremely destructive, leading to abandonment and even death. The world was a dangerous place for a woman, and anyone foolish or unfortunate enough to venture out alone was doomed to personal and moral failure.

Another dramatic contrast with Post fiction, which rarely featured mothers, was True Story's concentration on motherhood as the only route to happiness and self-actualization. Childless women were desperate beings filled with panic over their failure fully to achieve their sexual identity. A good example of the torment such women undergo is the suffering of an office-worker wife in "Motherhood by Proxy: Diary of a Test-Tube Mother" (April 1941). She marries a man who she is convinced will enable her to have the family she has desired with an intensity that verges on obsession: "When I look at him and see how fine and strong he is, when I know what fine children he will have, I feel so humble that I could lie down and let him walk over me." Upon discovering that he is sterile, she confides in a career-oriented friend, who nearly destroys her marriage by helping her get artificially inseminated. In torment over her rash act, the heroine finally confesses it to her husband. While he is initially distraught, all ends well when the baby arrives and they find they can love him as their own.

The major themes of True Story narratives before the recruitment campaign, then, were that self-abnegation, sexual fidelity, and domesticity were the ingredients of a happy life. The ideal heroine based her identity on marriage and motherhood. Careers or ambitions other than homemaking led heroines into disastrous courses of action while miscarriages, abortions, and infertility were signs of immaturity and irresponsibility. The clear message of these stories is that children are necessary for a successful life and essential for a woman's identity. In addition, prerecruitment stories were characterized by hardships of truly nightmarish proportions as heroines were subjected to rape, mental abuse, and material deprivation whenever they tried to make their way in the world. They frequently had to endure loss of loved ones through accident, fatal illness, homicide, or suicide. The torments they suffered from bad luck were compounded by the tragic consequences of their own misguided actions.

Buffeted about by external forces over which she had no control and by internal drives of which she had only the vaguest understanding, the confessions heroine of the early forties found refuge in stoic resignation and the dim hope that her patient virtue would someday be rewarded by the love of a good man. As we shall see, the confessions' emphasis on passive suffering and domesticity would place some restrictions on propagandists and would be incompatible with much of the government's womanpower program; indeed, the confessions portrait of war workers did not share the heroic qualities of the figure created by popular artists of the middle class.

Women's Changing Status during the War
and the Confession Formula

Unlike the *Post*, which failed to publish fiction concerning war workers until 1943, pieces concerning women in various phases of war work started appearing in *True Story* as early as the fall of 1941. Although it is possible that such stories resulted purely from social conditions, their overbearing patriotic themes suggest that editors contacted government officials for information on how magazines should handle the country's increasing involvement in the war. They appear to confirm Dorothy Ducas's reports that pulp editors had been trying to gear their material to government policy goals before OWI was organized, were frustrated by the lack of resources available to them for this purpose, and thought the establishment of regular communication between magazines and federal war agencies in mid-1942 was "long overdue."[13]

While they were not as comprehensive or well organized as OWI, there were a number of agencies that *True Story* could have consulted between the fall of 1941 and 1942. For instance, the Office of Emergency Management had set up a Division of Information in May of 1940, which was charged with disseminating war information to the media. In fact, the working relationship that had been established between federal agencies and the media through this office was eventually transferred to OWI along with its staff. Another agency that dealt with the media was the Office of Government Reports, formed in September 1939 to keep the president informed of public response to policies of federal programs. It was joined by the Office of Facts and Figures in October 1941.[14] Both OGR and OFF had special divisions for magazines. It appears that *True Story* contacted these agencies to get information on how the economy was being affected by conversion to war production, most likely to see how magazines would fare and to gauge the effect of such a shift on its readers.

These early stories employed several propaganda techniques, which were later refined by the more systematic organization of the media in 1943. One of these was the heroine's identification with the country's role as a defender of freedom. She saw herself as part of a great national enterprise to preserve democratic principles. In "We Shall Build Good Ships" (November 1941), for instance, the heroine's initial resentment of the anonymity, noise, and confusion in the shipyard gives way to a deep-felt respect for the work she is doing after an undercover FBI agent carefully explains why America needs to help Europe. He asks her if she loves her country, and she thinks to herself: "I think that in all the twenty-two years of my existence I had never asked myself that question, or let other things slip out of my mind while I thought of its greatness, its glory and beauty, the blessing its way of life was, its goodness. For the first time I was conscious of a little tingling thrill that came to me with the words 'my country.'" With her awakened sense of patriotism, she finds a new sense of pride in being part of the yard she had despised: "The sense of slavery to the yards dropped away, and an unaccustomed pride took its place. Slowly I opened my purse and took out my badge. . . . It wasn't a badge of servitude after all! It was a mark of distinction, of privilege!" A similar feeling of pride in her country motivates a coal miner's daughter to join the Army Nurse Corps: "in my purse was a picture, clipped from a newspaper, of an Army nurse. I studied the trim, neat uniform. Very soon I would look like this earnest girl!" ("Army Nurse," September 1941).

As with middle-class romances, these confession narratives focused on a developing love affair between the working heroine and a man she impresses while doing her job. The nurse finds that the army does not destroy a woman's sexual attractiveness when a movie star on her ward falls in love with her. The shipyard clerical worker marries a riveter. A small-town typist finds a job in a federal agency and is courted by the head of the Office of Production Management, eventually marrying one of the lawyers who regularly comes through her office ("Miss Smith Goes to Washington," December 1941).

Another characteristic that these early stories share with those of the later period is that the heroine earns the love of a good man by doing her best to let nothing interfere with performing her duty. A clerk who does volunteer civil defense war work after she leaves a department store earns the admiration of a male volunteer when they subdue a thief: "I love her because she's so calm and serene. Because she's the kind of girl we need in America today, the kind of girl who doesn't get hysterical or let her own private feelings get in the way of the job to be done. In a crisis, with two guns threatening her life, she remained just as cool and level-headed as Sergeant Jones down at camp in Virginia" ("Air-Raid Warden (Girl) Meets Air-Raid Warden (Boy)," March 1942). Another clerk who volunteers her services to the Office of Civil Defense is similarly described as being able to rise to the occasion because her country depended on her: "I used to be so tired after selling gloves at Palmer's from 9 to 5 every day that I went home from work ready to flop into bed. But now that there was something to be done, something that would help even a tiny bit the men who were helping us so much, I seemed to have energy to spare" ("Ten-Day Honeymoon," April 1942).

What these stories indicate is that the pulps were at least as eager as the government to develop a spirit of "war-mindedness" in the public and that writers were able to fashion romances around patriotic themes without explicit plot suggestions. Indeed, as early as December 1942 the supplements designed for pulp writers ceased providing detailed plot suggestions appropriate for various popular formulas because editors informed OWI that they had worked out ways to use the material in their special fields.[15] Though the Magazine Bureau felt it necessary to guide writers carefully toward proper fictional treatment of home-front campaigns during the early stages of its activities, the primary way it affected popular fiction was to inform writers of campaign goals and to define broadly ideological needs.

The lack of a comprehensive propaganda organization before the fall of 1942 did result in some confusion, however, about how the subject of war work ought to be handled.[16] This lack of coordination is reflected in these early stories. The major difference between the early and the later stories concerning war work is that the 1941 pieces deal with brutal personal tragedies, the stock-in-trade of the prewar confessions formula. The shipyard secretary of "We Shall Build Good Ships" is seduced and abandoned by an irresponsible fellow worker whose mother is described as a "tramp." In addition, she almost loses him to a sexually active woman living alone in company housing. The clerical worker in "Miss Smith Goes to Washington" rooms with two other women, one of whom gets pregnant by a married man and the other of whom engages in casual affairs. More-

A patriotic shipyard worker. From "We Shall Build Good Ships,"
True Story, November 1941. Copyright © 1941 by *True Story*. Reprinted by permission.

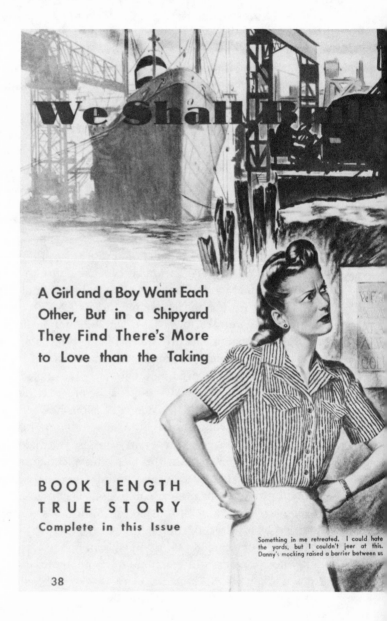

We Shall Bu...

A Girl and a Boy Want Each
Other, But in a Shipyard
They Find There's More
to Love than the Taking

BOOK LENGTH
TRUE STORY
Complete in this Issue

Something in me retreated. I could hate
the yards, but I couldn't jeer at this.
Danny's mocking raised a barrier between us

38

od Ships

ABOVE THE whitecaps on the river the spidery steel trellises over the shipways were black against the sky as I struggled homeward, my head down, my futile umbrella pushed hard against the driving rain which rushed like an avalanche before the wind that swept across Hampton Roads. Behind me, ahead of me and on both sides, crowded other workers from the shipyard office. A little ahead the men from the yards, pushing up the incline to the gate, merged with us office workers—almost all girls—on Washington Avenue, making a solid mass, all drenched now. There wasn't room to keep an umbrella up in the mob. I was about to close mine as useless, when a gust of wind saved me the trouble by taking it out of my hand, turning it inside out, and whipping it away. It was that way about everything here. A mighty force—stronger than that wind and rain even—had everyone here in its grip, forcing him to do its will.

But I wasn't going to stand it any longer! I had made up my mind that day. Three weeks was enough. I was through!

It wasn't that I minded the rain, itself. Under other circumstances I might have enjoyed this challenging struggle with elemental wrath. But somehow it seemed to emphasize the fact that I wasn't an individual here. I was simply one of the seventeen thousand nameless cogs in the great grinding, crashing, hissing, banging shipbuilding machine at Newport News. Ever since the President had declared a national emergency, the machine's tempo had been increasing. In less than a year, 7,000 new employees had rushed in to help speed the defense program—a new battleship, the *Indiana*, on the ways, eight new aircraft carriers, and heaven knew how many cargo vessels, tankers, and other ships on order. All the decent houses and apartments in Newport News (and a lot that weren't decent) were filled, and some of the men were driving more than forty miles to work every day. I felt less and less a person, more and more a mechanical unit subjected to an implacable, soulless power.

Well, I didn't have to put up with it. I could always go

39

over, the roommate who dates several men is raped and beaten unconscious during the course of the story.

Because the government thought it would reflect badly on war workers as a whole if women in war jobs were shown engaging in questionable sexual activities, the Magazine Bureau cautioned confessions writers to create heroines who would set a positive example for readers. Officials were afraid that stories placing war workers in compromising positions would turn public opinion against them and perhaps inhibit women from entering occupations where they were needed: "May we suggest that care be observed not to create the impression that women engaged in any phase of war work, whether with the military services, in civilian war agencies or in war industry, are more tempted or more susceptible to extra-marital dalliance than others? *War service, rather, should be depicted as a regenerative influence,* by example. The whole subject of wartime temptation to loose living should be treated circumspectly in fiction dealing with any war activity in which girls, women, or young men are engaged."[17]

The people who put together the supplement for the confessions urged writers to be aware of how damaging negative portrayals of war jobs could be. In regard to the recruitment of clerical workers for federal agencies, for example, the supplement chastised writers for showing Washington as a dangerous place for single women: "Certain writers, probably thoughtlessly rather than malevolently, have seized on this situation [the housing problems in Washington] to portray conditions in the capital as so deplorable that the necessary recruitment of girls for war work in Washington in some cases has been hampered seriously. Efforts must be concentrated on counteracting the false and damaging impression that has been created."[18]

As part of this strategy to depict war workers in a positive light, stories during the recruitment period featured narrators who have a relatively trauma-free life, and women in war jobs were always portrayed as respectable, dependable, dutiful wives, sweethearts, or daughters. While heroines were frequently orphans or children of divorce and perhaps had suffered the death of a parent, the nightmarish hardship of 1941 stories was noticeably diminished. To a large extent, the more positive tone of recruitment stories resulted from the absence of

True Story's previous sensationalistic treatment of sexuality and violence. Prior to the magazine's association with the Magazine Bureau, stories routinely dealt with such topics as abortion, premarital sex, adultery, rape, artificial insemination, suicide, and homicide. Stories concerning war workers, however, remained scrupulously free of such references. *True Story*'s more efficient communication with the government resulted in its toning down the more sensational aspects of the confessions formula, presumably because sex and violence were perceived as disruptive to the community and to the development of a spirit of unity. The government also attempted to eliminate prejudices against women in blue-collar work, and since working in male-dominated occupations was considered damaging to a woman's reputation, reinforcing that image interfered with the purpose of the enterprise.

Searching for a way to integrate the propaganda goals of attracting women to male blue-collar fields and creating an upstanding role model of production workers with a formula that concentrated on redemption from moral error, writers featured heroines who gained maturity and respectability from their war jobs. The following story, for instance, concerns a twenty-year-old factory worker whose job is making precision instruments. The narrator, like many confessions heroines, comes from a broken home and is shunned by the community because of the disreputable life style of her family. She has lived with her father since the scandalous desertion of her mother, who ran off with another man when the narrator was six years old. Her older sister has reinforced the town's negative opinion of the women in her family by indiscreet sexual activity and by divorcing her husband even though she was pregnant. Though the narrator must endure the twin burdens of poverty and social ostracism, she is loyal to her family and of high moral character, yet her true value is only recognized when she takes a war job at the plant. Not only do her neighbors come to respect her, but the boss's son falls in love with her ("Not Good Enough . . . ," August 1944). The story shows that factory work, far from encouraging sexual experimentation, was a positive influence on women taking blue-collar jobs. It demonstrates that readers can elevate their status in the community, escape their past by entering a war industry, and become self-disciplined, self-respecting people.

As the communication network between Washington and the media became better organized, True Story's treatment of the womanpower campaign reflected a more sophisticated awareness of such ideological subtleties and their impact on the recruitment effort. The major effect, then, of the Magazine Bureau was to provide a clearer direction for the confessions through keeping them informed of where women were needed, to which market magazines should address themselves, and which broad thematic approaches would be the most helpful. The more systematic contact is reflected in the plethora of stories about war workers that appear in True Story during the period of heavy recruitment. For example, nine of the twelve lead stories that featured war workers during the war years appeared between March 1943 and June 1944. We also see the impact of the 1943 "Women in Necessary Services" campaign in the five stories of the September issue (out of ten) with patriotic themes about female war workers. One concerns a married teacher who becomes pregnant and decides nevertheless to work in a copper refinery, "where they need women." Another features a high school graduate who abandons her college dreams for an aircraft plant, and a third is about a married nurse who joins the Army Nurse Corps. In addition, the cover of that issue features a female taxi driver and displays the womanpower recruitment symbol. Out of twenty-nine stories from my sample that had war-working heroines from 1941 to 1944, nine appeared in the months of the fall campaign, the largest number of any similar period during those years.[19]

As we have seen, OWI wished to encourage an overall attitude of dedication and stoicism in the population. One of its main goals was to cut down on absenteeism, job turnover, and work slowdowns in vital industries. A fictional technique employed by popular writers of the Post to create a dramatic home-front situation was to feature blue-collar workers defeating saboteurs, a plot that had been recommended by the Magazine Bureau, which urged that worker inefficiency be equated with treason.[20] It also asked editors to emphasize "the contributions of labor to victory . . . a new kind of teamwork between labor unions and industry."[21] Confessions writers were specifically asked to combine romantic allure with stoic, patriotic job performance in order to encourage maximum efficiency and appropriate civilian attitudes:

> In stories, in heart-to-heart talks and in reader's service pages the women's magazines can remind their readers that the nation's cheerful acceptance of the very real hardships we face in the year ahead is largely dependent on them. . . . fictional treatment of this theme [toughening up for war], with the romantic element, may be found in the influx of young women from sheltered homes into war industry. The personnel of war plants are nothing if not cosmopolitan, and there are many chances for variations of this theme:—the intolerant girl scornful of a lover from a different social background or the reverse, misunderstandings between lovers arising out of one or the other's intolerant attitudes, etc. The solution of [sic] the situation might perhaps come through some crisis in the plant that makes it clear to the erring person that all are Americans, giving of their best for the democracy that is the essence of America.[22]

One way confessions writers appear to have responded to this desire for a cooperative, diligent work force was to feature a romance between a working-class war worker and an employer in a defense plant who set her on the right path of service to her country. Whereas *Post* heroines usually won soldiers through their patriotic attitude, those in *True Story* fell in love with the bosses for whom they worked or with the boss's son, and it is through their involvement with this representative of management that they learn to do enthusiastically whatever their country demands of them. This theme is illustrated in "Young Girl's Secret" (October 1943). The narrator is a disgruntled secretary at an aircraft plant who resents her transfer from a high-paying assembly line job to the office. Because her new job is less glamorous and interesting than what she had been doing before, it is difficult for her to feel much enthusiasm for her work. Gradually, however, her supervisor's appreciation of her importance sheds new light on the situation, and her excitement mounts as she comes to feel part of a worthy cause: "All the world seemed filled with high endeavor; the noise of the factory an articulate voice, saying: more planes, more planes, more planes—we're making them, we're building them, we're sending them out. I looked with pride at the lists which came into my hands, and often I would glance up and see the pride in Courtney Atwell's eyes." As a result, she adopts a willingness to do whatever she is asked in order to help her country: "Wherever I'm most needed, wherever I can be the most help—that's all I want." Pleased with her subordination of her own wishes to those of the company, the boss approvingly replies: "That's the spirit . . . that will win this war."

It is not surprising that confession stories frequently contained fantasies about marrying the boss, the most likely way a working-class woman could imagine escape from her low socioeconomic situation. This upward-mobility fantasy was coupled with developing cooperation in working-class women through featuring heroines who gladly responded to the wise words of a supervisor or company owner concerning the importance of every person's role in the work force.

Another way stories during the recruitment period encouraged a feeling of solidarity between workers and the country as a whole was to convey the idea that to be a member of the working class was a mark of distinction because blue-collar workers were in the forefront of the economic struggle to defeat the enemies of democracy. This was in line with OWI's recommendation that writers emphasize the valuable contributions of the working class to securing victory: "Those who have made it possible for men at the fighting fronts to receive enough and superior equipment to do their tough and dangerous jobs and those who are keeping the wheels of our civilian economy turning until the boys come home again deserve recognition."[23] Just as heroines developed maturity in jobs requiring self-discipline, so too did they proudly affirm their working-class identities through understanding the importance of their war jobs.

An office worker narrates the story of her love affair with a college graduate in "The Pink Dress" (May 1943), for instance, while describing how she sheds her elitist prejudice against her working-class family. The narrator is so ashamed of her factory-worker brother and father and her hardworking mother that she lies to her boyfriend about her class background. He is the boss's son, and she is afraid he will reject her if he knows about her humble origins. Fortuitously, the boyfriend and brother become good friends in the army, and the heroine is caught in her elaborate fabrication when the brother brings her sweetheart home with him on furlough. She suddenly understands how wrong she was to devalue her own people and makes a spirited speech in which she characterizes them as the backbone of the nation. Pleased to see that the heroine has developed a proper appreciation of her family, the boyfriend proposes.

The positive perspective such characters adopted toward their working-class origins partially resulted from writers' looking for ways to develop "war-mindedness" and feelings of solidarity with the nation as a whole in pulp readers. The Magazine Bureau alerted writers to the fact that not all women felt a part of the struggle, asking them "to make the love book readers aware of [the womanpower question] and of their own place in its solution." To draw working-class women into a nationalistic spirit that identified their interests with the country's, it recommended further that writers portray women from the lowest social strata as valuable defenders of democracy: "Fictional treatment should be directed towards emphasizing the angle that the question is one for every reader, that it reaches into every stratum of society, that it touches, poignantly and personally, every woman and girl no matter what her position in life, her environment, her history of work and leisure."[24]

Characters who responded to their nation's distress call found a better sense of self, heightened self-esteem, and a new lease on life because their war jobs brought to them an opportunity to do something worthwhile, to be part of a noble enterprise. As a result, stories of the recruitment period show a marked change from those in 1941 and 1942, which rarely dealt with the narrator's feelings about her job and concentrated on love as the primary source of meaning in her life. While war-worker heroines continued to fall in love and patiently worked to resolve romantic problems, they were much more likely to be shown at the workplace, and their attitude toward the job was an important element in the story line. Writers took great pains to describe the enormous fulfillment war worker heroines experienced in their clerical, nursing, or factory positions.

Whereas women in the Post shed their upper-class snobbery for patriotic humility through taking war jobs, the confessions war worker gained a new sense of pride in herself and her origins as a result of her work. A homemaker who joins the assembly line in an aircraft plant after being inspired to serve her country by a Memorial Day parade glowingly relates her feelings about factory work: "It was part of me and I was part of it, fulfilled, content, finding new reserves of strength" ("In Love with America," June 1943). Another aircraft worker exuberantly describes her important role in helping soldiers: "I was so thrilled to be learning aircraft production that I didn't know anything else existed. The big Commanche Training Center . . . was the most glamorous place in the world to me. I thought nothing could be more deeply satisfying than to shape a piece of shining aluminum—carefully, conscientiously—knowing that a man's life might depend on the skill of my hands. . . . When my class finished the basic training I was so proud I thought I'd burst" ("Each Moment a Memory," March 1943). A nurse describes the transporting effects of her career in "The Army Takes Over" (September 1943): "It was that magnificent sense of a good and important and thrilling job of life-saving service rendered to a human being and the human race—a job perfectly done with all the science and skill of my nursing craft—that lifted me out of my plain little self and made my life and my work seem to take on the touch of divinity."

Another important goal of the recruitment campaign was to change negative attitudes toward employed women, especially married workers. The *Magazine War Guide* informed writers that fictional characters ought not to be shown as thinking that marriage was their "only career in wartime," and the supplement for confessions advised them to tackle the problem of male resistance to working wives: "In terms of the confession magazines' formula, we suggest that stories be written depicting the changing and changed women-world as affecting boy-girl relationships and perhaps the more mature relationships of young wife and husband. Some men, despite the advances of the past decades and despite the war, still cling to the tradition that 'woman's place is in the home,' and here we have a setting for misunderstanding and conflict."[25]

The following stories demonstrate the way writers tried to dramatize conflicts over the issue of working wives and to resolve them in ways compatible with recruitment goals. The aircraft worker in "Each Moment a Memory" has passed her training course with flying colors and is one of the first women in her plant to take a skilled job performed by men. During an air raid drill she meets another worker with whom she falls in love. Problems arise when he finds a better job in another city, as he wants to get married so that she can be with him there. The heroine balks even though she loves him, saying her training has made her indispensable at the plant. Though he is initially angry over her desire to keep working, they eventually agree that she will move with him and find another aircraft job.

A further complication develops, however, when the president of her plant singles her out for praise, saying that she has proven women can handle any job in the factory. As a sign of his trust in women, he assigns her to a top-secret job in the research section. The narrator is torn between her wedding plans and her responsibility to remain where she is. She is afraid that if she leaves employers will hesitate to depend on women again. When she points out to her fiancé that he would stay were the situation reversed, he angrily replies that it would be different for him. The narrator emphatically disagrees: "It isn't, not any more. Things have changed. Women have as much responsibility to war work as men have!" Finally persuaded that she is right, the fiancé agrees to marry and live separately. Though they do not look forward to being apart, they realize that duty to country requires women to work wherever they are needed: "We didn't say good-by. We said, 'Keep 'em flying!' For we must turn out our hopes in shining aluminum. Build our dreams into winged weapons for our fighting men." Whereas the normal outcome of a conflict between love and work would have been for the narrator to give up her job, this story shows her sense of responsibility to the company as a laudable quality, one that strengthens her fiancé's love. She is not punished for refusing to do what he wants but rather brings him to a better understanding of the role women play in the war. The reader, then, is being shown that loyalty to a man ought not to supersede dedication to the cause.

The second story ("In Love with America") concerns a housewife who takes a job in an aircraft plant when a Memorial Day parade reminds her of the need for women in the labor force. Though she loves being part of the national struggle and enjoys

An aircraft worker falls in love on the job. From "Each Moment A Memory," *True Story*, March 1943. Copyright © 1943 by *True Story*. Reprinted by permission.

I'll always remember the eerie din of an air raid siren, for that's how I met Jim

her financial independence, her husband pressures her to stay home because he feels threatened by her earning nearly as much as he does and because their adolescent son begins to skip school. Her husband complains that she is neglecting her household duties as well as her maternal responsibilities. The conflict comes to a head when the boy runs away. The narrator pursues him, suffers from exposure when her car stalls in a snowstorm, and finds herself in the hospital. After chastising herself for hurting her family, she finally sees a way to serve it and her country both: involve the children in the war effort by having them do emergency housework for the duration. Because the boy feels he is supporting soldiers through filling in for his mother, the truancy stops, and the husband is satisfied that the home is running smoothly. The story supports the recruitment of married older women into war production by showing how resistant husbands can be mollified and by demonstrating how working women can combine housework with a full-time job.[26]

Not only were wives able to work out problems associated with their war jobs, but frequently they found their marriages were rejuvenated by the altered conditions of wartime. In "Straight from the Shoulder" (March 1944), for example, a young aircraft worker's marriage is saved by the changes her job makes in her. Because the work is exhausting and she has never had to take care of herself or learn how to push herself to meet challenges, she has difficulty adjusting to her job as a grinder in an aircraft plant. Her husband, who is stationed overseas, is distressed by her negative attitude and considers divorce. Gradually the heroine comes to understand how important it is that she do her best to cope with wartime conditions and gains a new appreciation of the work she is doing: "I felt a new something—was it pride in accomplishment?—stirring inside me." Her husband is delighted when he sees her transformation; his child bride has become a strong, dependable adult, and he happily acknowledges the new equality in their relationship: "We never talked this way before, did we, Donna? Straight from the shoulder, one guy to another."

Young couples grappling with adjustment problems or older couples stifled by boredom found their relationships revivified by the changes wartime brought. A dull marriage of fifteen years is enlivened when the husband is drafted in "Once upon a Time" (May 1944). A young couple with a small baby quarrels over money and is burdened with debts due to the husband's extravagant purchases until his work in a shipyard settles him down while her clerical job at the yard cements their relationship in "Secret behind a Love Story" (January 1944). A new mother is forced to support the family because her unemployed mate loses all his self-confidence until he enlists and returns a strong man in "It's Time to Remember" (October 1943). Thus, the regenerative aspects of war work cut two ways: working-class heroines were redeemed or renewed by war jobs, and those who were married enjoyed more rewarding relationships with their husbands.

The imperatives of the recruitment campaign resulted in a strengthening of heroines' work identities and the portrayal of war work as a palliative to their sense of personal inadequacy, but the traditional focus of the confessions on domestic life as the source of women's happiness created restraints on *True Story*'s support of the womanpower drive. As a result, contradictory messages about how women could find fulfillment appeared throughout the war years. Unlike the *Post*, which completely dropped the conflict of marriage and career theme so typical of the 1930s, anticareer messages sporadically appeared in *True Story* as did the prerecruitment glorification of motherhood. Although they were in the minority, heroines continued to have babies, mourn miscarriages and infant deaths, overcome fear of maternal responsibilities, and devote themselves to their families. These stories coexisted with war-related ones portraying women primarily as workers or as wives and mothers competently handling two sets of responsibilities. Married working women did not suffer quite as much, nor did the driven woman of ambition appear as often. However, these stereotypes never disappeared entirely. The major change brought on by the war was that a distinction was made between married women working to support the war effort and those who were doing so to satisfy their own ambition. The latter continued to suffer and repent while the former managed to bear healthy children and maintain their marriages.

An example of a story in which the demands of war work are reconciled with those of homemaking is "Make-Believe Mar-

riage" (October 1944). A war-working wife narrates her difficulties in trying to keep her husband happy while working full
time. She asserts that she would like to stay home but feels a
duty to stick with the job. She does not suffer the tribulations of
a career wife, however, because she is in a war job and because
she clearly recognizes that her problem will be solved when the
war ends and she can take up housekeeping. The narrator of "A
Solemn Promise" (April 1944) does not fare so well because her
position as chief surgical nurse in a hospital is not one she has
achieved through patriotic motives but rather is the culmina-
tion of a burning ambition passed on to her by her mother, who
was embittered by an unhappy marriage: "At 23, I had no life
beyond the great walls of mercy—desired none. My work was
meat and drink to my soul."

The nurse's career obsession becomes a problem for her after
she falls in love with and marries one of her patients, a test pilot
who is forced to take a job in an aircraft plant due to his inju-
ries. Though he wants her to resign when they marry and start a
family, she refuses, saying that being superintendent of nurses
means more to her than children. As a result, the marriage dete-
riorates: "We might have prolonged the rapture of our honeymoon indefinitely had I stayed in the shining little rooms and
devoted my time to making a real home." The situation worsens
when she discovers she is pregnant, quits work with a great deal
of bitterness, and expresses her resentment by sloppy housekeeping. As is typical of confessions heroines who put career
before family, this narrator is shown the error of her ways when
she loses her baby and almost loses her husband. He enlists because she has made life miserable for him, an estrangement she
exacerbates by resuming her career. The crisis that finally puts
her on the path of domesticity occurs when the husband is
severely burned while rescuing a student pilot from a plane
crash. Vowing to abandon her selfish ways, the narrator declares she will give up her career obsession, nurse him back
to health, and content herself with a volunteer Red Cross job
when he is well.

Writers accommodated the need for women in war industries
by portraying the positive effects such jobs had on heroines
who found a new sense of purpose in going to work and whose
relationships with men improved as a result of their participat-

ing in wartime service. However, they supported the employment of women within the traditional confessions framework of self-blame, punishment for self-assertion, reliance on a male rescuer, and fulfillment through self-abnegation to a greater cause, whether that was home or country. The major change brought about by the recruitment campaign was that narrators engaged in war work developed strong work and class identities through their heightened self-esteem, but this pride in their work resulted from feeling part of the nation's battle to produce war material. Characters who did not subordinate personal dreams to husband or country were led into disastrous crises, whereas patriotic heroines avoided them and improved their social status. While narrators continued to suffer the deprivations of poverty, broken homes, and unsatisfying marriages, these were mitigated by the regenerative effects of war work.

A story that contains most of the major themes of the recruitment period and that serves as a model of how writers integrated OWI campaign goals into the confession formula is "Education of John Manley by a Girl" (September 1943). It appeared as part of the "Women in Necessary Services" campaign conducted by the Magazine Bureau in the fall of 1943 and addresses itself to absenteeism, working-class patriotism, womanpower, and the housing shortage in boomtowns. The bureau made repeated requests for writers to encourage workers to stay on the job and homeowners to rent rooms to war workers. For instance, the confessions supplement suggested integrating the housing problem into love fantasies: "Patriotic decision to open cloistered homes to young men and young women war workers may be the background for romance." Another supplement wanted pulp magazines to create reader sympathy for the problems that caused war workers to stay away from work in order to motivate them to help out in some way.[27] This story reflects both of these issues as well as the larger one of developing a patriotic spirit in confessions readers.

A working-class family is trying to adjust to the changes brought into their lives through the establishment of war industries in their community. The mother is against taking a roomer due to her prejudices against the incoming migrants but is opposed by her husband, who insists they do their civic duty by relieving the strain on community services brought about by the massive influx. The mother's class prejudice is further revealed when she urges her daughter to pay more attention to her appearance because she does not want people to know that her parents are "factory folks" (the father is a toolmaker). Her husband hotly retorts that factory workers are running the country, and they have nothing of which to be ashamed. Overruled, she agrees to take in a boarder, a skilled toolmaker named John Manley.[28]

The heroine falls in love with him, but her pride is hurt when John chastises her for planning to go to college when she should be taking a war job: "You'd learn plenty in a factory . . . thrift—efficiency—discipline—stamina—self-control. . . . You're willing to feed on your defense-worker of a father, while you're acquiring a synthetic polish." Stung by his criticism, she takes a job at the local defense plant and comes home covered with grease, exhausted, yet with her head held high. When her mother warns her that she is missing a golden opportunity to go to college and will later regret her decision, the heroine reminds her that American soldiers mean more to her than social success: "You can't frame the spirit that's back of the Stars and Stripes! And the boys in the trenches, the ones that are fighting and dying, aren't asking for a diploma!"

The narrator proudly identifies herself as a working-class woman, and her response to the job is typical of the nationalistic fervor that grips war-working heroines: "suddenly the patriotism that John had publicized awoke in me and flamed in a flower of radiance. When I stood beside a machine, the machine achieved not only vitality but immortality, and gadgets that I passed to the operator of the machine became the food with which it was nourished, and I told myself that when it had been fed sufficiently it would have the strength to gobble up opposition—yellow opposition with slanted eyes, square-headed, ruthless opposition that spoke in gutturals. As I felt muscles tightening in my grease-covered arms, I felt something intangible tightening in the arms of my spirit." The narrator's enthusiasm for serving the cause keeps her from giving in to the temptation to quit when the work gets discouragingly hard. It also leads her to tackle John's drinking problem, which is keeping him away from work too many days. Since he is a toolmaker, she reminds him of the shortage of skilled metalworkers and how much his knowledge is needed at the plant. Inspired by her own dedication, he stops drinking.

The story is characteristic of working-class propaganda in that it glorifies defense jobs for women as an opportunity to safeguard democratic ideals. It also features a heroine who temporarily delays her dreams in order to take a war job and who thereby achieves a new sense of her class background as something of which to be proud. The narrator's dedication to the job is meant to serve as a model of responsibility while her nationalistic spirit leads her to challenge the class-biased attitudes of her mother and the narcissistic despair of her boyfriend. She is above all a sterling representative of the factory woman—civic-minded, hardworking, virtuous, and patriotic. Like most war-worker heroines of confessions stories, she serves as a moral inspiration to those around her, affirms the important contribution of the working class to the war effort, and makes it clear that the welfare of her country is her primary consideration.

These, then, were the prominent themes of the early war years. Narrators during the period of intensive OWI recruitment from March 1943 to June 1944 were involved with work far more than those of the period before the government's campaign. They found fulfillment in being part of the national struggle to defeat the enemies of democracy and felt proud to be a member of the great working class upon whom victory depended. Confessions writers quickly adapted to the propaganda needs of the government yet were constrained from developing an image of women as men's equals by the major features of the formula: stoic endurance of disappointment, broken homes, female subordination (to male authority figures or to country), and reliance on love, whether sexual or maternal, for meaning.

The sin-suffer-repent formula with its passive female victim and its focus on domestic happiness was not abandoned during the recruitment campaign; it was merely modified to produce a more positive image of working women. Once the campaign ended, however, stories again placed problems with men and childlessness at the forefront of narrators' concerns. Toward the middle of 1944 through 1945 and early 1946, heroines underwent traumas associated with widowhood, adjustment to returning veterans, and problems with maternity. A typical story of this period is "The Return of Johnny Williams" (April 1945), which is narrated by a veteran. He has difficulty adjusting to civilian life; everything seems different to him, he cannot find a comfortable role, and it is especially hard for him to accept being a mere assembly line worker after having been an army captain. Though he has a devoted wife and a healthy baby, life appears dull and meaningless until the help of a friend allows him to reorient himself. Many stories during the reconversion period dealt with relations between women and veterans wherein the focus was on males' confusion over their peacetime identity rather than on adjustment of working women to losing their war jobs.

Stories that featured women most often concerned heroines' feelings about marriage and motherhood. In some of these we see an older woman, childless and lonely, who expresses her pain at not having a family. The narrator of "There Was Another Girl" (March 1946) resents bitterly the fact that another woman has stolen two men from her. In another story, a sixty-year-old former actress contemplates suicide in her twilight years. The only man she ever loved married another woman because he tired of waiting for her to give up her career. To underline how mistaken she was to refuse him, we are told that his widow lives comfortably from the money he has left her. The narrator—penniless, unloved—finds no solace in her memories of former greatness ("Great Lady," July 1945).

The major theme of the postrecruitment period was that marriage and children were essential for female fulfillment. The emphasis on fertility as the definitive characteristic of femininity, a primary feature of stories in 1941, never was dropped altogether during the war years but was overshadowed by work-centered romances in which the narrator's connection to a great cause substituted for earlier domestic fantasies. When the recruitment campaign ended, stories no longer put work in a central role but focused once more on the tragedies of childless women or on the way young wives overcame their fear of motherhood. Whereas wartime romances equated immaturity with unwillingness to tackle a demanding war job, reconversion pieces identified female fear of growing up with childlessness.

A story that illustrates the shift back to heroines who resist assuming the responsibilities of motherhood is "From Us to You—a Christmas Gift" (January 1945). The narrator's loveless childhood has made her wary of involvement with men. Her divorced mother's bitterness over her father's infidelities has given her a warped view of intimacy. Because she was raised in a boarding school, abandoned by her irresponsible rake of a father, and left totally alone by the death of her mother, the narrator has had no experience with warm family life; therefore she has no interest in becoming a homemaker herself. Even after she falls in love with her employer, she declares to him that a family is the farthest thing from her mind. One evening, however, she finds the three children who live across the hall are unattended and, in spite of herself, her maternal nature comes to the fore: "To my complete surprise, I found myself scooping the child up under one elbow and piloting her to the next room and taking off a wet romper and wet pants putting on dry ones which I somehow, and purely by instinct, managed to locate." As the evening progresses, her resistance to family life dissipates under the influence of the charming domestic scene into which she has accidentally stumbled: "And suddenly I knew why I'd felt so stiff, so rigid, so defiant while I was waiting for Gregg. I'd felt that way because I didn't want to give in to the truth. . . . I loved Gregory Chase and I'd loved him ever since I'd started working for him." After realizing that her antipathy to marriage was a defense against past hurt, she sees that she was wrong to not want a family and to deny the normal expression of her femininity.

There were no stories that showed women war workers returning to the home after the war as there were in the *Post*. Heroines in war work did not dream of full-time homemaking and motherhood, nor was there the same anticipation of postwar domesticity on the part of the soldiers. Similarly, confession stories did not show women leaving war work for female jobs, although when heroines worked—and fewer did than in 1943 or 1944—the job served only as a backdrop for romance (see below, table 5). A possible explanation for the failure of *True Story* to address itself more explicitly to the postwar role shift to domesticity and female jobs is that war work had coexisted with homemaking during the recruitment period. War-working heroines were often wives with husbands present, in contrast to the *Post*, which was more likely to portray service wives in war work with husbands overseas or single women. This made

inappropriate the anticipation of domestic bliss found in heroines of *Post* stories. The changes in roles brought on by the war
were taken in stride in that working women continued to bear
children and live with husbands, undoubtedly reflecting the
greater likelihood that the working-class reader was an employed wife of a blue-collar worker deferred for war work.

We need to ask, as we did in the case of the *Post*, to what extent these thematic changes were due to government direction
and to the imperatives of the recruitment campaign. Since the
popularity of confession magazines has depended on the ability
of writers to reflect the lives of their readers, we have to conclude that the narratives of *True Story* were to some degree a
mirror of working-class conditions. We have seen, for instance,
that narrators during the recruitment period continued to suffer
from mistaken notions about how to find happiness and from
the hardships of poverty but that their tribulations were not as
painful as those of the previous years. The isolation and self-
blame of confessions heroines were similarly not as prominent.
This change in part grew out of the government's desire to
create a positive image of war workers, one that encouraged
working-class women to enter male occupations. But the shift
in emphasis from tragedy to moral uplift through war jobs may
also have been partly due to the fact that objective economic
conditions were better for *True Story* readers during the war
years than they were during the Depression.[29] With high-paying
work available in the booming wartime economy, psychic stress
was lessened for the working-class woman, and we see this
change reflected in the more benign atmosphere of stories following Pearl Harbor.

It is also possible that the heightened self-esteem experienced by narrators who took war jobs was an accurate reflection
of how war work affected women in reality. Since working-class
women were able to earn high wages in heavy industry, could
apply themselves to tasks that were relatively more interesting
than those normally performed by women, and were aware of
how important their products were to the nation, it is likely that
they felt an increased sense of pride in themselves. Their work
was perhaps less alienating than housework or the tedious,
poorly paid jobs in the female job ghetto.[30]

Sherna Gluck's interviews with former aircraft workers from

the Los Angeles area indicate that war work was indeed a liberating experience for many working-class women. Although there was a range of meaning for those entering nontraditional jobs, feelings of pride and accomplishment were reported by most of Gluck's respondents when asked what impact the war had on their lives. Even the young single women for whom the war tended to be merely an interlude in their plans to become homemakers felt proud to be a part of the war effort. The older married women and single mothers declare as well that their aircraft jobs gave them self-confidence, a new sense of their capabilities, and more power over their lives.[31] Therefore, the upstanding, self-respecting heroine of wartime recruitment stories who found a better life through taking a war job mirrored many readers' perceptions of their new roles.

At the same time, it is clear from an examination of OWI recommendations to confessions writers that the positive identification of *True Story* narrators with their class origins and their feelings about their war jobs to a large degree resulted from propagandists' attempts to marshal public support for homefront programs, especially for workers in war industries. Pulp editors billed themselves as shapers of their readers' views in order to prove they were deserving of economic support. The way confession magazines reflected the mutual desire of the pulp industry and OWI to encourage worker solidarity with soldiers was to feature heroines who were transported from ordinary, dissatisfying lives to a world that held more joy and purpose than any they had known before. Even less glamorous jobs like clerical work and nursing were described in glorified terms clearly designed to demonstrate how vital they were to the national interest. Writers both reflected genuine feelings of *True Story* readers and tried to channel them in directions they thought would be useful to the wartime economy. There was, however, no contradiction between *True Story*'s entertainment and propaganda functions, between its reading of the audience and its cooperation with the government. Propaganda groups did not disrupt the activities of such magazines so much as make it easier for them to absorb labor force changes into an ideology that supported wartime goals.

Nonfiction

The connection between OWI and *True Story* is also evident in other features of the magazine. We can see here, as we can in the fiction, how it encouraged women to enter nontraditional fields and to combine home duties with wage work. Three regular columns dealt with the life-style changes and attitude shifts required by the employment of women in war production. The first of these was entitled "Home Problems Forum" and concerned readers' family conflicts. Letters of advice were solicited from other readers, who won prize money if their letters were chosen for publication. By examining the nature of the problems in this column and the advice letters chosen for resolving them, it is possible to see to what extent they followed OWI guidelines. Prior to the intensive drive initiated by the Magazine Bureau in the fall of 1942, the editor published letters from readers upset about family conflicts and sexual difficulties. An unwed pregnant teenager refuses to marry her irresponsible boyfriend, another teenager elopes but then discovers she is not ready for sex, a young bride confesses her previous affairs to her husband, an office worker asks for advice about a love affair with her married boss, a brother is shocked by his sister's sexual experimentation.

In keeping with the policy to upgrade images of working women and to encourage readers to focus their energy on work rather than sex, letters after the summer of 1942 did not concern these kinds of sexual problems. They instead dealt with issues arising from a homemaker's war job or her indecision about entering the labor force. Several letters dealt with conflicts women experienced between their homemaking role and their participation in war work. The first of these appeared in September 1942, from a mother of three in her thirties who possessed mechanical skills learned while working in her husband's machine shop. She wrote to ask if she should find work in a defense plant or remain a homemaker, as her husband wished, and do volunteer work. Both prizewinning responses support the recruitment effort by urging her to take a job because the country needed skilled workers. The editor's selection of this letter and those that recommended that this homemaker enter a defense plant is consistent with the War Manpower Commission's desire to bring women into skilled metal trades, one of the fields most desperately in need of workers.[32]

Another letter from a homemaker with previous factory experience and mechanical skills was printed in June 1943. The writer is thirty-five years old, childless, and the nurse for her invalid mother. Her husband and mother think she should enter a war production factory, but she is reluctant because it will mean, she fears, putting her mother in a nursing home. She wonders what she should put first, her country or her home. All three responses side with the mother and husband, advising the homemaker that her primary duty is to serve her country by taking a war job. Again, the decision to publish this letter with responses recommending factory work reflects the Magazine Bureau's publicizing of the desirability of getting older women without young children into the labor force, especially those with previous training.[33]

Most problems concerning war jobs focused on home responsibilities and were resolved through suggesting ways the war worker could meet those responsibilities without quitting her job. Readers advised married women throughout 1942 and 1943 to engage in factory work despite the objections of husbands and the disruption to family life. While homemaking was perceived as important work and the responsibility of women only, strategies were suggested for circumventing the housewife's full-time role, such as having older children take on household chores. One of the issues addressed by this column was how to handle recalcitrant husbands, a problem of special concern to the Magazine Bureau since government surveys identified the objections of husbands as the foremost reason women were not entering the labor force.[34] A letter from a factory worker published in November 1943 provided *True Story* with an opportunity to advise women how to deal with this problem. The writer says she entered a defense plant because "she had a real flair for mechanics" but that her high salary is creating difficulties with her husband, who is earning less money than she is. He wants her to quit in order to take care of their children and run the household because, since her mother took over these responsibilities, things have not gone well. He feels that "running a happy and healthy home is just as important and patriotic job as working in a war plant." The war worker believes she is facing a problem typical of many in her situation and that she has become "a symbol of all women in this country." The first-prize letter strongly supports the continued employment of this working wife, suggesting ways the couple can correct some of the things that are making the husband unhappy. It also includes a reassuring message to the husband that his home life will not always be so disrupted: "Do you think for one moment that she will be a machinist for the remainder of her natural life? You know how feminine she is, don't you?"

After this peak year of the womanpower drive, letters for the most part concerned problems with child rearing, many of which identified juvenile delinquency as a source of family friction. They no longer dealt with how employed homemakers could balance their responsibilities but instead took up other matters such as in-law interference or marital stress over children. By 1945, the column's support for working homemakers ceased. The following case, signaling the shift from approval of factory work to encouraging work in the home, concerns a returned veteran who wants his wife to quit her war job and take care of their child. She, however, disagrees with him. The first-prize letter is from a woman who had refused to quit working until peace was declared, and she relates that she was finally moved to return home when her husband read their marriage vows to her with tears in his eyes, advising the war-working wife to resume homemaking: "It is not normal to allow your mother to care for the baby. . . . It is unfair to deny your baby the mother's love that is his heritage. Lastly, hasn't Arthur earned the right to a full-time wife, companion and refuge of strength? If you fail to observe that right, and your first obligation, you are endangering the very rights for which men and women are fighting all over the world" (January 1945).

The second regular feature that encouraged women to engage in war production was "The Victory Homemaker," which began in October 1942 and was edited by Esther Kimmel, a frequent guest at the Magazine Bureau's meetings for magazine editors. Supporting the policies of the War Manpower Commission by asking single women and married women without children under fourteen to find a job, it also advised that mothers of young children should bear primary responsibility for their welfare. This column suggested ways to streamline housekeeping and to involve husbands and children in housework by featuring households of women in war work that successfully coped with the added stresses of a female breadwinner. It made clear that the participation of other family members in housework was not only workable but beneficial to individual self-esteem and family spirit.

One way the Magazine Bureau helped magazines publicize war jobs was to arrange for editors to visit defense plants where they could gather material at first hand on what factory work was like. It was undoubtedly just such an arrangement that produced an eight-page article for the "Victory Homemaker" column in April 1943. Kimmel interviewed four General Electric workers in Bridgeport, Connecticut: a supervisor, a clerical worker, an inspector, and a welder. All were photographed on the job and described as being very happy with their new positions. The women were carefully selected to make war work look like an appropriate activity for wholesome women since all enjoyed solid family lives. The feature also makes a point of saying that though the women like their jobs they will leave them eventually. For instance, the inspector, who left a position as clerk in a department store, is reported to have said that she vastly prefers her new job to her old one, but the article informs us that she will someday give it up "for [Eunice] is an intelligent girl who realizes that some day the war will be over, and she intends to doff her working clothes and be none the worse for factory dirt, dust, and grime."

Finally, a series of portraits of notable American women appeared in February 1944 to replace a column entitled "Great Romances." It was called "Women Who Served America" and ran for twenty-four issues until December 1945.[35] The figures chosen from American history to represent the strength, courage, and determination to win the war of modern women fell into three categories. One, predictably enough, was service in wartime. Nurses and legendary figures from the Revolution and the Civil War were spotlighted for their bravery. The second, pioneer women, emphasized the hardy qualities of those who helped their men settle the West. The third, social reformers and activists, were women strong enough to fight for their beliefs and for American ideals of freedom and social equality. Feminists appeared as well as groundbreakers like Mary Lyon and Elizabeth Blackwell. Significantly, all of the women featured were figures who predated World War I, a choice intended to emphasize the long tradition of female dependability in times of stress and to avoid, perhaps, more controversial selections from the contemporary scene. Many of the descriptions emphasized female heroism, achievement, and assertiveness, but the thrust of the series was patriotic service to one's country. The ideal of self-sacrifice that dominated the magazine, therefore, overshadowed its egalitarian overtones. This series was replaced by one in January 1946 called "Today's Children," which solicited letters from readers describing an experience in which they had successfully guided a child. The shift from romance to heroism to maternity illustrates the capacity of popular culture to both reflect and help shape dramatic ideological changes within a short period of time.

Nonfiction features of *True Story* were less ideologically complex than the fiction, but they served the important function of accurately identifying OWI campaign goals which the fiction sometimes did not. Stories failed, for example, to encourage the use of child care centers, and did not portray women in male occupations very frequently. The other sections of the magazine, however, reiterated WMC directives and supported nearly all of the major propaganda activities: salvage, farm labor, military recruitment, employment of older women, streamlined housekeeping, jobs in service and trade. The demands of a dramatic story made the fiction a more cumbersome framework for conveying propaganda while advertising and advice columns were better suited for explicit didactic messages. Another factor that made the fiction less reflective of OWI programs is the difficulty of organizing hundreds of free-lance writers and coordinating their activities with campaign schedules. Special editors and advertisers, on the other hand, enjoyed clearer lines of communication with Washington and could therefore transmit more accurately wartime policies.

True Story advertisements were not as elaborate as those of the *Post*. This was because the confessions had difficulty attracting advertising revenue due to the low purchasing power of their audience.[36] Major companies with high profit margins such as the auto manufacturers producing airplanes, the railroads, and producers of household consumer goods that had converted to war material did not advertise in *True Story*. Those who did buy space—food processors, soap manufacturers, household cleaner businesses, makers of paper products—operated on low profit margins and were therefore unable to hire the kinds of advertising service available to more prosperous industries. Heavy industry ignored the confessions market, which means that the ideological treatment of war workers was much less comprehensive in *True Story* than was true of the *Post*. Wartime prosperity, however, drew advertisers to *True Story* in great numbers, and they devoted a great deal of space to the recruitment of women into the labor force. Pond's, for example, portrayed college students in war work in nearly every issue from November 1942 to August 1945. Camel and Chesterfield had frequent ads supporting military recruitment and factory work, as did Kleenex, which carried appeals for women to enter the labor force.

While not as ideologically complex as those of the *Post*, advertisements contained many of the same themes. For example, they similarly praised female stoicism and showed hardy, capable women workers who could tackle any job successfully. A Kotex ad typifies the wartime emphasis on female strength: "Remember when the boys used to say that girls are made of sugar and spice and all things nice? Those days are gone forever . . . you're no sissy now! . . . You've learned how to be a good soldier . . . to keep going, keep smiling . . . no matter what!" (August 1942). Similarly, femininity was altered to discourage images of frailty. Beautyrest described slumbering women as resting after "doing a man-sized job," while Camel featured fashion designers turned blueprint artists and debutantes transformed into intelligence specialists. *True Story* also aroused guilt over soldier casualties and emphasized patriotic service as the primary appeals to get women into the labor force. For example, a perfume ad pictures a young woman with lunch box and factory overalls being thanked for taking a war job by an older woman who has lost a son (Bourgeois, October 1944). In another ad, a full-page portrait of a soldier's face is captioned "How Long to Live?" (Listerine, November 1944). Rita Hayworth is pictured saluting in a Naval Aid Auxiliary uniform with the title "In the Nation's Service" (Oneida, December 1943) while a war bond ad from the Treasury Department shows a soldier contemplating his fiancée's picture with the message: "The Man you're going to Marry is asking your Help . . . right now!" (June 1943). Thus, women were portrayed in both magazines as able to fill a man's shoes, but the egalitarian implications of that idea were muted by the focus on patriotic service to a man overseas.

Advertising filled the gap left by the fiction in its support of military recruitment. Though many companies ran identical ads in both magazines, the *Post* used family appeals and portrayed women in uniform in the company of men, whereas *True Story* featured servicewomen in isolation from men and families. Because cosmetic companies advertised more extensively in *True Story* and carried a large share of the military campaign, their choice of rather static images of glamor set the tone for that part of the campaign and illustrates the relatively shallow approach of all confessions advertisers. Both magazines did, however, use military imagery extensively in their portrayal of women. Nail polish was characterized as "a red badge of courage for every fingertip" (Cutex, September 1942) and given names such as "At Ease," "On Duty," and "Alert." A model pledges "to guard every bit of beauty that he cherishes in me" (Palmolive, July 1942). The intertwining of decorative femininity with militarism arose from the identification of women as domestic freedom fighters, and it simultaneously reflected their continued sexual objectification.

Three advertising themes contributed to the eventual disappearance of positive nontraditional models. One of these was the maintenance of homemaker images throughout the war. Even at the height of the recruitment period, housewives and mothers in ads constituted 45 percent of the total number of women portrayed. Though not as dramatic as the *Post's* emphasis on housewives as guardians of the nation, *True Story's* ads similarly equated housework with war work by including housewives in the company of servicewomen, welders, and riveters. Other ads anticipated domesticity by shifting from recruitment to traditional images throughout 1945. Kotex switched from showing a teenager sticking to her factory job to depicting one being counseled on housework; 7-Up ceased claiming it could produce a good disposition in women in order for them to win a better job to boasting it could help them be happy homemakers; Beautyrest replaced its exhausted war workers with a mother tucking her child into bed.

Finally, ads of the reconversion period began featuring babies, even for products that had nothing to do with infant care. Sunkist, for example, advertised oranges with a toddler and the caption "Little ones are mighty sweet now!" (October 1945). Babies were cast in adult roles and featured as counselors, authorities, and monarchs, symbolizing the new orientation the country was taking, one that placed children at the center of life. Ivory and Ipana showed infants helping teenagers with romance problems, while tuna fish fed to a toddler was described as "A Royal Dish to set before a King." Johnson and Johnson Products depicted an adult-sized baby scolding an infant-sized mother for not diapering him properly.

These images were due to a glorification of domesticity as well as to the postwar baby boom. True Story initiated National Baby Week as early as May 1944 and ran a contest in August of that year offering a war bond to the winner's favorite baby. Covers picturing mothers and their infants began in January 1944, and by May a "Beauty for Baby" column was instituted. Of course, readers were bearing children during this period of domestic glorification, but evidence from the stories and columns suggests that many readers were mothers in 1942 and 1943 yet no images of children appeared in ads of those years. Motherhood was an important, indeed a crucial, facet of the female role even at the height of the war, and the proliferation of baby images from 1944 through 1946 grew out of that emphasis. They served much the same function as Post images of wedded bliss in that they reflected widespread desires for prosperity.

The recruitment campaign produced a number of salutary effects on the True Story formula during the war years: women's class identities were heightened as was their sense of themselves as workers; it was made clear that everyone had a valuable role to play in winning a noble cause and that, no matter how sordid one's past, it was possible to redeem oneself through war work; finally, women gained a greater sense of their own power to create a decent life for themselves and were able to avoid the nightmares of passivity and self-doubt. What True Story readers saw, for the first time in the magazine, were women like themselves, who garnered respect from communities and desirable men because they were strong, self-disciplined, and courageous, who were able to meet the challenges of unfamiliar tasks, and who served as models of admiration for others. They were told that it was possible to be proud of being working-class women and that whatever shame they had acquired from violating social taboos was something they could put behind them. These positive messages both reflected the improvement of objective conditions for the working class during the war and grew out of the propaganda effort to draw women into war production.

At the same time, the potential of these messages to alter permanently the essentially patriarchal perspective of the confessions formula was undermined by key narrative elements. One of these was the continued glorification of self-abnegation as patriotic heroines asked nothing for themselves but focused only on what they could do for their country. Another was female dependence on male authority figures for direction and approval as war-working narrators were brought to a proper understanding of their role as citizens. Yet a third was the notion that disruptions to family life would be resolved when the war ended and women could resume full-time homemaking, an option that was not possible for most employed women but which reminded them that they were responsible for two jobs. Most important, *True Story* readers found in the magazine's pages no affirmation of working women's desires to keep their war jobs and were prevented from understanding the true significance of the war period for female labor patterns: that women were ordinarily denied access to positions in heavy industry, not because they were incapable of filling them but because employers preferred that they not do so.

4 Class Differences in the Portrayal of Women War Workers

IT is clear that both the *Saturday Evening Post* and *True Story* disseminated government messages to their readers through subtle emotional appeals, but what effect did their class orientation have on the ways war workers were presented? By examining the similarities and differences in the images of women propagated by magazines with clear class-based ideologies, we can better understand not only the influences on women during the 1940s but the degree to which women's positions were separated by class or linked by gender.

One of the most important similarities in the images of war workers produced by both magazines is that women were portrayed more positively than at any time before the war with the notable exception of blacks or other minorities. They were praised for bravery, loyalty to soldiers, intelligence, steadfastness, and competence. The egocentric, manipulative gold digger of prewar *Post* fiction virtually disappeared, as did *True Story*'s flirtatious heartbreaker. Negative images persisted, in the form of slackers and women driven by ambition or bitterness to their downfall, but these were counteracted by characters with positive qualities, and they were presented sympathetically for the most part. To a significant degree, negative stereotypes of women gave way to images of strength, dependability, and compassion.[1]

In addition, both magazines dropped major story formulas that depended on damaging stereotypes of women. The *Post* avoided the marriage-career conflict, while the trials of heroines who engaged in disapproved sexual activities disappeared from *True Story*. A good case can be made that these story types disappeared because the editors deemed them inappropriate for wartime conditions. The marriage-career conflict theme undermined the government's attempt to recruit homemakers into war production. Similarly, the sexual activity and violent overtones of the confessions seemed incompatible with the wartime emphasis on community spirit and the need to overcome prejudice against women in blue-collar occupations.

Related to this overall improvement in the image of women was the increase in egalitarian images of women's role in society. The *Post* had portrayed egalitarian relationships in romances of the thirties in which competent, assertive heroines matched wits with suitors, and these images carried over into the war years. But the equality of women with men was further emphasized in its wartime fiction by the image of women blazing trails as a group rather than as individuals. Not only were women considered equally capable of shouldering work roles vacated by men, but women's work was depicted equally as important as men's work. The same glorification of women's work occurred in *True Story*. Although egalitarian themes in confession stories were much less pronounced than in the *Post*, writers portrayed women as equal contributors to and shapers of the nation. Information on and support of the Equal Rights Amendment appeared, for instance, signaling the extent to which the war moved even a conservative magazine like *True Story* in a progressive direction.

Though the dominant image of working women in both magazines was that of the self-sacrificing patriot who would return to traditional female concerns at the end of the war, women's war work produced strong egalitarian images that competed with these traditional ones. A story appeared in *True Story* in September 1945, for instance, that was totally out of character for a confession magazine. It concerned a female doctor who is attractive, hardworking, and trusted by nurses. She marries a surgeon, and they team up in private practice. When she becomes pregnant, he insists she quit working, but she refuses out of a desire to maintain her identity: "I ached with longing for a perfect harmony we had never had, except in rare moments when I was willing to submerge my real self so completely that I practically became subservient to Dennis. And that wasn't harmony, if you looked at it squarely, but merely bondage" ("Dear Patient"). Ordinarily, this heroine would suffer from and repent of her audacious decision to leave her husband, but this story ends with the heroine assuming her husband's practice while he recovers from a serious illness. It is he who has been punished and who asks forgiveness, agreeing to reconcile on her terms, which include her following a career in medicine.

Similarly, ads appeared in both magazines that were favorable to career women. Singer sewing machine featured a businesswoman and the caption "I'm a success!" in the September 1945 issue of *True Story*, while Nescafé featured a congresswoman in March of 1946. A Listerine ad in the same issue portrayed a sixteen-year-old contemplating her future: "Whether it's marriage you're after, or a career, or both—always put your best foot forward." Likewise, the *Post* ran a Mutual Benefit Insurance ad in October 1944 in which a daughter informed her mother that she planned to marry, keep her job, and buy a life insurance policy designed for women. These anomalous ads and stories were atypical of the reconversion period. However, they point out the complexity of sex-role ideology during the forties. Traditional and egalitarian images coexisted during the war, and though images of domesticity in the reconversion period overwhelmed those that fostered expanded roles for women the impetus given by war work to changing conceptions of women in the postwar world was very great.

Another characteristic of wartime female images with egalitarian potential was that women's work identity was strengthened. Advertisements were far more likely to portray women at work or in factory clothes than in the pre- or postwar years. In fiction, the feelings of heroines toward their work were more likely to surface than before the war, and they were often the subject of the story. Women in the stories obtained great satisfaction from their jobs, even physically and emotionally demanding ones. War jobs heightened the self-esteem of heroines in both magazines and made them feel independent. This was in dramatic contrast to prewar fiction when work created problems for married women.

Another way writers from both magazines made war jobs look attractive was to dramatize the transformation of heroines into women who enjoyed a keener awareness of themselves as important because they were performing a crucial service for the country. The theme of moral regeneration through war work was a major one as women in factories developed into mature, strong adults through meeting the challenge of long hours and hard physical labor. In *Post* fiction, young women from middle-class families were faced with assuming the responsibilities of a wage earner for the first time when they entered a defense industry. Because they had been pampered by protective parents and had enjoyed the luxuries of class privilege, their initial attitudes toward not only the womanpower campaign but the home front as a whole revealed a selfish immaturity that rendered them useless to the war effort. Through their romantic relationships with soldiers they were forced to leave behind their childish dependency and egocentricity, while through their defense jobs they acquired self-discipline. As a result, they became civic-minded and grew into the kind of women soldiers found suitable as adult marriage partners.

True Story heroines were similarly transformed but from social inferiors into proud representatives of the working class. Initially plagued with an unhappy marriage, a tragic past, or a soiled reputation, working-class heroines were able to make a new beginning and were given a clean slate when they entered a defense job. Unlike the *Post* heroine, who was chastened by her assumption of civic responsibilities, the confessions war worker gained a heady sense of her own importance to the nation and was thereby exonerated. Her shame at having been born of humble origins was replaced by pride in herself as a woman of the laboring class, the very foundation of American democracy and strength. One of the positive effects of the recruitment campaign was that the characterization of war work as redemptive provided working-class women with a fantasy in which they could fashion a better self through their own actions.

Propaganda groups affected female images in another way as well: positive messages about the white working class abounded, especially about working-class women. Stories and advertisements glorified factory work as psychologically rewarding, as emotionally exciting, and as leading to success in love. Both magazines combated class prejudice against factory work by portraying working-class men and women as diligent, patriotic, wholesome people. The *Post* fostered positive images of blue-collar work by describing the intellectual challenges of problem solving and praising American ingenuity involved in war production.[2] Working-class women were resourceful, respectable, warmhearted, and resilient. In *True Story*, characters experienced pride in their working-class origins and were glad to be an important part of the nation.

In addition, to recruit married women into the labor force, both magazines modified the career-marriage conflict of prewar fiction. Whereas working married women of the thirties and early forties were selfish and destructive to their families, wartime fiction contained many heroines who successfully coped with both family and work responsibilities. The change was most marked in the *Post*, which dropped the marriage-career conflict theme entirely. The married woman possessed by the devil of ambition persisted in *True Story* but with a distinction between working for self and working for country; heroines who engaged in war work were not plagued with the difficulties of those caught up in personal careers. Both magazines featured more married working women as major characters during the war, a reflection of the marriage boom of 1942, the increased participation of married women in the labor force, and the influence of the recruitment campaign.

Both story formulas accommodated the need for women in war production within the limits of those formulas. The *Post* adapted plot devices to wartime needs by showing women war workers as winners in love and as successful business managers. The egalitarian romances from the thirties, in which self-confident, competent heroines verbally fenced with men, continued through the war years and featured women in uniform or entering male domains in the work force. The *Post's* support of the recruitment effort was limited, however, by the necessity of using adventurous young women in fiction for entertainment purposes. This meant that the target group and the goals of government recruitment drives were frequently ignored. Similarly, the confessions formula of "sin-suffer-repent" was adapted to wartime needs with repentant heroines entering war work, becoming "war-minded," and being spared some of the more painful consequences suffered by prewar heroines. The hazards of love were intertwined with the forced separations and role dislocations of war, and love was temporarily made subordinate to patriotic duty. At the same time, *True Story's* emphasis on self-abnegation and traditional family values limited the extent to which it could feature women in male work roles.

There are many differences between the treatment of war workers in *True Story* and in the *Post* that demonstrate that both kinds of formulas shaped propaganda as much as they were transformed by OWI campaign goals. One of the most striking is that few heroines in *True Story* were in male occupations, even in factory work, while the *Post* contained many women who were pilots, policewomen, taxi drivers, engineers, and factory workers. Women in *True Story* were concentrated in female occupations such as office work, sales, teaching, and nursing. While *True Story* glorified war work as much as the *Post* did, the role shifts in its stories and articles were not nearly as extensive. The *Post* featured women in high-paying professional, managerial, and skilled occupations vacated by men, whereas in *True Story* the upward mobility of working-class women was confined to assembly line jobs in war factories.

During the peak years of the recruitment campaign, 1943 and 1944, the proportion of heroines from stories of the *Post* who were in male occupations was 28 percent and 36 percent, respectively, while those in female occupations (including homemaking) comprised 33 percent of the total in 1943 and only 21 percent in 1944. This represented a dramatic decrease in traditional work roles from 1941 when a mere 15 percent of all characters were in atypical wage work and 44 percent were cast as teachers, office workers, housewives, and other categories identified as female work.

In contrast, the proportion of *True Story* heroines from stories of 1944 in male jobs was 23 percent with 47 percent in the traditional roles of office worker, clerk, teacher, and homemaker. Although this was a significant increase over the number of women in male occupations in 1941 (5 percent), it was nevertheless much lower than one would expect given the impact of the recruitment campaign on the *Post*. Only in 1943, the peak year of the womanpower campaign, did the number of *True Story* heroines in male occupations approximate that of the *Post*, and even these figures are misleading since characters featured as factory workers were mostly in semiskilled assembly line jobs whereas *Post* women were in skilled ones (see table 5).

Table 5   Occupations of Female Characters in the *Saturday Evening Post* and *True Story*, from All Stories in Sample

Year	Male occupations, servicewoman		Female occupations, homemakers		No occupation, student, volunteer war worker		Other	
	Post	TS	*Post*	TS	*Post*	TS	*Post*	TS
1941	15%	5%	44%	58%	29%	21%	12%	16%
1943	28	27	33	45	29	20	10	8
1944	36	23	21	47	29	24	14	6

These figures indicate that *Post* heroines were far more likely to be shown in high-wage or high-status work while those in *True Story* were concentrated in "pink-collar" jobs even when working in war industries.

Related to the less radical departure from female roles of *True Story* heroines is the absence of stories devoted to women in uniform. Only three stories from this sample concerned women in the military, none of which placed the heroines in combat. The *Post*, by contrast, ran sixteen such stories with several placed in combat zones. This difference is again due to the limitations of the confessions formula, which emphasized erotic rather than physical adventure, female passivity, and strict demarcation between men and women. The woman in uniform as a symbol of wartime was thus featured in advertisements, but the rest of the magazine gave little encouragement to blue-collar women to join the service.

It is for these reasons too that *True Story* gave more support to the nursing campaign than did the *Post*. Because nursing, like teaching, was an accessible profession for working-class women and because it involved the nurturant aspects of the female role, *True Story* could easily accommodate nurse recruitment within its traditional outlook. Ministering to the needs of others has been within the province of women's activities, so nursing was not inconsistent with the magazine's conservative orientation.

Another characteristic distinguishing the two periodicals is that *True Story* defined motherhood as the essential feature of a well-integrated adult female whereas the *Post* did not. Characters of the *Post* did not begin to desire children until the recon-

In support of nurse recruitment. From "My Beloved Nurse," *True Story*, March 1943. Copyright © 1943 by *True Story*. Reprinted by permission.

■ "Oh, you beautiful little dope, how could you fall for a mug like me?" I asked Peggy softly

version period, whereas those in *True Story*, despite the war-time focus on women in wage work, were frequently faced with the painful disappointments of miscarriage, infertility, or babies who were born dead. They were, in addition, more likely to be mothers than their middle-class counterparts who, if they were cast as parents, were older women without the intense maternal responsibilities of *True Story* heroines. It is perhaps because motherhood was a marker of female maturity and a prerequisite to happiness that *True Story* gave very little support to the child care program. While *Post* writers integrated day care centers into romantic comedies, *True Story* narratives refrained from any reference to institutionalized child care, even though its heroines were more likely to be employed mothers than those of the *Post*. The "Victory Homemaker" column did urge women without children to work in nurseries but stated that it was the primary duty of young mothers to care for their children at home, and it failed to feature even one war-working mother who made use of a defense plant center.

Though the Lanham Act made inadequate provisions for working mothers, evidence from *True Story* suggests that the failure of many women to place their children in government centers may have been partly due to their desire to see that they were cared for properly, which meant that they felt more comfortable calling on the services of a mother, mother-in-law, sister, or neighbor. Even in recent times, with the positive publicity that has been given to the concept of day care, sociologists have found that working-class women are more reluctant to hand over their children to nonfamily members than are middle-class mothers.[3]

Aside from *True Story*'s emphasis on motherhood and its more frequent portrayal of women in traditional work roles, the feature that set it apart most clearly from *Post* fiction was the nature of the ideal heroine. For both magazines, she was usually a twenty-year-old woman involved in a romance that ended with engagement or marriage. While both focused on love, the confusion about sexual attraction characteristic of the confessions heroine was not present in *Post* stories. Although the recruitment campaign produced a significantly healthier image of women, characters in *True Story* still tended to be indecisive, torn by contradictory feelings, whereas women of the *Post* generally knew who they were and what they wanted. Similarly, working-class heroines were buffeted about by sudden mood changes and by catastrophes. They were also more fearful of getting hurt, being deserted or punished, and losing love.

The passivity and fear at the base of the working-class heroine's personality stood in stark contrast to the competent, assertive heroine who overcame hurdles with self-confidence and wit, so typical of the *Post*. *Post* women were distinguished by an ability to wield authority in an emergency or prod a self-doubting male into action, and possessed humor that functioned as character armor. The women of *True Story*, on the other hand, experienced crises as punishment for wrongdoing, succumbed to flattery and wild living when in positions of authority, and viewed life with unrelieved seriousness. Though stoicism and strength were valued in both heroines, *Post* women demonstrated those qualities through decisive action, whereas those in *True Story* did so through patience, resignation, and endurance.

Though the regenerative nature of war work mitigated the suffering of confessions heroines during the recruitment campaign, they were more likely than their *Post* counterparts to endure cruel twists of fate, to feel inferior to men, and to experience fulfillment through directing their energies toward a cause they thought worthier than their own ambition, such as husband or employer. Whereas *Post* war workers tackled their new jobs with zest and authority, those in *True Story* enjoyed only the feeling of helping their country to win the war. The negative self-image of the working-class heroine was partially offset by her pride in performing war work, but her inability to wield anything except moral authority stood in stark contrast to the competent, assertive *Post* heroine who met the challenges of war work with self-confidence and wit. The confessions heroine suffered more blows from the outside world and the torments of self-doubt.

The fundamental differences between the middle-class and the working-class heroines of the war years as well as the divergent class values that affected the recruitment campaign are best demonstrated by comparing stories from the two magazines that contain similar plots. While the following stories encouraged the participation of women in war work, they did so within the particular formula established for each audience. The first pair illustrates the tendency of True Story to locate female identity in motherhood rather than in outside employment. Stories before, during, and after the recruiting effort frequently dealt with a narrator whose barrenness symbolized her selfishness, immaturity, or failure to accept her womanly nature. In addition, women who put themselves before their husbands or who failed to live by the middle-class values of domestic respectability were punished by miscarriages, stillborn children, or infertility. Even though True Story's cooperation with the government resulted in work-centered stories, the centrality of mothering in the magazine's definition of fulfillment remained. The following story, albeit aimed at getting women into the labor force, subtly reinforces this ideology.

"Big Sister" (September 1943) appeared during the Magazine Bureau's fall campaign in 1943, which inundated the public with appeals for women to take war jobs. It is narrated by a young woman who has had to assume maternal responsibilities for a younger brother due to the death of both parents. Such family situations were common for True Story heroines in 1941 and 1942, and this story is making use of that early convention. The narrator's problem is that her brother has joined the marines and no longer needs her. Consequently, even though she has a good job at a forge plant as personnel manager, her life seems empty and meaningless. Her identity crisis is resolved, not by reorienting herself to a career but by mothering the people at the office who come to her for advice about personal problems.

The writer weaves propaganda goals into this maternal emphasis through the kinds of difficulties that the narrator, Solomon-like, straightens out. For example, a young woman distraught over her boyfriend's attraction to another woman asks the heroine what she should do to get him back. She is told that it is imperative for her not to talk about her war job to her boyfriend because the woman he is dating is untrustworthy and might reveal important information to an enemy agent, a warning intended to remind workers that they were responsible for national security. She also provides insight into the boyfriend's behavior by saying that he is probably jealous of the woman's war job as he is helping run the family store rather than producing military equipment. The narrator advises her coworker to tell him that all jobs are war jobs and as important as the production of bombs or bullets. Thus, the story puts across three propaganda messages while maintaining *True Story*'s emphasis on motherhood: antirumor, the characterization of civilians as home-front soldiers, and the encouragement for women to enter factory work, especially those without family responsibilities.

The *Post*, on the other hand, placed work at the center of female identity, at least before marriage, and showed how fulfilling meeting the challenges of demanding professions could be. As we have seen, work adventure romances were a staple of *Post* fiction even during the Depression. Motherhood was the farthest thing from these heroines' minds as they applied themselves to flying an airplane, getting a story, or learning how to rivet. Their work was important to them because they could transcend their limitations and be independent. A story that shows the contrast between the two magazines' treatment of maternal and work roles is "The Wall Between" (Margaret Craven, 25 September 1943), which likewise was published during the fall campaign. Similarly, too, it features a heroine hired to fill a man's managerial job in a war plant and is designed in part to draw women into such positions. Like the *True Story* narrator, Ann Burkett has had to shoulder a great deal of responsibility because her husband has died in battle and she must support a daughter and mother-in-law. Both characters have adjustment problems as they try to fashion new identities through their war jobs. The confession story, however, shows the heroine's alienation from her work coming to an end when she is able to recast her managerial functions in maternal terms, while Ann's difficulties stem from the antipathy of her male coworkers and are resolved when she proves herself their equal. Though Ann is a mother, we do not see her taking care of her child, nor does she take a maternal interest in people at the office. The story, rather, is concerned about the acceptance of women as equals as they enter jobs with authority and status.

Ann's patient endurance of prejudice as she competently executes her work is intended to show the reader how unfair it is to discriminate against women in the workplace. The heroine's large investment in gaining acceptance for her sex as well as her desire to perform her job well are indicative of the commitment *Post* characters made to their work and contrast sharply with *True Story* narrators' investment in children. The two stories, then, show the differing approaches each magazine used to get women into nontraditional work: the *Post* conveyed the message that irrational prejudice needed to be eliminated in order to allow women to assume their rightful place in the war economy, whereas *True Story* ignored egalitarian appeals in favor of those that echoed familial roles.

We find another example of *True Story's* more conservative interpretation of proper female behavior in contrasting the following stories, which also dealt with the womanpower issue. The *Post's* "Rough Turn" (Ray Millholland, 7 August 1943) attempts to combat male prejudice against women in male jobs by describing the successful efforts of a personnel manager to integrate female machinists into the plant. The story provides an image of women in skilled blue-collar work as socially respectable (the mayor's daughter is working on the line), technically proficient, and tough enough to handle the harassment of hostile workers. One of the key sources of this positive image is Maizie Grebb, the working-class daughter of a janitor who has been performing skilled labor in a ball bearing factory for three years. Maizie is put in charge of the other women and is able to resolve the conflict because she is perceptive, well organized, and confident that women can do the job.

True Story's "Not Good Enough . . ." (August 1944) also attempts to eliminate prejudice against women in blue-collar jobs but does so without broaching the egalitarian message of the *Post* story that women are capable of performing skilled blue-collar work and without showing women engaged in male tasks. The narrator is meant to provide, as does Maizie Grebb, a positive image of war workers to the reader, but whereas Maizie gains our respect by acting decisively and wisely, the heroine of this story acquires respectability by her refusal to follow the sordid examples of her mother and sister who have become social outcasts as a result of their irregular sexual behavior. The mother deserted her family for another man, and the sister divorced her husband while pregnant.

Both stories concern themselves with the destructive myth that women in factories are immoral, but the *Post* gives us a skilled worker who can handle authority wisely and who is interested in the work she is doing rather than in romance whereas *True Story*'s war worker is not a skilled worker (we know only that she works on the assembly line making parts for precision instruments), is admirable for her *failure* to act (engage in sexual activity), and falls in love with the boss's son. The confession story places importance on illicit sexuality and morally proper behavior for women while focusing on romance rather than on the rewards of nontraditional occupations.

Similarly, "Young Girl's Secret" (October 1943) tries to tackle some of the womanpower issues addressed by the *Post* story but within a more conservative perspective. The narrator's good moral character is established when we learn that she lives with her family while she works in an aircraft plant. We are also encouraged to view women in durable goods industries as able to perform their work competently. As was true of many confessions war workers, however, this narrator is in a pink-collar job—clerical work—and it is her romantic relationship with her employer that assumes center stage. It is his praise that inspires her to do whatever her country asks. *Post* war workers never became involved with employers or supervisors; indeed, they often occupied such positions themselves. Those in *True Story*, in contrast, frequently attracted the attention of an employer or his son. Though the work identity of confessions heroines was strengthened as a result of the propaganda to get women into war jobs, the *Post* emphasized the enjoyment women got from welding, riveting, or running a business, dealt with the key question of how women could be integrated into the male work force, and showed that fulfillment came from work, not motherhood or even romance.

One of the reasons *True Story* did not feature many women in male roles is that the confessions heroine could not handle authority nor was she capable of acting heroically. Her principal characteristic was that her moves toward independence or power in the public world led her to make unwise decisions, to behave insensitively to those she loves, and to become increasingly selfish. In short, her desire to participate as an equal in the world of men caused her to lose her femininity along with the love of men and children. Prior to the postwar feminine mystique, however, *Post* heroines garnered the affection of men through their independent pursuit of an exciting career; female autonomy was equated with dependability, not egocentricity (except in the case of married women). This dramatic difference in attitudes toward female power meant that the *Post* ran recruitment stories that glamorized women in managerial or military positions while *True Story* failed to show war workers taking heroic action.

Two stories that supported the campaign to get women into the armed forces illustrate the effect of class on portrayals of assertive women. "The Lady and the Flat-Top" (Stanley Washburn, Jr., 17 March 1945) exemplifies the *Post's* positive treatment of war workers in dangerous situations as they cope admirably with crisis. Lieutenant Childs is a member of the Army Air Evacuation Nurse Corps and is stationed in combat areas in the Pacific. Her position as senior ward nurse in battle zones requires that she be able to make fast decisions about life-and-death matters under stressful conditions and that she command a great deal of authority. Her responsibilities are extensive enough that she sometimes performs the tasks of chief surgeon.

Childs's ability to act appropriately in a crisis is clearly evident in the climax of the story, which occurs when a plane filled with wounded soldiers develops engine trouble over the Pacific. The pilot has already angered her by flying at such a high altitude that one of her patients dies (the first soldier she has lost), but when he tells her that it is impossible to avoid a crash landing, she explodes: "'Impossible,' she spoke contemptuously. 'We've been doing the impossible out here for eight months.'" We see further indications of the lieutenant's strength as she talks the pilot into landing aboard a carrier that is within reach: "She spoke as if she were forcing fate aside by sheer will power alone." Ultimately convinced that her plan is worth the risk, the pilot makes the landing, thereby saving all on board, and extends to her his admiration and gratitude.

True Story's "One Hour" (March 1944) also concerns a servicewoman who is faced with a critical, life-or-death situation and who similarly deals with a combat pilot forced to make a crash landing. Although she is a WAVES air traffic controller, a job with much responsibility, and is described as "disciplined," "calm," "efficient," the story does not cast the narrator in a heroic role. She is, for one thing, not in the middle of combat as is

Heroic women in combat. From "The Lady and the Flat-Top," reprinted from *Saturday Evening Post*, 17 March 1945. © 1945 The Curtis Publishing Company.

Lieutenant Childs; the story takes place at an air base in the United States where pilots are testing planes and acquiring training. The second element making this a nonheroic role for the narrator is the nature of the crisis and her part in it. As is typical of the confessions formula, the heroine suffers from a mistake she has made: in this case, our WAVE hesitates to accept the pilot's marriage proposal even though she is strongly attracted to him. The catastrophic event that shows her what choice she should have made occurs in this story when the pilot's plane experiences a mechanical breakdown while she is guiding it in for a landing. The narrator watches helplessly in terror as the plane flies out of control, and her horrified reaction reveals to her how much she needs this man. Unlike the *Post* nurse who acts decisively to resolve a similar crisis, the *True Story* character passively awaits the outcome and can only hope that her dreams will not be shattered before her very eyes. Though women were praised in *True Story* for their strength and dependability as part of the recruiting effort, the prohibition on assertiveness meant that strength would be seen as dedication, not as female ability to assume a man's leadership position.

It is for this reason that only one story in my *True Story* sample cast the narrator in an executive role, whereas one of the major techniques *Post* writers employed during the recruitment campaign was to replace an injured male businessman with a woman who ran the operation until he recovered. In "Nine Days' Leave" (*True Story*, August 1943), we see how problematic wielding power, even temporarily, is for women, according to the confessions. The heroine is a secretary at a small printing press who is promoted to assistant manager when it blossoms into a large-scale enterprise printing war posters and pamphlets for the government. We get early indications that this character is not meant to be a positive figure of identification for the reader when we see that she is unfaithful to her childhood sweetheart, who not only is of princely character and totally in love with her but is a soldier. Her symbolic betrayal of her country is a sign that she is not to be trusted with the authority she has acquired in her new position. The central scene of the story takes place when the narrator is sent to New York to place an order for the company and is propositioned by a high-level executive. At first, she is thrilled to be treated as an important person in her business dealings, but the affair with this sophisticated bachelor leaves her brokenhearted and repentant. The heroine has been punished for her hubristic exercise of power, and we see that she was wrong to reject the sweet home life offered by her sweetheart in favor of the tantalizing prospects of high-status career as a businesswoman.

Whereas her position of authority brings this heroine a great deal of trouble, *Post* characters in identical roles resolved crises, never let the pleasures of the position interfere with performance, and managed simultaneously to win at romance. The wisecracking heroine of "Heart on Her Sleeve" (Clarence Budington Kelland, 29 March 1943), for instance, baffles men with her chatter while she manages her father's war plant. The crisis provoked by saboteurs brings out the best in her, and the resistance to her romantic overtures of the man she desires merely strengthens her resolve to win him over.

Both stories end well in that the heroines succeed in love, but one is chastened and forgiven by her man while the other wins him because she has demonstrated how competent she is at taking charge of things. Powerlessness in the world external to the family has been one of the chief characteristics of confessions heroines, and though the recruitment of readers into war work resulted in stories of women who were able to gain self-respect through performing a key service for their country, the notion that women are doomed to suffer tribulations passively remained a staple of the formula.

One pair of stories that illustrate the degree to which confessions heroines suffered from powerlessness concern shipyard secretaries who have lost parents, find romance with a worker in the yard, and defeat sabotage. The working-class secretary in *True Story*, however, experiences greater deprivation than her *Post* sister. She bears the scars of her parents' bitter divorce and has lived most of her life apart from her father. When her mother dies, she returns to her father and resigns herself to work in the shipyard, which she hates. She falls in love with an irresponsible riveter who seduces and abandons her and endures his desertion stoically until he returns.

The *Post*'s middle-class heroine is also a person who has experienced financial hardship and whose father worked at the yard. However, though she is an orphan, she has enjoyed a happy home life, and the manager of the shipping operation has taken her under his wing. Unlike her working-class counterpart, she loves the shipyard and is fascinated by the technology of shipbuilding. Her competence and intelligence attract a rootless innovator who helps her battle saboteurs when she is thrust into managing the business. Whereas the *True Story* secretary suffered the consequences of seduction, the *Post* heroine resists temptation when forced to spend the night with her coworker. In addition, he is as much a source of support to her as the *True Story* riveter is a source of pain. Passive stoicism contrasts with self-confident assertiveness in the two women, as does the fact that one remains in a female work role while the other becomes a supervisor.[4]

Finally, the formula and value differences of the magazines can be seen in two stories that encouraged the employment of housewives with older children. Both concern the resistance of husbands and children to the heroine's taking a war job and resolve the conflict in favor of the wife's leaving home. In the *True Story* plot, however, the working mother feels guilty about the family havoc created by her aircraft job and suffers from exposure to the cold when she tries to find her runaway son in a snowstorm. Though she manages to end her son's truancy and win the approval of her factory-worker husband, she does so with difficulty and without any moral support. The husband of the *Post* story is a lawyer who objects to his wife's taking a factory job on the grounds that their two children need a full-time mother. While the heroine encounters marital conflict when she enrolls in a training course, she suffers none of the traumas of the *True Story* character, nor must she handle her husband's objections alone. Her children and her sister support her, until her husband cheerfully accepts her new role.[5]

There are a number of possible explanations for the more traditional image of war workers found in *True Story*. One is that the confessions audience was young, undoubtedly much younger than that of the *Post*, and since many school-age women who entered the labor force went into clerical work, the large number of office-worker heroines reflected the labor-force activity of the readers.[6] On the other hand, nearly as many women left school to take jobs in factories, yet they were underrepresented.[7] The relatively low visibility of welders and shipyard workers, as well as of women in male jobs within trade and transportation, however, did not mirror the fact that such jobs were actually accessible to working-class women and were filled by them in record numbers. Then, too, if we are going to posit that the magazines reflected the occupations of their readers, how do we account for the large number of *Post* characters in factory work when labor statistics show that women war workers were predominantly from the working class while the *Post's* audience was largely middle-class?

One, more convincing, reason for the failure of *True Story* to feature as many women in authoritative, nontraditional roles is that its readers were extremely unlikely to find managerial or professional positions in the real world. Their fantasies of upward mobility, therefore, depended on male authority figures who could lift them out of their clerical or sales jobs into a higher socioeconomic bracket through marriage. Thus, we find many romances wherein bosses fall in love with their secretaries. If they were to fantasize about professional success, the only realistic avenues open to them would have been the traditional female fields of teaching, dress designing, or nursing, all of which were regular occupations in fiction of the war years. It is for this reason that *True Story* was able to give more support to OWI's campaigns to recruit nurses and service workers than it was to those for white-collar executive jobs.

In addition, the two kinds of heroines grew out of formulas that predated the recruitment campaign. The *Post* had featured assertive, risk-taking women all through the 1930s whereas the confession formula relied on a drama pitting a helpless victim of fate against overwhelming forces that she is unable to understand or control. George Gerbner has characterized her plight very well: "Buffeted by events she cannot understand and is not permitted to wrest about to suit herself, the heroine's headlong flight down the line of least resistance leads to her inevitable 'sin.' . . . Her suffering is a spine-tingling object lesson in bearing up under relentless blows of half-understood events. Through her agony comes not insight into the circumstances of her act, transcending the immediate causes of her misfortune, but, if anything, a more remote glimpse of such 'happiness' as might be had in coming to terms with an unbending, punitive, and invisible code of justice."[8] Because she believes her actions have been largely responsible for her predicament, the confessions narrator takes refuge in passivity, leaving it to fate to provide her with a rescuer. Middle-class heroines were able to resolve problems for themselves through their actions, but *True Story* characters created more by trying to realize their dreams or wield power.

The central act of these stories—the confession—is a self-debasing one as opposed to the self-transcending actions of women in work adventure romances. It is the focus on redemption from error that places the confessions narrator in a position of passive suffering as she patiently waits for the right moment in which she can cleanse her soul. As Penni Stewart says, the heroine does not grow more powerful as a result of her painful learning experiences but rather saves herself through dependent bonding to someone stronger than she to whom she confesses her sins: "The plea is the classic stratified model of confession derived from the religious tradition of prayer in which the penitent humbly begs forgiveness from her confessor, and voluntarily submits to, or may even seek, the punishment expected or rendered. The purpose of the plea is to restore respectability, the usual place in the existing social order. . . . there is little scope for self-growth with the plea."[9]

The beneficial impact of propaganda designed to inspire the blue-collar labor force and the working-class housewife was that the war-worker heroine could redeem herself through taking an important job. She served as a model of rectitude and thereby avoided the most painful consequences of following dangerous illusions. However, she shared with her prewar predecessor a debilitating lack of confidence in her own powers, a fear that her safe world would come tumbling down, and a dependence on male authority for direction. Given that the appeal of confession magazines has lain in their mirroring female anxieties about entering the adult world, then promising relief through the love of a forgiving man, it makes sense that wartime heroines would continue to make mistakes and find salvation in a strong provider.

Of course, the source of appeal for these two models of women was the audience's need for an appropriate figure of identification. Readers of the *Post* found it satisfying to follow the adventures of a stouthearted, clever young woman whose idealism was tempered by shrewd awareness of human nature. She was endearingly self-confident, driven by a desire to command her destiny, and blessed with the intelligence, health, and fortitude to make her dreams a reality. As a woman, her efforts and successes were especially admirable since she had to battle extra odds to make it in a male world. Such a heroine fit well into the *Post*'s conception of America as a place where anyone with will, imagination, and the capacity for hard work could achieve his or her goals. Its heroes were self-made men and women who refused to let obstacles defeat them; instead, they took difficulties on as a challenge and welcomed the opportunity to exercise their powers.

George Horace Lorimer, editor of the *Post* from 1899 to 1936, admired such people and indeed saw them as the backbone of the country, the driving force behind America's greatness. Consequently, he aimed his publication at an imagined ideal reader, one who shared his enthusiasm for individual enterprise: "the gray-haired President with young brains, the never-say-die salesman, the up-and-coming clerks, the get-ahead cubs . . . the men who win cases and save lives, who fight for clean politics, and a better America . . . the professor who can interest his classes in a dry-as-dust subject . . . the clear-eyed, upstanding women who think in terms of something besides cup custards and sex stories."[10] Lorimer's ideals were direct descendants of the Horatio Alger myth, which posited that Americans were blessed with the freedom to rise by their own merits to whatever level they deserved and that the end result was a democratic aristocracy whose power flowed from character strength and idealism.

The wartime image of war workers reflects this perspective as enterprising women gamely entered the unfamiliar setting of noisy factories or fields of combat to defeat the enemy. Undeterred by their lack of training or small size, such women were the embodiment of American ingenuity. That they could rise to the occasion boded well for the country's survival. Women's competent performance of men's work was reassuring rather than threatening, as it was undertaken to show the world that Americans could tackle any job. Anyone who objected was allowing rigid, unreasonable, Old World traditionalism to get in the way of that at which Americans had always excelled: taking an open-minded, creative approach to problems in order to progress. The assertive, efficient woman in pants or uniform was a symbol of this indefatigable forward-looking spirit.

The confessions formula struck a very different chord. Unlike the *Post*, which celebrated triumph over obstacles, *True Story* and its sister publications showed that life was cruel and largely uncontrollable. Geared to the woman at the bottom of the socioeconomic ladder, its appeal lay in reflecting the hardships she experienced as a person struggling to attain financial security, middle-class stability, and self-respect. Postwar interviews with working-class women provide some insight into the attraction such an approach has for them. One study revealed that women trying to hold families together on meager budgets and who have grown up in similar households have an understandable tendency to feel insecure about their livelihood: "the working-class wife's outlook is shaded by a fairly pervasive anxiety over possible fundamental deprivations. . . . She is anxious about her physical safety, stability of affection, dependable income."[11] These fears of disaster are mirrored in the confessions' focus on traumatic crises such as accidents, desertion, betrayal, and forced separations of lovers, all of which the heroine endures with as much faith as she can muster that her fortunes will change for the better.

Lillian Rubin attributes the fatalism we find mirrored in the confessions to repeated and overwhelming disappointment in working-class life: "Imagine . . . an environment in which . . . paucity of choices is the reality of most lives—no friends or relations around who see a future with plenty of possibilities stretching before them; no one who expects very much because experience has taught them that such expectations end painfully. Such is the fertile field in which the fatalism, passivity, and resignation of the working-class grow—qualities so often remarked upon by professional middle-class investigators."[12] The *Post* heroine's belief in her own efficacy, on the other hand, arises from the relatively greater autonomy of the middle-class woman, who has been given both more tools with which to achieve her goals and a more privileged life style, which protects her from many of the harsh realities encountered by the working class.

Rubin's observations also provide insight into the guilt, self-hatred, and passivity of *True Story* heroines when she comments on the tendency of working-class people to blame themselves for their problems: "turning inward with self-blame is common among [working-class] women and men . . . a product, in part, of the individualist ethic in the American society which fixes responsibility for any failure to achieve the American dream in individual inadequacy."[13] The confessions formula reflects these feelings of powerlessness and personal inadequacy through its depiction of women who are overwhelmed by the consequences of their misguided acts: wives who refuse to accept their responsibilities are cursed with infant deaths, alienated children, or enfeebled husbands; women who put themselves before their mates are abandoned or faced with a terrible accident; immature women who break men's hearts are trapped in miserable marriages and shunned by the community. Because her acts bring her pain, the confessions heroine depends for her survival on the guidance of a strong man who can protect her from her own mistakes and redeem her with his love.

It is the promise of redemption that makes bearable the hideous nightmares contained in these magazines. They provide the hopeful message that any woman, no matter how great her weakness or how painful her burden, can cleanse her soul through admitting her mistakes and thereby put her life in order. The reward of a happy home life awaits the young woman who can overcome her sexual yearnings, her immaturity, and her selfish, unrealistic ambition. The attraction of a solid family and home of one's own found in wartime confessions is partially explained by the tendency of working-class adolescents to seek independence from parents through getting married and having children. As a working-class wife expressed her adolescent dreams to Lillian Rubin, "All I wanted was just to grow up and get out of there. I used to dream about how I'd grow up and get married and live in one of those big, beautiful houses like they show in magazines—you know, magazines like *House Beautiful*. God, all the hours I spent looking at those magazines, and dreaming about how I would live in one of those houses with all that beautiful furniture, and everything just right; and how my husband would come home at night; and how I'd look beautiful waiting for him; and how the kids would be pretty and good; and how we'd all be happy together."[14] Confession stories about infertility or early pregnancy reflect the tendency of working-class young women to rely on starting families of their own as one route to the privileges of adulthood. Because the kinds of jobs such women can generally get are dull, dead-end ones with little status or promise of psychological reward, Rubin concludes that they seize upon motherhood as the ticket to social acceptance and personal happiness. It is through her family that the working-class woman expects to acquire respect and power, not through employment.[15]

All of these factors contributed to a more traditional, less heroic image of war workers in *True Story*. In addition, propagandists developed different strategies for making war work look attractive to the two audiences, which resulted in the *Post's* greater abundance of women in authoritative roles. Middle-class women needed to be persuaded that it was worth their while to take a step down and enter the blue-collar world, one which carried less status than the bourgeois life style to which people in a capitalist society aspire. One of the recommendations made to the Magazine Bureau by polltakers investigating sources of female resistance to government pleas to take war jobs was that propagandists build up the prestige of factory work as women who did not have to work for economic reasons were reluctant to associate themselves with blue-collar occupations: "The type of work [the war worker] does and the conditions under which he works are too often regarded as characteristic of the lower classes."[16] To do this, *Post* writers placed war-worker heroines in managerial and supervisory positions or in blue-collar jobs requiring technical skill, which enhanced the appeal of factory work for a middle-class audience. Women were thus featured in the most prestigious blue-collar fields and in roles where they wielded power over men, especially working-class men. Such a portrayal maintained middle-class superiority, which balanced the loss of social status inherent in entering blue-collar work.

We can speculate that working-class women, on the other hand, would have been put in a more problematic situation by such a strategy as they would have been competing with men of their own class for power.[17] In addition, war work for them meant some measure of social advancement, as it provided higher wages than female occupations and garnered praise for them as leaders of the production front. Two primary themes used in the campaign appear to address these issues. One was to convey the message that all confessions readers, no matter how trouble-filled their lives, had something valuable to contribute to the war effort and would personally benefit from participation in it.[18] Hence, many confession stories show war work as a redeeming influence on the heroine rather than as an opportunity to exercise power over men. The other goal was to strengthen the connection between readers, the working class as a whole, and the interests of the country by featuring war workers who placed national or company goals before their own and whose self-esteem stemmed from feelings of solidarity with a strong working-class army rather than from pride in the achievements of women. Both approaches avoided exacerbating possible tensions between working-class men and women while encouraging confident, energetic, and enthusiastic attitudes toward war work in women.

Thus, the stoic confessions heroine whose only hope for salvation lay in subordinating self to a greater good functioned as a patriotic model of the dutiful worker, and the goals of the recruiting effort led to a class rather than a gender emphasis in *True Story*. The function of middle-class images of war workers was slightly different: to reassure the public that women were capable of winning the production battle essential to victory and of taking care of things on the home front. They served the important role of reminding civilians that war was being waged by women in the factories as well as by men on the battlefield.

The redefining of female abilities necessitated by the labor shortage produced strong female characters in middle-class popular fiction who could defeat an enemy agent, run a drill press, work sixty-hour weeks, or build a bomber. However, working-class literature for women failed to adequately reflect the new occupations women were performing because its ideology and the treatment of class in propaganda limited the degree to which such redefinition could occur. The Rosie the Riveter who could handle a rivet gun, weld a ship's hull, or test parachutes was primarily a middle-class image. The working-class picture of Rosie was that of a self-effacing though proud patriot in semiskilled assembly line jobs or clerical work, who was prone to making tragic mistakes that damaged her relationships with men.

To a certain extent, the portrait of women workers in *True Story* was the more accurate one in that most women were employed in traditional female fields and those that entered war plants mainly performed unskilled or semiskilled work.[19] But it appears that its more conservative treatment resulted from audience dreams of security and status in combination with propaganda needs for a respectable, well-disciplined image of blue-collar workers. The *Post's* portrayal of war workers contained a strong feminist dimension, in contrast, because of the strategies followed by its writers for meeting the various goals of the propaganda effort and because its readers were moved by different visions.

Conclusion

SEVERAL lessons can be drawn from an analysis of the way propaganda, gender norms, and class values interacted during World War II to produce the complex image of women we find in magazine fiction and advertising. Perhaps the most basic of these is that we are provided with an example of how quickly images can change when the media, government, and industry are mobilized to accomplish a goal. Specifically, comprehensive social change was undertaken to facilitate the employment of women in nontraditional jobs and to bring housewives into the labor force. The media were viewed as a crucial component of this undertaking, and the messages they relayed about women workers were scrutinized more carefully than at any time in American history, with the possible exception of the contemporary women's movement and its attention to demeaning stereotypes. Certainly the propaganda campaign of World War II was the most comprehensive, well-organized effort this society has made toward ending prejudice against women in male occupations and toward legitimizing the notion that women belong in the paid labor force. Of course, propagandists were constrained by the cultural context in which they operated, but within those limits they created a partially progressive image of women as competent workers in all fields, equal to the tasks set before them. Their success is an object lesson in how rapidly messages change when it benefits capitalists to have women play a larger role in public life.

In contrast, today's movement for feminist social change has had a relatively smaller impact on the media. Despite some progress, particularly in women's magazines, there are fewer positive images of women in nontraditional or professional roles than there were during the war.[1] The gains feminists have made in eliminating negative stereotypes of women and replacing them with inspirational ones have not been insignificant, but they have been hard-won and difficult to keep. It can be argued that social change emanating from the bottom is ultimately more successful in that it is controlled by the people who benefit from it. Certainly the dismantling of the progressive structure erected during the recruitment campaign demonstrates the crucial importance of goals in any social experiment as well as the input of the people it affects. Such change is, however, slower to produce significant alterations in media portrayals without the support of political and economic institutions.

The constraints that operated on the recruitment campaign are also revealing, for they indicate the limits to which entertainment formulas and advertising techniques can be stretched in attempting widespread attitude shaping. Propagandists had to work within a familiar set of values and myths in order to gain the attention of an audience operating in a capitalist society, which meant that certain aspects of OWI's program were left undeveloped while others received wider treatment than the government wished, sometimes resulting in misleading impressions or failing to provide targeted groups with needed information. Advertisers and fiction writers, for instance, neglected to publicize or make attractive the many jobs available in service, trade, or transportation while overemphasizing the armed forces and aircraft factories. Similarly, the subject of sabotage was a staple of wartime fiction even though it did not surface in reality, yet coping with crowded public transportation was not addressed sufficiently though it was a major problem.

Popular artists chose subjects they felt would lend themselves to dramatic treatment and, moreover, used figures of identification to which the public had become accustomed and through which it could live out private fantasies. Therefore, while the target group for recruitment propaganda was older women with children in school, the media focused on young single women with no economic incentive for seeking employment. Even the heroines of *True Story* took war jobs for reasons other than economic necessity, though they came from working-class families: to serve a noble cause, heal a broken heart, or fulfill a private dream. In part, this treatment grew out of propaganda goals to inspire unselfish service. But it also resulted from artists' tendency to use as models of identification people who were independent, successful, glamorous, or candidates for romance. Such figures were romantic and outside the realm of daily life where budgets had to be kept, youthful dreams discarded, and unpleasant responsibilities faced. War workers functioned as symbols of youthful energy, fresh beginnings, and an adventurous spirit, untethered by children or economic hardship.

Yet another dimension of the media's portrayal of women revealed by this study is that formulas developed for middle-class and working-class audiences emphasized different aspects of OWI's program and fashioned rather different portraits of war workers. The confession formula was based on the fantasy of personal renewal through exorcism of one's inner devils, with the reward being domestic happiness. The confession heroine was normally a battered victim of cruel forces beyond her control, which made a strong male leader upon whom she could depend for strength an attractive source of salvation. This kind of story line was largely incompatible with feminist aspects of the recruitment campaign, focusing as it did on female helplessness, dependence on a man for survival, and seeking identity through motherhood. Though writers showed war workers as strong moral beings, they were followers rather than leaders of men and retained full responsibility for rearing children. Writers were able to support the OWI goals of encouraging stoicism, dedication to the job, combining marriage with wage work, but their attempts to demonstrate that women could perform a man's role were rather unsuccessful.

The *Post*, in contrast, relied on a romance formula that contained the fantasy of overcoming all obstacles through wit, pluck, and determination. The adventures it portrayed were not erotic ones as in *True Story* but forays into the world of business and glamorous careers. Heroines were trailblazers, proving that a woman could do anything on which she set her mind. The fantasy was one of self-actualization through confident tackling of problems rather than the confessions object lesson in self-immolation with eventual rebirth into a safe world. This framework was much more hospitable to the propaganda goal of providing home-front heroes and eliminating prejudice against women in nontraditional work. As a result, the confessions heroine became a respresentative of the patriotic blue-collar worker who found self-esteem through a man appreciative of her class background and good work habits, while the Post war worker represented her gender, demonstrating that men could rely on women to get the job done.

These variations raise questions about the degree to which portrayals of women are affected by the audience's class or ethnic status. The wartime contrast suggests that images of female experience as filtered through the media are greatly influenced by the socioeconomic level of the group at which they are aimed. It appears that the bourgeois ethic that informed the Post during the war years fostered egalitarian views of women. In the same time period, however, working-class women's magazines took a more conservative approach, perhaps reflecting the reader's greater need for the trappings of middle-class success —a solid home life, a male provider, and a non-wage-earning wife. The faith in individual achievement and glorification of professional success reflected in the Post were obviously inappropriate for an audience without the resources to risk such ventures in reality. This is not to say that there are no correspondences in women's literature, but the differences in wartime magazines ought to sensitize us to the fact that the fantasies, aspirations, and self-images of women depend on more than their gender. In addition, the racist treatment of black women in propaganda demonstrates that their gender failed to outweigh the negative stereotypes attached to their race. Even in propaganda devised specifically for the working class, a category into which most black women fell, they were completely ignored. We are provided here with a lesson in the meaningless nature for minorities of improving images for women when it is not accompanied by a concerted effort to attack racism as well.

Finally, the propaganda operation highlights a truth about images of women in the media during World War II that has been overlooked: that ideas about and models of women were shaped by larger cultural forces reinforced by propaganda groups for their own agenda. Though it is certainly true that their media portrayal in the postwar years reflected women's losses in the labor market, the precise nature of that portrayal was determined by other factors that came into play during the war period and its immediate aftermath, a major one of which was the campaign to mobilize the civilian population. Images are, in a fundamental sense, dependent upon economic and political structures, but it is too simplistic to say that the media treatment of war workers was chiefly designed to manipulate women into and out of the labor market. Propagandists were certainly operating from sexist notions about the meaning paid employment held for women, but they were also attempting to bring the war home to the public. To do that, they developed several propaganda strategies that exerted a profound influence on the public's perception of war workers.

One of these fostered a progressive view of women as strong workers, well equipped to play an equal part in public life. This was the creation of an inspirational figure with which the country as a whole could identify in order to have the courage and faith to believe in and work toward victory. The woman doing a man's work filled this role as she symbolized American adaptability and hardiness. She became the standard-bearer for all civilians who were taking on new tasks, challenging themselves to expand their limits, and shedding old habits in order to move forward. Similarly, the belief in heroic achievement against all odds, one reinforced by the woman making it in a man's world, served as a comforting reminder that America produced winners.

This part of the campaign also had a salutary effect on beliefs about white working-class women. Because the working class was glorified as the backbone of the production army, blue-collar women, especially those in factory jobs, were heralded as upstanding, reliable people able to carry a heavy load. They became models of American efficiency and proletarian strength. The pride they had in their country and their class was reciprocated in the lavish praise bestowed upon them by admiring supervisors or soldiers.

Other strategies, however, undermined these positive notions. The identification of working women with the country and its representatives, for instance, blurred the distinctions between nontraditional and female occupations while it masked the benefits women received from moving into male spheres. As defenders of liberty, women were cast into a selfless role that conflicted with the concept of female self-actualization through new work opportunities. This was especially pronounced in working-class propaganda, which encouraged class pride but largely ignored the issue of female advancement. Moreover, the campaign goal to increase production produced the reactionary message that capitalists and workers had the same interests.

Finally, the nuclear family came to represent the values of all Americans and was used as a symbol of unity. It also stood for the survival of decency and humanity in a world rent by suffering. The nostalgic view of the family that gained such strength during the war years reflected widespread yearning for familiar rituals, childhood innocence, and physical comfort, but within a context that attempted to stir the passions of civilians. As the war drew to a close, this view grew stronger, and women became the chief heralders of peace just as they had been the militant home-front fighters in battle. The desire for rest, tranquillity, comfort fed easily into the depiction of women in a traditional helping role, and they were idealized as healers who would salve men's wounds while nurturing the generation that would harvest the rich fruit of postwar prosperity.

One of the benefits of studying propaganda is that it articulates ideas that are deeply rooted in American mythology. An examination of its use during World War II reveals that at least two major models of American womanhood inspire great numbers of people. One is the guardian of the hearth, who represents vulnerability, spirituality, and nurturance. The other is the tough fighter who can work beside men as an equal. The former is the bourgeois ideal that inhibits the full integration of women into public life, whereas the latter, perhaps stemming from the value we place on self-reliance, fosters the entry of women into leadership positions and all walks of life. This egalitarian impulse will not prevail, however, until we make a commitment to the principle that women of all races ought to be engaged in the world outside the home because it benefits society as a whole, not just in emergencies but as a vital thread in the social fabric we weave every day.

Appendix A: Sampling Procedure

Ole Holsti states in *Content Analysis for the Social Sciences and Humanities* (Reading, Mass.: Addison-Wesley, 1969) that the major problem an investigator must address when devising sampling procedures is whether the sample accurately represents the material under analysis in terms of the purposes of the study (p. 132). Specifically, the analyst must guard against selecting a sample that distorts the content of the material under consideration: "in preparing a sampling design the analyst must ensure that his [or her] sample of documents, whatever its size, is free of idiosyncracies which may bias his findings" (p. 133). I selected the *Saturday Evening Post* and *True Story* because they were bestselling magazines during World War II and could be counted on to represent the most popular themes of their day for their respective markets (middle-class in the case of the *Post*, working-class in the case of *True Story*). Though they undoubtedly possessed unique qualities, I did not feel that these would distort the aim of the study, which was to investigate the representation of women and war workers as it reflected the themes of the propaganda operation. My aim was not to do a comprehensive analysis of popular culture but rather to examine the interface between home-front propaganda and images of women during the war years.

Faced with a massive amount of fiction (the *Post* averaged six stories per issue and *True Story* ten), I decided to establish sampling reliability by reading the first story from each issue and basing the tables on those stories only. The exception is table 5 which includes all stories in the sample because the number of lead pieces from *True Story* (a monthly) was too small to be representative of the kinds of jobs heroines had during the recruitment period. In addition, all tables are drawn from those stories with at least one prominent adult female character. To be considered prominent, a woman had to play a vital role in the plot, be essential to its resolution, and carry the main weight of the story. This criterion excluded many *Post* pieces such as those that focused on male combat or sea lore, were sagas of self-made entrepreneurs or frontiersmen, were mysteries with a male detective, or dealt with religious prophets, male business rivals, children and adolescents, swashbucklers, and animals. All of the confession stories featured a prominent female character.

The information coded for each story was: occupation, age, marital status, and number of children of main female character (the heroine), attitude of main female character toward her occupation and toward the war effort, attitude of other characters in the story toward the heroine. The occupation of the heroine was categorized in two ways: (a) war work or job not considered part of the war effort; and (b) traditional female occupation or nontraditional role. What a heroine did was considered war work if she worked in a defense plant (in either a blue- or white-collar capacity), was a member of the armed forces, performed volunteer services such as Red Cross work or block warden duties, or occupied one of the positions identified by the government as those for which workers should be recruited (nursing, service and trade fields, clerical jobs in federal agencies, lumber mills, mines, farms). Housework was not considered war work nor were such activities as acting and free-lance writing. Occupations were judged traditionally female if they fell into pink-collar categories: secretary, waitress, librarian, nurse, teacher below the college level, stewardess, cashier, maid. Housework was counted as a traditional female occupation. Nontraditional types of jobs included positions in which women in the labor force were rarely or never found before the war: business executive, factory worker in durable goods, police officer, college teacher, shipyard worker, editor, engineer, doctor, gas station attendant, servicewoman, pilot, psychologist, commercial artist.

According to Earl Babbie (*Research Methods in the Social Sciences* [Belmont, Calif.: Wadsworth, 1980], p. 240), the best way to insure content reliability and validity is to code both the manifest and the latent content of communication. Manifest content refers to that which can be quantified and objectively categorized whereas latent content is that which the researcher characterizes in a more subjective way. The former is more reliable, but the latter is better designed for thematic analysis and validity. I incorporated both methods by coding the objective categories into which characters fell while relying on an intuitive, wholistic approach for describing the major themes. For the latter, I felt free to use stories gathered in a random sampling of material from other parts of the magazines.

Finally, I evaluated the validity of the sample by referring to what Ole Holsti calls "face validity" (*Content Analysis*, p. 143). He states that this method is most frequently used for descriptive research and is established through the informed judgment of the investigator. Are the results plausible, given what the researcher knows about the material, the historical period, and the problem under investigation? Using this criterion, I judged the sample of fiction to be consistent with the historical record and the editorial policies of these two periodicals.

The total sample consists of 266 lead (6 were missing) and 206 nonlead stories from the *Post* and 63 lead supplemented by 58 nonlead stories from *True Story*. The time period was January 1941 through March 1946. There are many more stories from the *Post*, both because it was a weekly and *True Story* was a monthly and because I had access to the *True Story* material only during business hours for two weeks, at the insistence of the publishers, The Macfadden Group, Inc. To provide myself with a sample of stories from the prerecruitment period, I relied on the years 1941 and 1942. For the *Post*, I was able to analyze an additional 160 stories from the years 1931 through 1939 because I had completed the research for a previous study. I ended the sample in March

1946 because the propaganda operation had come to a close in August 1945 and the reconversion period was virtually over.

Because the advertisements were not as time consuming to analyze, I was able to code all those that contained women. Information coded included the occupation, activity, and dress of all women in any advertisement in which they appeared. If a woman's clothing or activity did not reflect her employment as either wage worker or housewife, she was placed in the category "no occupation." The occupational status was coded in the same way as it was for the fiction: traditional pink-collar roles (including housewife) or nontraditional jobs (including male occupations and the armed services); and war work (including volunteer activities) or employment unrelated to the war effort (housework was placed in this category). Products being advertised and company names were noted for all advertisements picturing women. If children appeared in the ad or if reference was made to a woman's family, she was considered a mother. In addition, I noted the attitude expressed toward the woman's role in the illustration, text, and caption, i.e., how her activity was presented to the reader, how her contribution to the war effort was interpreted, and what motivation she was pictured as having for playing the role in which she was cast.

Advertisements containing women were categorized into two major groupings: those that concerned war workers and those that did not. An ad was judged to be in the former category if it featured at least one woman in clothing appropriate for factory work, ship construction, the armed forces, male service and transportation jobs, farm labor, and volunteer services, or if the work she did was clearly identified as paid employment that was related to the war effort (such as clerical worker, nurse, child care supervisor, telephone operator, draftsperson, or service and trade worker). Advertisements that featured women but did not describe them as having paid employment (in home roles, planting victory gardens, buying goods, or serving as decorative figures) were not considered to be about war work. Finally, the size of the advertisement was noted, whether it was a full, half, or quarter page. Full page ads were given more weight in the analysis than the others that did not yield as much cultural information and were judged to have less of an impact on the reader.

Appendix B: Magazine Fiction Identified by the Magazine Bureau of the Office of War Information as Propaganda for the Recruitment Campaign

Saturday Evening Post

"The Seventh WAVE" by Agnes Burke Hale, 4 March 1944, p. 14.
"A WAVE for Mac" by Sidney Herschel Small, 11 March 1944, p. 24.
"A WAC at West Point" by Frank Bunce, 1 July 1944, p. 22.
"You Can't Do That" by Frank Bunce, 16 December 1944, p. 28.
"The Lady and the Flat-Top" by Stanley Washburn, Jr., 17 March 1945, p. 24.

Confession Magazines

"Fair Weather Sweetheart," True Love and Romance, November 1943.
"So I Married the Farmer," Real Story, July 1943.
"Taxi Girl," Real Story, September 1943.
"I, Too, Serve," Personal Romances, July 1943.
"A WAAC and a Soldier," Personal Romances, September 1943.
"Never to Call You Mine," Personal Romances, August 1943.
"If It Should Be You," Personal Romances, October 1943.
"Love Was the Answer," Personal Romances, November 1943.
"Dearest, Do You Miss Me?" Personal Romances, May 1945.
"Absent without Leave," Real Confessions, October 1943.
"Too Selfish to Care," Real Confessions, October 1943.
"The Heart of Pvt. Julie Hall," True Experiences, April 1944.
"Absentee Sweetheart," True Experiences, November 1943.
"Absentee Girl," Modern Romances, July 1943.
"I Lied to Save a Soldier," Modern Romances, October 1943.

Other Magazines

"The Lt. Meets the WAAC," Cosmopolitan, July 1943.
"Gravy Guy," Collier's, July 1943.

"Scared Stiff," *Girl's Companion*, June 1943.

"Turnips or Typewriters," *Girl's Companion*, August 1943.

"Rivet Bucker," *Girl's Companion*, September 1943.

"Kiss Me Good-by," *Ladies' Home Journal*, December 1943.

"Such Little Faith," *Ladies' Home Journal*, February 1945.

"The Lt. Changed His Mind," *Family Circle*, 13 April 1945.

"I'm Alive Again," *Redbook*, July 1945.

"Punch-in Susie," *Scholastic*, 1 November 1943.

"Glitter Girl," *Farm Journal* and *Farmer's Wife*, January 1944.

"Ma Dunnaway, Recruiter," *Farm Journal*, September 1944.

"Hospital Ship," *Hygeia*, July 1944.

"Mystery in Ward 13," *Calling All Girls*, September 1944.

"Underwater Wave," *Calling All Girls*, September 1944.

"Miss Ellen Grinds Dovetails," *Woman's Day*, March 1945.

"Furlough," *Radio Mirror*, March 1945.

"We'll Never Give Enough," *Radio Romances*, April 1945.

Notes

Introduction

1   Karen Anderson summarizes the literature on this question in *Wartime Women: Sex Roles, Family Relations, and the Status of Women during World War II* (Westport, Conn.: Greenwood Press, 1981), pp. 8–11.

2   William Chafe, *The American Woman: Her Changing Social, Economic, and Political Roles, 1920–1970* (New York: Oxford University Press, 1972), p. 181; Leila Rupp, *Mobilizing Women for War: German and American Propaganda, 1939–1945* (Princeton, N.J.: Princeton University Press, 1978), p. 176.

3   Anderson, *Wartime Women*, pp. 173–74.

4   Susan Hartmann, *The Home Front and Beyond: American Women in the 1940s* (Boston: Twayne, 1982), p. 216.

5   Eleanor Straub discusses the exclusion of women from policy-making bodies in "U.S. Government Policy toward Civilian Women during World War II," *Prologue* 5 (Winter 1973): 240–54. Evidence that employers viewed women as temporary workers is provided in Anderson, *Wartime Women*, p. 53. Sheila Tobias and Lisa Anderson document the failure of unions to protect women's rights during reconversion in "What Really Happened to Rosie the Riveter: Demobilization and the Female Labor Force, 1945–47" (New York: MSS Modular Publications, module 9, 1974), pp. 1–36. See also Lyn Goldfarb, *Separate and Unequal: Discrimination against Women Workers after World War II* (Washington, D.C.: Union of Radical Political Economists, n.d.); and Anderson, *Wartime Women*, pp. 53–60.

6   Betty Friedan, *The Feminine Mystique* (New York: Dell, 1963).

7   Ibid., p. 36.

8   Ibid., p. 186.

9   Ibid., p. 207.

10 Rupp, *Mobilizing Women*.

11 Ibid., pp. 146–52.

12 Ibid., p. 151.

13 Ruth Milkman, "Redefining 'Women's Work': The Sexual Division of Labor in the Auto Industry during World War II," *Feminist Studies* 8, no. 2 (Summer 1982): 337–72; J. E. Trey, "Women in the War Economy—World War II," *Review of Radical Political Economics* 4 (July 1972): 41–57.

14 Rupp, *Mobilizing Women*, p. 174.

15   Anderson, *Wartime Women*, p. 177.

16   Susan Hartmann, "Prescriptions for Penelope: Literature on Women's Obligations to Returning World War II Veterans," *Women's Studies* 5, no. 3 (1978): 223–39; Hartmann, *Home Front*, p. 204; Anderson, *Wartime Women*, p. 178.

17   A summary of research that shares this perspective is provided in Frank Fox, *Madison Avenue Goes to War: The Strange Military Career of American Advertising, 1941–1945* (Provo, Utah: Brigham Young University Press, 1975), p. 11.

18   Wilbur Schramm, "The Nature of Communication between Humans," in Wilbur Schramm and Donald Roberts, eds., *The Process and Effects of Mass Communication* (Urbana: University of Illinois Press, 1971).

19   Ibid.

20   Rupp, *Mobilizing Women*, p. 168.

21   Hartmann, *Home Front*, p. 205.

22   John Cawelti, *Adventure, Mystery, and Romance: Formula Stories as Art and Popular Culture* (Chicago: University of Chicago Press, 1976), p. 34.

23   Ibid., p. 23.

24   Government surveys of 1944 showed that up to 80 percent of the women in war production plants wanted to be rehired at comparable rates of pay and in comparable jobs after reconversion. U.S. Department of Labor, Women's Bureau, *Women Workers in Ten War Production Areas and Their Postwar Employment Plans*, bulletin 209 (Washington, D.C.: Government Printing Office, 1946). Evidence of war workers' resistance to being channeled into female fields is provided in idem, *Employment of Women in the Early Postwar Period*, bulletin 211 (Washington, D.C.: Government Printing Office, 1946). Protests made by aircraft workers who had been laid off are recorded in Tobias and Anderson, "What Really Happened."

25   Susan Griffin, *Pornography and Silence* (New York: Harper and Row, 1981), p. 107.

26   For a study of film, see Melva Joyce Baker, "Images of Women: The War Years, 1941–1945" (Ph.D. diss., University of California–Santa Barbara, 1978); for a discussion of radio, see Raymond Stedman, *Serials: Suspense and Drama by Installment* (Norman: University of Oklahoma Press, 1971); a general overview of popular culture, but without much reference to women, is Richard Lingeman, *Don't You Know There's a War On? The American Home Front, 1941–1945* (New York: G. P. Putnam's Sons, 1970).

27   An authoritative history of the importance of early twentieth-century magazines is provided by Theodore Peterson, *Magazines in the Twentieth Century* (Urbana: University of Illinois Press, 1964).

28   With a subscriber circulation of three million during the war years, Theodore Peterson has called the *Post* the most successful family magazine of its type in the early twentieth century (ibid., p. 183); *True Story* had a subscriber circulation of two million, and Peterson documents its leadership position in the confessions field (ibid., p. 302).

29   Records of the Office of War Information's Magazine Bureau indicate that magazine editors were publishing stories, articles, and editorials in line

with government propaganda requests and carefully reading the bureau's bimonthly *Magazine War Guide*, which outlined images and themes the government wanted stressed. See below, chapter 1, for description and discussion of this data.

30 For a description of these groups, see chapter 1.

31 Martin Martel and George McCall, "Reality-Orientation and the Pleasure Principle: A Study of American Mass-Periodical Fiction (1890–1955)," in *People, Society, and Mass Communications*, ed. Lewis Dexter and David Manning White (Glencoe, Ill.: Free Press, 1964).

32 For a discussion of Lorimer, his philosophy, and his impact on the *Post*, see John Tebbel, *George Horace Lorimer and the "Saturday Evening Post"* (Garden City, N.Y.: Doubleday, 1948).

33 The following studies have documented the fact that confession magazines are read primarily by women from blue-collar families and that middle-class women have a negative image of the confessions and so avoid them: Lee Rainwater, Richard Coleman, and Gerald Handel, *Workingman's Wife* (New York: Oceana, 1959); George Gerbner, "The Social Role of the Confession Magazine," *Social Problems* 6 (Summer 1958): 29–40; Cornelia Butler-Flora, "The Passive Female: Her Comparative Image by Class and Culture in Women's Magazine Fiction," *Journal of Marriage and the Family* 33 (August 1971): 435–44; Pamela McCallum, "World without Conflict: Magazines for Working Class Women," *Canadian Forum* 55 (September 1975): 42–44.

34 Bernard Berelson and Patricia J. Salter, "Majority and Minority Americans: An Analysis of Magazine Fiction," *Public Opinion Quarterly* 10 (1946): 168–97; Milton Albrecht, "Does Literature Reflect Common Values?" *American Sociological Review* 21 (1956): 722–29.

35 Cawelti, *Adventure*, p. 35.

36 Patricke Johns-Heine and Hans Gerth, "Values in Mass Periodical Fiction, 1921–1940," *Public Opinion Quarterly* 13 (Spring 1949): 105–13.

37 There are many studies of advertising as a reflection of dominant American values. Examples of the best of these include Leo Bogart, *Strategy in Advertising* (New York: Harcourt, Brace and World, 1967); and David Potter, *People of Plenty: Economic Abundance and the American Character* (Chicago: University of Chicago Press, 1954). Studies that focus on the image of women in advertising are Trevor Millum, *Images of Woman: Advertising in Women's Magazines* (Totowa, N.J.: Rowman and Littlefield, 1975); and Erving Goffman, *Gender Advertisements* (New York: Harper and Row, 1976). Analysts who criticize advertising for exploiting the American consumer include Vance Packard, *The Hidden Persuaders* (New York: David McKay, 1957); and Stuart Ewen, *Captains of Consciousness: Advertising and the Social Roots of the Consumer Culture* (New York: McGraw-Hill, 1976). A good history of advertising in magazines is provided by Frank Luther Mott, *A History of American Magazines, 1885–1905* (Cambridge: Harvard University Press, 1957).

38 I referred to the following sources for my sampling procedures: Ole Holsti, *Content Analysis for the Social Sciences and Humanities* (Reading, Mass.:

Addison-Wesley, 1969); and Earl Babbie, *Research Methods in the Social Sciences* (Belmont, Calif.: Wadsworth, 1980).

39   I read a total of 472 stories from the *Post* and 121 stories from *True Story* covering a period of five years and three months, from January 1941 through March 1946. I read the lead story from every issue and randomly selected stories from other sections of the magazines. The *Post* sample is larger because it was a weekly whereas *True Story* was a monthly and because I had access to the *True Story* collection for only two weeks, at the publisher's request. Johns-Heine and Gerth ("Values") base their conclusions on a total of 728 stories covering a twenty-year period; Butler-Flora's sample ("Passive Female") consisted of 202 randomly selected stories; David Sonenschein read 73 stories from confession magazines for his analysis of sexual themes in "Love and Sex in the Romance Magazines," *Journal of Popular Culture* 4, no. 2 (1970): 398–409; and Wilbur Schramm based his analysis of the confessions on a random sample of 100 stories, stating that his results had stabilized after 30 had been read; this 1955 study is cited in Gerbner, "Social Role."

1   Creation of the Myth

1   Tobias and Anderson, "What Really Happened"; Paddy Quick, "Rosie the Riveter: Myths and Realities," *Radical America* 9 (July 1975): 115–32; Chafe, *American Woman*; Anderson, *Wartime Women*; Trey, "Women in the War Economy."

2   U.S. Women's Bureau, *Women Workers*, p. 4. Chafe posits that only 5 percent of women war workers joined the labor force for the first time during the war years (*American Woman*, p. 52).

3   U.S. Women's Bureau, *Women Workers*, p. 4.

4   Ibid., p. 18. For an analysis of racial discrimination against black women in war industries, see Karen Anderson, "Last Hired, First Fired: Black Women Workers during World War II," *Journal of American History* 69 (June 1982): 82–97.

5   U.S. Department of Labor, Women's Bureau, *Changes in Women's Employment during the War*, special bulletin 20 (Washington, D.C.: Government Printing Office, 1944), p. 13.

6   U.S. Department of Labor, Women's Bureau, *Employment Goals of the World Plan of Action: Developments and Issues in the United States* (Washington, D.C.: Government Printing Office, July 1980), table 11, pp. 9, 8.

7   U.S. Department of Labor, Women's Bureau, *Women at Work: A Century of Industrial Change*, bulletin 161 (Washington, D.C.: Government Printing Office, 1939), p. 12. The following are overviews and analyses of sexual segregation in the work force: Valerie Oppenheimer, *The Female Labor Force in the United States*, Population Monograph Series, no. 5 (Berkeley: University of California Press, 1970); Martha Blaxall and Barbara Reagan, eds., *Women and the Workplace* (Chicago: University of Chicago Press, 1976); Zillah Eisenstein, *Capitalist Patriarchy and the Case for Socialist Feminism* (New York: Monthly Review Press, 1979); Cynthia Lloyd and

Beth Niemi, *The Economics of Sex Differentials* (New York: Columbia University Press, 1979); Cynthia Lloyd, Emily Andrews, and Curtis Gilroy, eds., *Women in the Labor Market* (New York: Columbia University Press, 1979); W. Elliott and Mary M. Brownlee, *Women in the American Economy: A Documentary History 1675–1976* (New Haven: Yale University Press, 1976); Rosalynn Baxandall, Linda Gordon, and Susan Reverby, eds., *America's Working Women: A Documentary History—1600 to the Present* (New York: Vintage Books, 1976). For an excellent review of women's labor force patterns from 1870 to 1940, see U.S. Department of Labor, Women's Bureau, *Women's Occupations through Seven Decades*, bulletin 218 (Washington, D.C.: Government Printing Office, 1947).

8   *Industrial Mobilization for War: History of the War Production Board and Predecessor Agencies, 1940–1945*, vol. 1 (Washington, D.C.: Government Printing Office, 1947). Other studies that stress the importance of American productive capacity are Eliot Janeway, *The Struggle for Survival: A Chronicle of Economic Mobilization in World War II* (New Haven: Yale University Press, 1951); and Sumner Slichter, *Economic Factors Affecting Industrial Relations Policy in National Defense*, Industrial Relations Monograph, no. 6 (New York: Industrial Relations Counselors, 1941).

9   U.S. Department of Labor, Bureau of Labor Statistics, *Handbook of Labor Statistics*, bulletin 916 (Washington, D.C.: Government Printing Office, 1947), p. 17.

10   U.S. Department of Labor, Bureau of Labor Statistics, "Postwar Labor Turn-Over among Women Factory Workers," by Clara Schloss and Ella Polinsky, *Monthly Labor Review* 64 (March 1947): 411–19.

11   Chester Gregory, *Women in Defense Work during World War II* (New York: Exposition Press, 1974), pp. 114, 95, 81, 130, 68.

12   U.S. Department of Labor, Bureau of Labor Statistics, "Recent Occupational Trends," by Harold Wool and Lester Pearlman, *Monthly Labor Review* 65 (August 1947): 139–47.

13   U.S. Women's Bureau, *Women Workers*, table III-1, pp. 8–9.

14   Ibid., p. 38.

15   Karen Anderson, "The Impact of World War II in the Puget Sound Area on the Status of Women and the Family" (Ph.D. diss., University of Washington, 1975), p. 32.

16   A moving account of the WASP, one based on interviews with its former members, is Sally Keil's *Those Wonderful Women in Their Flying Machines* (New York: Rawson, Wade, 1979).

17   U.S. Women's Bureau, *Women Workers*, pp. 11–12. New York State, Department of Labor Reprints, *Post-War Plans of Women Workers in New York State*, Women in Industry and Minimum Wage Series, August 1945; U.S. Department of Labor, Bureau of Labor Statistics, "Women in Industry," *Monthly Labor Review* 59 (September 1944): 585–91.

18   U.S. Department of Labor, Bureau of Labor Statistics, "Women Workers and Recent Economic Change," by Mary Pidgeon, *Monthly Labor Review* 65 (December 1947): 666–71.

19   U.S. Women's Bureau, *Employment in the Early Postwar Period*, p. 13. An-

other report that documents women's dissatisfaction with being laid off is U.S. Department of Labor, Women's Bureau, *A Preview as to Women Workers in Transition from War to Peace*, special bulletin 18 (Washington, D.C.: Government Printing Office, 1944).

20 U.S. Bureau of Labor Statistics, "Postwar Turnover," by Schloss and Polinsky, p. 413.

21 U.S. Bureau of Labor Statistics, "Recent Trends," by Wool and Pearlman, p. 145.

22 Anderson, "Last Hired, First Fired."

23 U.S. Bureau of Labor Statistics, "Recent Trends," by Wool and Pearlman, p. 140. U.S. Department of Labor, Women's Bureau, *Handbook of Facts on Women Workers*, bulletin 225 (Washington, D.C.: Government Printing Office, 1948) p. 3.

24 U.S. Department of Commerce, Bureau of the Census, *Sixteenth Census of the United States Population—the Labor Force: Employment and Family Characteristics of Women* (Washington, D.C.: Government Printing Office, 1943), p. 3.

25 Thelma McKelvey, *Women in War Production* (New York: Oxford University Press, 1942), p. 39. Other reports that expected that temporary employment of women not in the labor force at the time of Pearl Harbor would take care of the labor shortage are: Jerome Kidder, *Women in Factory Work*, Studies in Personnel Policy, no. 41 (New York: National Industrial Conference Board, 1942); M. L. Gainsbrugh and I. J. White, "Women as War Labor Reserves," *Conference Board Economic Record* 4 (February 1942): 47–50; and Harold Metz, *Is There Enough Manpower?* (Washington, D.C.: Brookings Institution, 1942).

26 Gainsbrugh and White, "War Labor Reserves."

27 McKelvey, *Women in War Production*, p. 36.

28 Anderson, "Puget Sound," p. 26.

29 Good analyses of the child care program are the following: Karen Beck Skold, "The Politics of Child Care during World War II: The Case of the Kaiser Child Care Centers" (Paper presented at the National Women's Studies Association, Bloomington, Ind., 1980); Howard Dratch, "The Politics of Child Care in the 1940s," *Science and Society* 38 (Summer 1974): 167–204; Anderson, *Wartime Women*, pp. 122–53.

30 U.S. Women's Bureau, *Women Workers*, pp. 23–25.

31 U.S. Women's Bureau, *Preview*, p. 22.

32 Straub, "U.S. Policy toward Civilian Women," *Prologue*, describes the unsuccessful efforts of women in the federal government to safeguard employed women's rights and discusses the inadequate enforcement of federal regulations to insure fair treatment of women in war plants.

33 Eleanor Straub, "U.S. Government Policy toward Civilian Women during World War II" (Ph.D. diss., Emory University, 1973), pp. 170, 33.

34 Allan Winkler, "Politics and Propaganda: The Office of War Information, 1942–1945" (Ph.D. diss., Yale University, 1974), pp. 1–46. This study was published by Yale University Press in 1978 under the title, *The Politics of Propaganda: The Office of War Information, 1942–1945*.

35 A brief account of this organization is given in George Creel, *How We Advertised America* (1920; rpt. New York: Arno Press, 1972). See also James Mock and Cedric Larson, eds., *Words that Won the War: The Story of the Committee on Public Information, 1917–1919* (Princeton, N.J.: Princeton University Press, 1939).

36 Fox, *Madison Avenue*, p. 68.

37 Winkler, "Politics and Propaganda," p. 47.

38 The best sources of information on OWI are Winkler's study and David Jones, "The U.S. Office of War Information and American Public Opinion during World War II, 1939–1945" (Ph.D. diss., State University of New York–Binghamton, 1976).

39 Fox, *Madison Avenue*, p. 22.

40 Richard Polenberg, *War and Society: The U.S., 1941–1945* (New York: J. B. Lippincott, 1972), p. 11.

41 Fox, *Madison Avenue*, p. 68.

42 Ibid., p. 50.

43 These extensive links are described in records of the Office of War Information. See Manpower Campaigns file and "Report from the War Advertising Council," September 1942, Record Group 208, entry 39, National Records Center, Suitland, Md. All subsequent references to archival material will be from this source.

44 Fox, *Madison Avenue*, p. 41.

45 Chester La Roche to Gardner Cowles, 13 January 1943, Young and Rubicam file, entry 20, box 15.

46 "Policy and Plan for the Total War Campaign of the Magazine Publishers Association," 31 December 1942, Young and Rubicam file, entry 20, box 15.

47 J. Walter Thompson was the advertising agency for the War Manpower Commission; "Words that Work for Victory," 1 March 1944–1 March 1945, "Report of the War Advertising Council," entry 90, box 588.

48 Women in the War Campaign file, entry 90, box 591.

49 Ibid. This is just a small sample of the amount of recruitment propaganda created and disseminated by the media under OWI direction. In 1944 alone, fifty radio programs on the "womanpower" campaign were broadcast each week for twenty-six weeks.

50 Memo, Dorothy Ducas to Ulric Bell, 11 May 1942, Magazine Bureau Organization file, entry 339, box 1695.

51 Memo, Ducas to Cowles, 4 August 1942, Magazine Bureau Organization file, entry 339, box 1695.

52 Report, Ducas to Harold Guinzburg, 25 March 1943, Magazine Bureau Organization file, entry 339, box 1695.

53 Memos, Ducas to F. Girardot, 17 September and 11 December 1943, Magazine Bureau Organization file, entry 339, box 1695.

54 Memo, Ducas to Elmer Davis, 23 September 1943, Magazine Bureau Organization file, entry 339, box 1695.

55 Report, Ducas, 16 December 1942; memos, Ducas to Bell, 19 May 1942, 30 June 1942, 11 May 1942, 21 December 1942, Magazine Bureau Organization file, entry 339, box 1695.

56   These directions are given in an undated memo to the Bureau of Campaigns from the War Manpower Commission, Womanpower Recruitment Campaign file, entry 90, box 587.

57   "National Magazine Covers in Support of the Womanpower Program," Publications on War Subjects, entry 340, box 1696.

58   "Women in Necessary Services," *Magazine War Guide* supplement, June–July 1943, entry 345, box 1700.

59   "Basic Program Plan for Womanpower," August 1943, Records of the Program Manager for the Recruitment of Women, entry 90, box 587.

60   "Results of This OWI Service to Magazines," 25 August 1943, Magazine Bureau Organization file, entry 339, box 1695.

61   Memo, Ducas, 25 June 1943, Magazine Bureau Organization file, entry 339, box 1695.

62   Memo, Genevieve Herrick to Mary Keeler, 20 December 1943, Magazine Bureau Organization file, entry 339, box 1695.

63   This listing shows that from March 1943 to August 1945 the following number of articles, stories and editorials were published: 433 on recruitment of women, 399 concerning women in the armed forces, 138 supporting the nurse campaign, 58 on child care facilities, and 26 publicizing streamlined housekeeping. Magazine Editorials, Articles, and Fiction Stories on Programs Being Promoted by OWI, entry 343, box 1699.

64   Ducas's request to enlarge the Magazine Bureau's operation was made in a memo to Cowles dated August 1942. Typical of her contacts with popular writers is the work she did with Katherine Brush, a well-known romance writer whom she guided through a story about a housewife who takes a factory job to help out her country. She also spoke to the Authors' League early in the war and asked writers to use themes suggested by her office. Report, Ducas, 30 October 1942. All of these memos are in the Magazine Bureau Organization file, entry 339, box 1695. Ducas's special request to the Magazine Advisory Committee to weaken prejudice against employed women was referred to in her memo to Palmer Hoyt, 17 September 1943, Magazine Advisory Committee file, entry 340, box 1696.

65   *Magazine War Guide*, November/December 1942, entry 345, box 1700.

66   *War Guide* Supplement for Confession Magazines, 15 October 1942, entry 345, box 1700.

67   *War Guide* Supplement for Love and Western Love Magazines, 15 October 1942, entry 345, box 1700.

68   Early analyses conducted by corporate leaders of what would be involved in shifting to a wartime economy stressed how critical was the cooperation of labor if productivity goals for military material were to be met: "Mobilizing the interest and intelligence of the workers is an important step in developing the efficiency of the defense program." Slichter, *Economic Factors*, p. 11.

69   "Editors' Conference Report," 5 April 1943, Meetings of Magazine Editors file, entry 339, box 1695. Ducas's remarks appear in a memo to Bell dated 15 July 1942, Historical Records file, entry 339, box 1695.

70   Memo, Ducas to Cowles, "Magazine Publishers' Protest against Discrimi-

nation by the Government," 12 November 1942, Magazine Bureau Organization file, entry 339, box 1695.

71 Ibid.

72 "First Visits to Editors," memo, Ducas to Bell, 11 May 1942, Magazine Bureau Organization file, entry 339, box 1695.

73 "First meeting of Magazine Advisory Committee," 17 September 1943, Meetings of Magazine Editors file, entry 339, box 1695.

74 Supplement for October 1942 and *War Guide* Supplement for Love and Western Love Magazines, 11 September 1942, entry 345, box 1700. Racist treatment of the Japanese was also suggested in the *Magazine War Guide*, reflecting the kind of attitudes that led to incarceration of Japanese-Americans on the West Coast. The following is an example of OWI's racist propaganda: "Understanding your enemies can be a weakness. Japanese upbringing, environment, and training have made them the ruthless, savage people they are. The magazines can do a great deal to portray the nature of our Eastern enemies to the American people"; *Magazine War Guide*, November/December 1942, entry 345, box 1700.

75 *War Guide* Supplement for Love and Western Love Magazines, 11 September 1942, entry 345, box 1700.

76 A most comprehensive source of information on this group is Robert Howell, "The Writers' War Board: Writers and World War II" (Ph.D. diss., Louisiana State and Agricultural and Mechanical College, 1971).

77 "First Annual Report," 9 December 1942, Writers' War Board file, entry 339, box 1695.

78 Howell, "Writers' War Board," pp. 499, 58, 62. Howell points out that Stout's claim is unverifiable since there are no financial records from the board later than 1942.

79 Ibid., p. 79.

80 In October 1944, OWI canceled many government propaganda efforts and asked the Writers' War Board to halt its activities. The board reacted with hostility to this request and continued to solicit propaganda pieces from popular writers. Howell states that 1944 was the most active year for the board because budget cutbacks threatened to make OWI less effective, and the WWB stepped up its activities to compensate; ibid., pp. 149, 135.

81 Memo, Ducas to Bell, 30 December 1942, Magazine Bureau Organization file, entry 339, box 1695.

82 See above, n. 64.

83 Supplement I, 3 September 1942, and Supplement III, 30 October 1942, entry 345, box 1700.

84 "Putting That College Education to Work," *Magazine War Guide*, August/September 1943, entry 345, box 1700.

85 "Housing War Workers," *Magazine War Guide*, June/July 1943, entry 345, box 1700.

86 *War Guide* Supplement for Love and Western Love Magazines, 11 September 1942, entry 345, box 1700.

87 Listed in Magazine Editorials, Articles, and Fiction Stories on Programs Being Promoted by OWI, entry 343, box 1699.

88   "War Production Drive," *Magazine War Guide*, December/January 1943, entry 345, box 1700; emphasis added.

89   *War Guide Supplement for Love and Western Love Magazines*," September 1942, entry 345, box 1700.

90   Ibid., 15 October 1942, entry 345, box 1700; *War Guide Supplement for Confession Magazines*, 15 October 1942, entry 345, box 1700.

91   *War Guide Supplement III for Confession Magazines*, 30 October 1942, entry 345, box 1700; emphasis added.

92   *War Guide Supplement for Love and Western Love Magazines*, 15 October 1942, entry 345, box 1700; *War Guide Supplement for Confession Magazines*, 15 October 1942, entry 345, box 1700.

93   "Toughening Up for War," *Magazine War Guide*, December/January 1943, entry 345, box 1700; "Discomfort," ibid., March/April 1943, entry 345, box 1700.

94   *War Guide Supplement for Confession Magazines*, 15 October 1942, entry 345, box 1700.

95   Ibid.

96   Anderson, "Last Hired, First Fired," 1982.

97   "Postwar," *Magazine War Guide*, June/July 1943, entry 345, box 1700.

98   These attacks on OWI's domestic branch began in the spring of 1943 when the House of Representatives recommended discontinuation of the entire domestic operation. David Jones explains this hostility as an attempt on the part of the Republican-dominated Congress to regain ground lost to the executive branch during the Roosevelt years and to Republican desires to dismantle the New Deal. Jones, "U.S. Office of War Information," pp. 442–500.

99   Memo, Allan Wilson to advertisers, undated, entry 90, box 587.

100 The advertising industry, for example, nearly doubled its magazine business from $197 million in 1940 to $364 million in 1945. Jones, "U.S. Office of War Information," p. 260.

2   Middle-Class Images of Women in Wartime

1   Regular contributors of fiction to the *Post* who were executive members of the Writers' War Board include Rita Halle Kleeman, J. P. Marquand, Stephen Vincent Benét, Walter D. Edmonds, Mary Roberts Rinehart, Kenneth Roberts, Sophie Kerr, Robert Pinkerton, and Paul Gallico. Although the authors of other stories with clear propaganda purposes were not members of the board's advisory committee, it is likely that they were asked by fellow writers to write stories for OWI campaigns. Though these writers do not appear on the rosters of board committees, the nature and quantity of the stories they wrote suggest contact with board members. Robert Carson, for example, wrote stories that glorified heroines in war work. Margaret Craven and Phyliss Duganne also contributed fiction with strong recruitment themes. Craven wrote about women working collectively to aid the war effort, the negative effects of prejudice against female war workers, and the maturation of a housewife performing volunteer work. Duganne

created romances that encouraged positive attitudes toward women in blue-collar work and toward day care centers.

2   See Appendix A for an explanation of which stories were selected for this study and how the selection was made.

3   Sidney Herschel Small, "A WAVE for Mac," 11 March 1944; and Agnes Burke Hale, "The Seventh WAVE," 4 March 1944. Both are cited in a memo from Cliff Sutter to Dave Fredericks, 23 March 1944, Records of the Program Manager for the Recruitment of Women, entry 90, box 588.

4   Magazine Editorials, Articles, and Fiction Stories on Programs Being Promoted by OWI, entry 343, box 1699. See Appendix B for a listing of all the fiction identified by OWI as propaganda for the recruitment campaign.

5   Of the lead stories with prominent female characters, 45 percent supported the womanpower campaign between March 1943 and July 1945. This does not include the many fiction stories that supported other home-front campaigns.

6   I read all the fiction from January 1931 through December 1939. This analysis is based on that material and on the lead stories from January to December 1941. Part of my discussion is drawn from Maureen Honey, "Images of Women in the *Saturday Evening Post*, 1931–1936," *Journal of Popular Culture* 10 (Fall 1976): 352–58. There is some evidence that this portrayal reflected the elevated status and authority of wives whose husbands were unemployed during the Depression. A case study of one family's adjustment to the husband's unemployment describes his wife's assumption of family authority; Wight Bakke, "Family Life," in Baxandall, Gordon, and Reverby, *America's Working Women*.

7   Friedan, *Feminine Mystique*, p. 38.

8   There are two good discussions of the autonomous thirties heroine as she appears in film: Molly Haskell, *From Reverence to Rape: The Treatment of Women in the Movies* (New York: Holt, Rinehart and Winston, 1974); and Marjorie Rosen, *Popcorn Venus* (New York: Avon, 1974).

9   The *Magazine War Guide* publicized the desperate need for women in skilled work and supervisory positions during the first half of 1943. The War Manpower Commission had provided the Magazine Bureau with a list of twenty-four occupational categories in skilled work that were critical to war industries and short of workers. This list was published in the April/May 1943 issue of the *Guide*, entry 345, box 1700.

10   *War Guide* Supplement for Love and Western Love Magazines, 11 September 1942, entry 345, box 1700.

11   U.S. Women's Bureau, *Handbook of Facts*.

12   *Magazine War Guide*, June/July 1943. These requests were made by Dorothy Ducas during her trips to New York and by other issues of the *Guide*. See, for example, the December/January 1943 issue, "Still More Nurses Needed," and the August/September 1943 issue, "Putting That College Education to Work," entry 345, box 1700.

13   Agnes Burke Hale, "The Seventh WAVE," 4 March 1944. This story is cited in Magazine Editorials, Articles, and Fiction Stories on Programs Being Promoted by OWI, entry 343, box 1699.

14   Surveys conducted by OWI's Special Services Bureau in May and June 1943 showed that women who were not in the labor force remained at home because their husbands wanted them to. "Resistance to Taking War Jobs in Three New England Cities," special memorandum no. 62, 24 June 1943, OWI Special Services Bureau, entry 118, box 706. OWI was trying to change negative attitudes about married employed women that had been prevalent during the Depression. In 1939 a Gallup poll found, for instance, that 78 percent of the public was opposed to married women taking a job; Ruth Shallcross, "Shall Married Women Work?" in Baxandall, Gordon, and Reverby, *America's Working Women.*

15   *Magazine War Guide,* January/February 1944, entry 345, box 1700.

16   Berelson and Salter, "Majority and Minority Americans."

17   Anderson, "Last Hired, First Fired."

18   Berelson and Salter, "Majority and Minority Americans."

19   This story is cited in Howell, "Writers' War Board."

20   See, for example, the May/June 1943 and August 1944 issues of the *Magazine War Guide,* entry 345, box 1700.

21   *War Guide* Supplement for Love and Western Love Magazines, 11 September 1942, entry 345, box 1700.

22   Ibid., 15 October 1942, entry 345, box 1700.

23   Hartmann, "Prescriptions for Penelope."

24   Ibid.

25   *Magazine War Guide,* February/March 1943, entry 345, box 1700.

26   Cawelti, *Adventure,* p. 6.

27   Other companies that devoted a great deal of advertising to recruitment were Camel cigarettes, General Electric, Beechnut Packing Company, Whitman's chocolates, Black and Decker, Budget hoists, Sal Hepatica, Dr. West's toothbrushes, Hammermill Bond paper and office supplies, and Smith-Corona.

28   La Roche to Cowles, 3 January 1943, Young and Rubicam file, entry 20, box 15; emphasis added.

29   Rupp, *Mobilizing Women,* p. 143.

30   Memo, Robert Simpson to Sutter, 4 September 1943, Records of the Program Manager for the Recruitment of Women, entry 90, box 588.

31   "WAVES Wanted," Records of the Program Manager for the Recruitment of Women, Womanpower file, entry 90, box 588.

32   Stanley Washburn, Jr., "The Lady and the Flat-Top," 17 March 1945; the Small story is cited in a memo from Sutter to Fredericks, 23 March 1944, Records of the Program Manager for the Recruitment of Women, entry 90, box 588. The Washburn story is cited in Magazine Editorials, Articles, and Fiction Stories on Programs Being Promoted by OWI, entry 343, box 1699.

33   Rupp, *Mobilizing Women,* p. 151.

34   This source of resistance is identified in the "Women in the War" campaign guide, Records of the Program Manager for the Recruitment of Women, Womanpower file, entry 90, box 588.

35   Agnes Burke Hale, "The Seventh WAVE," 4 March 1944; see p. 79.

36 Allan Bérubé, "Coming Out under Fire," *Mother Jones*, February–March 1983, pp. 23–29.

37 This is mentioned in the *Magazine War Guide*, June/July 1943, entry 345, box 1700.

38 *Magazine War Guide*, September/October 1943, entry 345, box 1700.

39 "Jobs for Returning Soldiers and Sailors," *Magazine War Guide*, September/October 1943, entry 345, box 1700.

40 "Women in Post-War Jobs," *Magazine War Guide*, January 1945, entry 345, box 1700.

41 In 1941, 47 percent of those ads featuring women portrayed them in no occupation; in 1946, 57 percent of such ads did, while in 1944, only 14 percent featured women in no work roles. These figures are drawn from all the ads in three issues per year for three years—1941 (prerecruitment), 1944 (recruitment period), and 1946 (reconversion period). The issues included in this sample were 4 October 1941; 8 November 1941; 13 December 1941; 29 April 1944; 13 May 1944; 24 June 1944; 5 January 1946; 9 February 1946; 16 March 1946.

42 U.S. Department of Labor, Women's Bureau, *Women's Wartime Hours of Work: The Effect on Their Factory Performance and Home Life*, bulletin 208 (Washington, D.C.: Government Printing Office, 1947).

43 U.S. Women's Bureau, *Women Workers*.

44 An example of the earlier campaign to demonstrate that married women could be employed too is "Streamlined Housekeeping," *Magazine War Guide*, June/July 1943, entry 345, box 1700.

45 "Policy and Plan for the Total War Campaign of the Magazine Publishers Association," 31 December 1942, Young and Rubicam file, entry 20, box 15.

46 "Give Us More Wacs . . . ," Records of the Program Manager for Homefront Campaigns, Nurses file, entry 84, box 569; "Waves Wanted," January 1944, Records of the Program Manager for the Recruitment of Women, Womanpower file, entry 90, box 588.

47 "Waves Wanted," January 1944, Records of the Program Manager for the Recruitment of Women, Womanpower file, entry 90, box 588.

48 Ibid.

49 Women in the War Campaign file, entry 90, box 588.

50 Rupp, *Mobilizing Women*, p. 152.

51 Ibid., p. 99.

52 Anderson, *Wartime Women*, p. 61.

53 Kidder, *Women in Factory Work*.

54 "Policy and Plan," 31 December 1942, Young and Rubicam file, entry 20, box 15.

55 Michele Shover, "Roles and Images of Women in World War I Propaganda," *Politics and Society* 5, no. 3 (1975): 469–89.

56 Barbara Welter, "The Cult of True Womanhood: 1820–1860," *American Quarterly* 18 (Summer 1960): 151–74.

57 Baker, "Images of Women."

58 *No Exceptions*, produced by 20th Century Fox, released 30 December 1943

by the War Activities Committee; script included in "Women in the War" campaign guide, January 1944, Records of the Program Manager for the Recruitment of Women, Women in the War file, entry 90, box 588.

59   This point is also made in Hartmann, "Prescriptions for Penelope."

60   For a discussion of the social forces that led toward a more restrictive role for women at the war's end, see Anderson, *Wartime Women*, pp. 75–121.

3   The Working-Class Woman and the Recruitment Campaign

1   Gerbner, "Social Role."

2   Ibid. Gerbner cites several articles from *Writer's Market* that support the conclusion that confession stories are written by professional writers. Theodore Peterson also states that editors of popular magazines relied primarily on professional writers at least from the 1920s; *Magazines in the Twentieth Century*, p. 125. These observations are confirmed by my own conversations with the editors of *True Story*, who indicated that most of the stories they accept for publication are written by people who have mastered the formula.

3   Muriel Cantor and Elizabeth Jones, "Creating Fiction for Women," *Communication Research* 10 (January 1983): 111–37.

4   These comments are from interviews with *True Story* readers cited in a 1959 study of working-class women. They were taken from Macfadden-sponsored interviews with 420 working-class housewives. Although it can be argued that the Macfadden study was biased, the sociologists who drew on its findings found them confirmed by their own interviews with readers of confession magazines; Rainwater, Coleman, and Handel, *Workingman's Wife*, p. 129. Unfortunately, we have no data from the war years concerning the attitudes of confessions readers, but it is reasonable to assume that the later evidence reflects a long-standing appeal of the formula.

5   Ibid., p. 132. The authors conclude that working-class readers of *True Story* believe that it is realistic, mirrors their problems, and is a good source of positive lessons for their lives; see "Morality and Hope: The Case of *True Story*," in Rainwater, Coleman, and Handel, *Workingman's Wife*.

6   Memo, Ducas to Ken Dyke, 3 September 1942; Ducas to Carroll Rheinstrom, 21 October 1942, Bureau of Campaigns file, entry 39, box unnumbered.

7   "Writers' War Board Annual Report," January 1944, entry 339, box 1695.

8   Magazine Editorials, Articles, and Fiction Stories on Programs Being Promoted by OWI, entry 343, box 1699. See Appendix A for sampling procedure.

9   Confessions writers cited in Gerbner, "Social Role."

10   Sonenschein, "Love and Sex."

11   Florence Palmer, "Six Ways to Successful Confessions," in *The Writer's Handbook*, ed. A. S. Burack (Boston: The Writer, 1974), pp. 126–32.

12   Jean Jackson, "The Changing Confession Market," *The Writer*, May 1975, p. 15.

13 Ducas's reports during this period are discussed in chapter 1. Unfortunately, The Macfadden Group Inc., publishers of *True Story*, have not kept records from the war period. Whatever correspondence may have taken place between its offices and Washington from 1939 to 1942 has been lost.

14 David Jones describes those information agencies that served as liaisons between the media and the government and preceded the Office of War Information in "U.S. Office of War Information."

15 Supplement IV for February/March 1943, 10 December 1942, entry 345, box 1700.

16 David Jones discusses the uneven nature of communication between the media and government information agencies at this time. "During the early months of the war a confusing relationship existed between the information program and the media. Newspapers and radio stations were swamped with requests from government agencies for time and space. In an attempt to rationalize this situation the OFF was directed to provide guidance for departments and agencies in their dealings with the radio industry. To that end, OFF developed a radio allocation plan. Lowell Mellett, the uncrowned czar of the information managers, favored strengthening the CWI [Committee on War Information] contacts with advertisers and initiating a program of government-paid advertising. He even suggested that 'possibly the government should take over the radio for the duration.' The networks received this threat coolly, although they recognized that nationalization was within the realm of possibility because of FCC licensing for commercial broadcasters." "U.S. Office of War Information," p. 109. It is clear that the media engaged in propaganda before the systemizing of campaigns under OWI, but the difficulties they experienced in getting information were considerable.

17 *War Guide* Supplement for Confession Magazines, 11 September 1942, entry 345, box 1700; emphasis added.

18 Ibid., 15 October 1942, entry 345, box 1700.

19 The sample of stories from which this study is drawn includes all the lead stories from January 1941 to March 1946 (sixty-three) and fifty-eight non-lead stories that appeared to concern employed women.

20 Supplement II, 15 October 1942, entry 345, box 1700.

21 *Magazine War Guide*, September/October 1943, entry 345, box 1700.

22 *War Guide* Supplement for Confession Magazines, 15 October 1942, entry 345, box 1700; emphasis added.

23 *Magazine War Guide*, September/October 1943, entry 345, box 1700.

24 *War Guide* Supplement III for Confession Magazines, 30 October 1942, entry 345, box 1700.

25 Ibid.

26 One of the major features of the womanpower drive was the campaign to cut housework down to four hours a day, which OWI dubbed "streamlined housekeeping." This story reflects one of the methods recommended for reducing housework—to put older children in charge of some home tasks.

27 *War Guide* Supplement III for Confession Magazines, 30 October 1942, and Supplement VII, May/June 1942, entry 345, box 1700.

28   Though this story concerns the prejudice of a homeowner against male mi-
      grants to war production centers, it was female workers who had trouble
      renting rooms, and surveys showed that people with rooms to let preferred
      male over female renters. U.S. Department of Labor, Women's Bureau,
      Progress Report on Women War Workers' Housing, special bulletin 17
      (Washington, D.C.: Government Printing Office, 1944).

29   Women were hit especially hard by the Depression. Women comprised 30
      percent of all persons on relief in 1934 even though they were only 22 per-
      cent of all workers in 1930. U.S. Department of Labor, Women's Bureau,
      Women in Industry, bulletin 164 (Washington, D.C.: Government Printing
      Office, 1938).

30   Lillian Rubin mentions the psychological benefits working-class women
      receive from performing even low-status, low-paying jobs in *Worlds of
      Pain: Life in the Working-Class Family* (New York: Basic Books, 1976):
      "Their attitudes toward their work are varied, but most find the work
      world a satisfying place—at least when compared to the world of the
      housewife. . . . Like men, they take pride in doing a good job, in feeling
      competent. They are glad to get some relief from the routines of house-
      wifery and mothering small children. They are pleased to earn some
      money, to feel more independent, more as if they have some ability to con-
      trol their own lives. There is, perhaps, no greater testimony to the deaden-
      ing and deadly quality of the tasks of the housewife than the fact that so
      many women find pleasure in working at jobs that by almost any definition
      would be called alienated labor—low-status, low-paying, dead-end work
      made up of dull, routine tasks" (p. 169). We can assume that, if Rubin's in-
      terviews with working-class women reveal that any kind of wage work
      raises self-esteem, it is reasonable to conclude that skilled, higher-paying
      work in war industries was even more rewarding. We have some docu-
      mentation of the positive self-images women received from war work in
      the film, *The Life and Times of Rosie the Riveter*, where we hear former
      workers in shipyards and aircraft plants discuss how much satisfaction
      they got from such work.

31   Sherna Gluck, "Interlude or Change: Women and the World War II Experi-
      ence," *International Journal of Oral History* 3 (June 1982): 92–113.

32   The Bureau of Labor Statistics estimated that one third of the new war jobs
      would be for skilled workers in metal trades since they would be concen-
      trated in metal goods industries, especially steel. It anticipated that the
      economy would require more than double the number of such workers by
      January of 1942 and that the limited number of available workers in this
      field would inhibit the production of not only steel but zinc, aluminum,
      nickel, and tungsten, which were all essential for weapons manufacture.
      Slichter, *Economic Factors*.

33   The *Magazine War Guide* identified this group of women as the most fa-
      vored for wartime employment in its first issue; *New Magazine War Guide*,
      November/December 1942, entry 345, box 1700.

34   In a poll taken in 1943, 55 percent of married men said they would be un-

willing to have their wives take full-time jobs running a machine in a war plant; Oppenheimer, *Female Labor Force*, table 2.10.

35 The women who were lauded in this series include: Pocahontas, Mary Ann Bickerdyke, Lydia Darragh, Narcissa Whitman, Clara Barton, Jane Addams, Anne Hutchinson, Susan B. Anthony, Dorothea Dix, Sacagawea, Frances E. Willard, Mother Seton, Martha Washington, Elizabeth Blackwell, Louisa May Alcott, Molly Pitcher, Betsy Ross, Abigail Adams, Mary Lindley Murray, Dolly Madison, Jemima Johnson, Mary Lyon.

36 Peterson, *Magazines in the Twentieth Century*, p. 302.

4   Class Differences in the Portrayal of Women War Workers

1 Eleanor Straub mentions that praise of women was a prominent feature of public wartime statements about the home front in "U.S. Policy toward Civilian Women," *Prologue*.

2 The *Post's* "South toward Home" (Margaret Weymouth Jackson, 19 April 1941) is a good example of how the magazine glorified American technological genius and practical efficiency. It concerns a small-town boy who takes a defense job in a metropolitan area. At first, he is alienated by the noise, the anonymity, and the harshness of his boss, but he eventually sees how the factory's output of army tanks is testimony to those qualities which have made America great: "American goods made by American cranks. This was the language that could be spoken everywhere . . . the language of precision."

3 Rubin, *Worlds of Pain*. Rubin concludes that the working-class distaste for institutionalized child care stems from parental fear that the children will acquire bad habits and that their moral precepts will be undermined: "Where nursery school attendance is a commonplace among the children of middle-class families, it is rare among those of the working-class—not primarily for financial reasons, nor because working-class parents value education less, but because they look with question and concern at the values that are propagated there" (p. 87).

4 "We Shall Build Good Ships," *True Story*, November 1941; Robert Pinkerton, "Dangerous Ways," *Saturday Evening Post*, 2 January 1943.

5 "In Love With America," *True Story*, June 1943; Isabella Holt, "The Belittling Parent," *Saturday Evening Post*, 11 September 1943.

6 There are no available data on the age of wartime readers. Before the war, the typical *True Story* reader was between eighteen and twenty-four; Johns-Heine and Gerth, "Values." There is evidence from the magazine, however, that readers spanned a wider age range than is indicated by the Johns-Heine and Gerth study. The readers featured in a column concerning home problems, for instance, ranged from eighteen to thirty-five.

7 Of all those who were clerical workers in major war production areas in 1944–45, 46 percent identified themselves as having been in school the week before Pearl Harbor, whereas of those who were employed in op-

erative work, 31 percent described themselves as former students. U.S. Women's Bureau, *Women Workers*, table II-6.

8   Gerbner, "Social Role."

9   Penni Stewart, "He Admits . . . but She Confesses," *Women's Studies International Quarterly* 3, no. 1 (1980): 105–14.

10   Tebbel, *Lorimer*, p. 226.

11   Rainwater, Coleman, and Handel, *Workingman's Wife*, p. 46.

12   Rubin, *Worlds of Pain*, p. 163.

13   Ibid., p. 19.

14   Ibid., p. 43. Rubin uses this explanation to account for the high rate of premarital pregnancy among the working-class women in her sample, of whom 44 percent were pregnant when they married. Further support for the conclusion that working-class women bear children earlier than those of the middle class is provided by Rainwater, Coleman, and Handel, *Workingman's Wife*, p. 69.

15   Rubin, *Worlds of Pain*, p. 168.

16   "Resistance to Taking War Jobs in Three New England Cities," special memorandum no. 62, 24 June 1943, OWI Special Services Bureau, entry 118, box 706.

17   Anderson concludes that the entry of women into male occupations exerted stress on working-class marriages when husbands felt their authority threatened; *Wartime Women*, p. 83.

18   See above, pp. 99–100.

19   In May of 1943, for example, only 3,062 of 14,435 women employed in the Puget Sound area were in semiskilled positions while a mere 109 were performing skilled work; Anderson, "Puget Sound," p. 60. Straub also mentions the underutilization of women in skilled jobs in war plants; "U.S. Policy toward Civilian Women, p. 162. Similarly, women were hired by the steel industry for the least skilled positions with black women getting the worst jobs; Gregory, *Women in Defense Work*, p. 186.

Conclusion

1   Despite the rising number of women in the work force and the heightened social awareness of discrimination against women in the labor market, images of women in the media are by and large traditional ones. For a review of the research on sexism in the media, see Matilda Butler and William Paisley, eds., *Women and the Mass Media* (New York: Human Sciences Press, 1980); and Leslie J. Friedman, *Sex Role Stereotyping in the Mass Media: An Annotated Bibliography* (New York: Garland, 1977). Gaye Tuchman discusses the invisibility of working women in the media and its negative impact on women's job opportunities in Gaye Tuchman, Arlene Kaplan Daniels, and James Benét, eds., *Hearth and Home: Images of Women in the Mass Media* (New York: Oxford University Press, 1978).

Bibliography

Books and Monographs

Abbott, Edith. *Women in Industry*. New York: Appleton, 1913.

Anderson, Karen. *Wartime Women: Sex Roles, Family Relations, and the Status of Women during World War II*. Westport, Conn.: Greenwood Press, 1981.

Babbie, Earl. *Research Methods in the Social Sciences*. Belmont, Calif.: Wadsworth, 1980.

Baker, Laura. *Wanted—Women in War Industry: The Complete Guide to a War Factory Job*. New York: E. P. Dutton, 1943.

Baxandall, Rosalynn; Linda Gordon; and Susan Reverby, eds. *America's Working Women: A Documentary History—1600 to the Present*. New York: Vintage Books, 1976.

Blaxall, Martha, and Barbara Reagan, eds. *Women and the Workplace*. Chicago: University of Chicago Press, 1976.

Bogart, Leo. *Strategy in Advertising*. New York: Harcourt, Brace and World, 1967.

Bowman, Constance. *Slacks and Callouses*. New York: Longmans, Green, 1944.

Breckinridge, Sophonisba. *Women in the Twentieth Century: A Study of Their Political, Social, and Economic Activities*. New York: McGraw-Hill, 1933.

Brownlee, W. Elliott, and Mary M. Brownlee. *Women in the American Economy: A Documentary History, 1675–1976*. New Haven: Yale University Press, 1976.

Bullard, Washington. *Women's Work in War Time*. Boston: Merchants National Bank, 1917.

Butler, Matilda, and William Paisley, eds. *Women and the Mass Media*. New York: Human Sciences Press, 1980.

Cawelti, John. *Adventure, Mystery, and Romance: Formula Stories as Art and Popular Culture*. Chicago: University of Chicago Press, 1976.

Chafe, William. *The American Woman: Her Changing Social, Economic, and Political Roles, 1920–1970*. New York: Oxford University Press, 1972.

———. *Women and Equality: Changing Patterns in American Culture*. New York: Oxford University Press, 1977.

Clawson, Augusta. *Shipyard Diary of a Woman Welder*. New York: Penguin Books, 1944.

Creedy, Brooks. *Women behind the Lines: YWCA Program with War Production Workers, 1940–1947*. New York: Woman's Press, 1949.

Creel, George. *How We Advertised America*. 1920; rpt. New York: Arno Press, 1972.

Eisenstein, Zillah. *Capitalist Patriarchy and the Case for Socialist Feminism*. New York: Monthly Review Press, 1979.

Ewen, Stuart. *Captains of Consciousness: Advertising and the Social Roots of the Consumer Culture*. New York: McGraw-Hill, 1976.

Fox, Frank. *Madison Avenue Goes to War: The Strange Military Career of American Advertising, 1941–1945*. Charles E. Merrill Monograph Series. Provo, Utah: Brigham Young University Press, 1975.

Friedan, Betty. *The Feminine Mystique*. New York: Dell, 1963.

Friedman, Leslie J. *Sex Role Stereotyping in the Mass Media: An Annotated Bibliography*. New York: Garland, 1977.

Goffman, Erving. *Gender Advertisements*. New York: Harper and Row, 1976.

Goldfarb, Lyn. *Separate and Unequal: Discrimination against Women Workers after World War II*. Washington, D.C.: Union of Radical Political Economists, n.d.

Greene, Theodore. *America's Heroes: The Changing Models of Success in American Magazines*. New York: Oxford University Press, 1970.

Gregory, Chester. *Women in Defense Work during World War II*. New York: Exposition Press, 1974.

Griffin, Susan. *Pornography and Silence*. New York: Harper and Row, 1981.

Hartmann, Susan. *The Home Front and Beyond: American Women in the 1940s*. Boston: Twayne, 1982.

Haskell, Molly. *From Reverence to Rape: The Treatment of Women in the Movies*. New York: Holt, Rinehart and Winston, 1974.

Hoggart, Richard. *The Uses of Literacy: Aspects of Working-Class Life*. London: Chatto and Windus, 1957.

Holsti, Ole. *Content Analysis for the Social Sciences and Humanities*. Reading, Mass.: Addison-Wesley, 1969.

Industrial Mobilization for War: History of the War Production Board and Predecessor Agencies, 1940–1945. Vol. 1. Washington, D.C.: Government Printing Office, 1947.

Janeway, Eliot. *The Struggle for Survival: A Chronicle of Economic Mobilization in World War II*. New Haven: Yale University Press, 1951.

Keil, Sally Van Wagenen. *Those Wonderful Women in Their Flying Machines*. New York: Rawson, Wade, 1979.

Komarovsky, Mirra. *Blue-Collar Marriage*. New York: Vintage Books, 1962.

Lingeman, Richard. *Don't You Know There's a War On? The American Home Front, 1941–1945*. New York: G. P. Putnam's Sons, 1970.

Lloyd, Cynthia, and Beth Niemi. *The Economics of Sex Differentials*. New York: Columbia University Press, 1979.

Lloyd, Cynthia; Emily Andrews; and Curtis Gilroy, eds. *Women in the Labor Market*. New York: Columbia University Press, 1979.

Lowenthal, Leo. *Literature, Popular Culture, and Society*. Englewood Cliffs, N.J.: Prentice-Hall, 1961.

McKelvey, Thelma. *Women in War Production*. New York: Oxford University Press, 1942.

Millum, Trevor. *Images of Woman: Advertising in Women's Magazines.* Totowa, N.J.: Rowman and Littlefield, 1975.

Mock, James, and Cedric Larson, eds. *Words that Won the War: The Story of the Committee on Public Information, 1917–1919.* Princeton, N.J.: Princeton University Press, 1939.

Mott, Frank Luther. *A History of American Magazines, 1885–1905.* Cambridge: Harvard University Press, 1957.

Oppenheimer, Valerie. *The Female Labor Force in the United States.* Population Monograph Series, no. 5. Berkeley: University of California Press, 1970.

Packard, Vance. *The Hidden Persuaders.* New York: David McKay, 1957.

Peterson, Theodore. *Magazines in the Twentieth Century.* Urbana: University of Illinois Press, 1964.

Pinchbeck, Ivy. *Women Workers and the Industrial Revolution, 1750–1850.* New York: F. S. Crofts, 1930.

Polenberg, Richard. *War and Society: The U.S., 1941–1945.* New York: J. B. Lippincott, 1972.

Potter, David. *People of Plenty: Economic Abundance and the American Character.* Chicago: University of Chicago Press, 1954.

Rainwater, Lee; Richard Coleman; and Gerald Handel. *Workingman's Wife.* New York: Oceana, 1959.

Robinson, Lillian. *Sex, Class, and Culture.* Bloomington: Indiana University Press, 1978.

Rose, Lisle. *Dubious Victory: The U.S. and the End of World War II.* Kent, Ohio: Kent State University Press, 1973.

Rosen, Marjorie. *Popcorn Venus.* New York: Avon, 1974.

Rothman, Sheila. *Woman's Proper Place: A History of Changing Ideals and Practices, 1870 to the Present.* New York: Basic Books, 1978.

Rubin, Lillian Breslow. *Worlds of Pain: Life in the Working-Class Family.* New York: Basic Books, 1976.

Rupp, Leila. *Mobilizing Women for War: German and American Propaganda, 1939–1945.* Princeton, N.J.: Princeton University Press, 1978.

Schramm, Wilbur, and Donald Roberts, eds. *The Process and Effects of Mass Communication.* Urbana: University of Illinois Press, 1971.

Slichter, Sumner. *Economic Factors Affecting Industrial Relations Policy in National Defense.* Industrial Relations Monograph, no. 6. New York: Industrial Relations Counselors, 1941.

Stedman, Raymond. *Serials: Suspense and Drama by Installment.* Norman: University of Oklahoma Press, 1971.

Tebbel, John. *George Horace Lorimer and the "Saturday Evening Post."* Garden City, N.Y.: Doubleday, 1948.

Tuchman, Gaye; Arlene Kaplan Daniels; and James Benét, eds. *Hearth and Home: Images of Women in the Mass Media.* New York: Oxford University Press, 1978.

War and Women's Employment: The Experience of the United Kingdom and the U.S. Montreal: International Labour Office, 1946.

Winkler, Allan. *The Politics of Propaganda: The Office of War Information, 1941–1945.* New Haven: Yale University Press, 1978.

Wood, James. *Magazines in the U.S.: Their Social and Economic Influence.*
New York: Ronald Press, 1971.

Articles, Reports, Papers, and Dissertations

Albrecht, Milton. "Does Literature Reflect Common Values?" *American Sociological Review* 21 (1956): 722–29.

Anderson, Karen. "The Black Woman War Worker." Paper presented at the National Women's Studies Association, Bloomington, Ind., May 1980.

———. "The Impact of World War II in the Puget Sound Area on the Status of
Women and the Family." Ph.D. diss., University of Washington, 1975.

———. "Last Hired, First Fired: Black Women Workers during World War II."
Journal of American History 69 (June 1982): 82–97.

Baker, Helen. *Women in War Industries.* Research Report Series, no. 66, Industrial Relations Section. Princeton, N.J.: Princeton University Press, 1942.

Baker, Melva Joyce. "Images of Women: The War Years, 1941–1945." Ph.D.
diss., University of California–Santa Barbara, 1978.

Benston, Margaret. "The Political Economy of Women's Liberation." *Monthly
Review* 21 (September 1969): 13–28.

Berelson, Bernard, and Patricia J. Salter. "Majority and Minority Americans:
An Analysis of Magazine Fiction." *Public Opinion Quarterly* 10 (1946):
168–97.

Bérubé, Allan. "Coming Out Under Fire." *Mother Jones* February–March (1983):
22–29.

Brewer, F. M. "Women Workers after the War." *Editorial Research Reports* 1
(22 April 1944): 285–300.

Butler-Flora, Cornelia. "The Passive Female: Her Comparative Image by Class
and Culture in Women's Magazine Fiction." *Journal of Marriage and the
Family* 33 (August 1971): 435–44.

Cantor, Muriel, and Elizabeth Jones. "Creating Fiction for Women." *Communication Research* 10 (January 1983): 111–37.

Cowan, Ruth. "Two Washes in the Morning and a Bridge Party at Night: The
American Housewife between the Wars." *Women's Studies* 3, no. 2 (1976):
147–72.

Dratch, Howard. "The Politics of Child Care in the 1940s." *Science and Society*
38 (Summer 1974): 167–204.

Gainsbrugh, M. L., and I. J. White. "Woman as War Labor Reserves." *Conference
Board Economic Record* 4 (February 1942): 47–50.

Gerbner, George. "The Social Role of the Confession Magazine." *Social Problems* 6 (Summer 1958): 29–40.

Gluck, Sherna. "Interlude or Change: Women and the World War II Experience." *International Journal of Oral History* 3 (June 1982): 92–113.

Hartmann, Heidi. "Capitalism, Patriarchy, and Job Segregation by Sex." In
Women and the Workplace, ed. Martha Blaxall and Barbara Reagan. Chicago: University of Chicago Press, 1976.

Hartmann, Susan. "Prescriptions for Penelope: Literature on Women's Obligations to Returning World War II Veterans." *Women's Studies* 5, no. 3 (1978): 223–39.

Honey, Maureen. "Images of Women in the *Saturday Evening Post*, 1931–1936." *Journal of Popular Culture* 10 (Fall 1976): 352–58.

Howell, Robert. "The Writers' War Board: Writers and World War II." Ph.D. diss., Louisiana State and Agricultural and Mechanical College, 1971.

Jackson, Jean. "The Changing Confession Market." *The Writer*, May 1975, p. 15.

Johns-Heine, Patricke, and Hans Gerth. "Values in Mass Periodical Fiction, 1921–1940." *Public Opinion Quarterly* 13 (Spring 1949): 105–13.

Jones, David. "The U.S. Office of War Information and American Public Opinion during World War II, 1939–1945." Ph.D. diss., State University of New York–Binghamton, 1976.

Kessler-Harris, Alice. "Women, Work, and the Social Order." In *Liberating Women's History*, ed. Berenice Carroll. Urbana: University of Illinois Press, 1976.

Kidder, Jerome. *Women in Factory Work.* Management Research Division, Studies in Personnel Policy, no. 41. New York: National Industrial Conference Board, 1942.

Lazarsfeld, Paul, and Rowena Wyant. "Magazines in Ninety Cities—Who Reads What?" *Public Opinion Quarterly* 1 (October 1937): 29–42.

Leman, Joy. "'The Advice of a Real Friend': Codes of Intimacy and Oppression in Women's Magazines, 1937–1955." *Women's Studies International Quarterly* 3, no. 1 (1980): 63–78.

Lipman-Blumen, Jean. "Role De-differentiation as a System Response to Crisis." *Sociological Inquiry* 43, no. 2 (1973): 105–29.

Lloyd, Charles. "American Society and Values in World War II from the Publications of the Office of War Information." Ph.D. diss., Georgetown University, 1975.

McCallum, Pamela. "World without Conflict: Magazines for Working Class Women." *Canadian Forum* 55 (September 1975): 42–44.

MacKay, Lamar. "Domestic Operations of the Office of War Information in World War II." Ph.D. diss., University of Wisconsin, 1966.

McKenzie, Vernon. "Treatment of War Themes in Magazine Fiction." *Public Opinion Quarterly* 5, no. 2 (1941): 227–32.

Martel, Martin, and George McCall. "Reality-Orientation and the Pleasure Principle: A Study of American Mass-Periodical Fiction (1890–1955)." In *People, Society, and Mass Communications*, ed. Lewis Dexter and David Manning White. Glencoe, Ill.: Free Press, 1964.

Metz, Harold. *Is There Enough Manpower?* Washington, D.C.: Brookings Institution, 1942.

Mezerik, A. G. "Getting Rid of the Women." *Atlantic Monthly* 175 (June 1945): 79–83.

Milkman, Ruth. "Redefining 'Women's Work': The Sexual Division of Labor in the Auto Industry during World War II." *Feminist Studies* 8, no. 2 (Summer 1982): 337–72.

Palmer, Florence. "Six Ways to Successful Confessions." In *The Writer's Handbook*, ed. A. S. Burack. Boston: The Writer, 1974.

Palmer, Gladys. "Women in the Post-War Labor Market." *Forum* 104 (October 1945): 130–34.

Pierson, Ruth. "Women's Emancipation and the Recruitment of Women into the Canadian Labour Force in World War II." Paper presented at the Canadian Historical Association, Quebec, 1976.

Quick, Paddy. "Rosie the Riveter: Myths and Realities." *Radical America* 9 (July 1975): 115–32.

Roe, Constance. "Can the Girls Hold Their Jobs in Peacetime?" *Saturday Evening Post*, 4 March 1944, p. 28.

Shover, Michele. "Roles and Images of Women in World War I Propaganda." *Politics and Society* 5, no. 3 (1975): 469–89.

Skold, Karen Beck. "The Job He Left Behind: American Women in the Shipyards during World War II." In *Women, War and Revolution*, ed. Carol Berkin and Clara Lovett. New York: Holmes-Meier, 1980.

———. "The Politics of Child Care during World War II: The Case of the Kaiser Child Care Centers." Paper presented at the National Women's Studies Association, Bloomington, Ind., May 1980.

Sonenschein, David. "Love and Sex in the Romance Magazines." *Journal of Popular Culture* 4, no. 2 (1970): 398–409.

Stewart, Maxwell. *The Coming Crisis in Manpower.* Public Affairs Pamphlet, no. 69 (1942), n.p.

Stewart, Penni. "He Admits . . . but She Confesses." *Women's Studies International Quarterly* 3, no. 1 (1980): 105–14.

Straub, Eleanor. "U.S. Government Policy toward Civilian Women during World War II." Ph.D. diss., Emory University, 1973. *Prologue* 5 (Winter 1973): 240–54.

Tobias, Sheila, and Lisa Anderson. "What Really Happened to Rosie the Riveter: Demobilization and the Female Labor Force, 1945–47." New York: MSS Modular Publications, module 9, 1974, pp. 1–36.

Trey, J. E. "Women in the War Economy—World War II." *Review of Radical Political Economics* 4 (July 1972): 41–57.

Welter, Barbara. "The Cult of True Womanhood: 1820–1860." *American Quarterly* 18 (Summer 1960): 151–74.

Winkler, Allan. "Politics and Propaganda: The Office of War Information, 1942–1945." Ph.D. diss., Yale University, 1974.

Archival Sources

Records of the Office of War Information. Record Group 208. National Records Center, Suitland, Md.

Government Documents

New York State Department of Labor Reprints, Division of Industrial Relations. Women in Industry and Minimum Wage Series. *Employers Post-War Plans for Women Workers*, January 1945. *Home Duties of Working Women in New*

York State, November 1945. *Post-War Plans of Women Workers in New York State*, August 1945. *What My War Job Means*, March 1944.

U.S. Department of Commerce, Bureau of the Census. *Money Income in 1977 of Families and Persons in the United States*. Current Population Reports Series P-60, no. 118. Washington, D.C.: Government Printing Office, 1979.

———. *Sixteenth Census of the United States: Population—the Labor Force: Employment and Family Characteristics of Women*. Washington, D.C.: Government Printing Office, 1943.

U.S. Department of Labor, Bureau of Labor Statistics. "Changes in Women's Employment during the War," by Mary Pidgeon. *Monthly Labor Review* 59 (November 1944): 1029–33.

———. "Effect of 'Cutbacks' on Women's Employment." *Monthly Labor Review* 59 (September 1944): 585–91.

———. *Handbook of Labor Statistics*. Bulletin 916. Washington, D.C.: Government Printing Office, 1947.

———. "Postwar Labor Turn-Over among Women Factory Workers," by Clara Schloss and Ella Polinsky. *Monthly Labor Review* 64 (March 1947): 411–19.

———. "Recent Occupational Trends," by Harold Wool and Lester Pearlman. *Monthly Labor Review* 65 (August 1947): 139–47.

———. "Recent Trends in the Labor Force," by Harold Wool. *Monthly Labor Review* 65 (December 1947): 638–47.

———. "Sources of Wartime Labor Supply in the U.S.," by Leonard Eskin. *Monthly Labor Review* 59 (August 1944): 264–78.

———. "Wartime and Postwar Trends Compared: An Appraisal of the Permanence of Recent Movements," by Harold Wool and Lester Pearlman. *Monthly Labor Review* 65 (August 1947): 139–47.

———. "Woman Workers in Two Wars," by Mary Robinson. *Monthly Labor Review* 57 (October 1943): 650–71.

———. "Women in Industry." *Monthly Labor Review* 59 (September 1944): 585–91.

———. "Women Workers and Recent Economic Change," by Mary Pidgeon. *Monthly Labor Review* 65 (December 1947): 666–71.

———. "Women's Work in Wartime," by Frances Perkins. *Monthly Labor Review* 56 (April 1943): 661–65.

U.S. Department of Labor, Women's Bureau. *The American Woman—Her Changing Role*. Bulletin 224. Washington, D.C.: Government Printing Office, 1944.

———. *Changes in Women's Employment during the War*. Special Bulletin 20. Washington, D.C.: Government Printing Office, 1944.

———. *Changes in Women's Occupations, 1940–1950*. Bulletin 253. Washington, D.C.: Government Printing Office, 1954.

———. *Employment Goals of the World Plan of Action: Developments and Issues in the United States*. Washington, D.C.: Government Printing Office, July 1980.

———. *Employment of Women in the Early Postwar Period*. Bulletin 211. Washington, D.C.: Government Printing Office, 1946.

————. *Employment of Women in an Emergency Period.* Bulletin 241. Washington, D.C.: Government Printing Office, 1952.

————. *Employment Opportunities in Characteristic Industrial Occupations of Women.* Bulletin 201. Washington, D.C.: Government Printing Office, 1944.

————. *"Equal Pay" for Women in War Industries.* Bulletin 196. Washington, D.C.: Government Printing Office, 1942.

————. *Handbook of Facts on Women Workers.* Bulletin 225. Washington, D.C.: Government Printing Office, 1948.

————. *Negro Women War Workers.* Bulletin 205. Washington, D.C.: Government Printing Office, 1945.

————. *The New Position of Women in American Industry.* Bulletin 12. Washington, D.C.: Government Printing Office, 1920.

————. *The Occupational Progress of Women, 1910–1930.* Bulletin 104. Washington, D.C.: Government Printing Office, 1933.

————. *A Preview as to Women Workers in Transition from War to Peace.* Special Bulletin 18. Washington, D.C.: Government Printing Office, 1944.

————. *Progress Report on Women War Workers' Housing.* Special Bulletin 17. Washington, D.C.: Government Printing Office, 1944.

————. *State Labor Laws for Women with Wartime Modifications.* Bulletin 202. Washington, D.C.: Government Printing Office, 1945–46.

————. *Technological Changes in Relation to Women's Employment.* Bulletin 107. Washington, D.C.: Government Printing Office, 1935.

————. *Womanpower Committees during World War II.* Bulletin 244. Washington, D.C.: Government Printing Office, 1953.

————. *Women at Work: A Century of Industrial Change.* Bulletin 161. Washington, D.C.: Government Printing Office, 1939.

————. *Women in Industry.* Bulletin 164. Washington, D.C.: Government Printing Office, 1938.

————. *Women's Occupations through Seven Decades.* Bulletin 218. Washington, D.C.: Government Printing Office, 1947.

————. *Women's Wartime Hours of Work: The Effect on Their Factory Performance and Home Life.* Bulletin 208. Washington, D.C.: Government Printing Office, 1947.

————. *Women Workers in Ten War Production Areas and Their Postwar Employment Plans.* Bulletin 209. Washington, D.C.: Government Printing Office, 1946.

————. *Women Workers in Their Family Environment.* Bulletin 183. Washington, D.C.: Government Printing Office, 1941.

Index